ON ANCIENT *Central-Asian* TRACKS

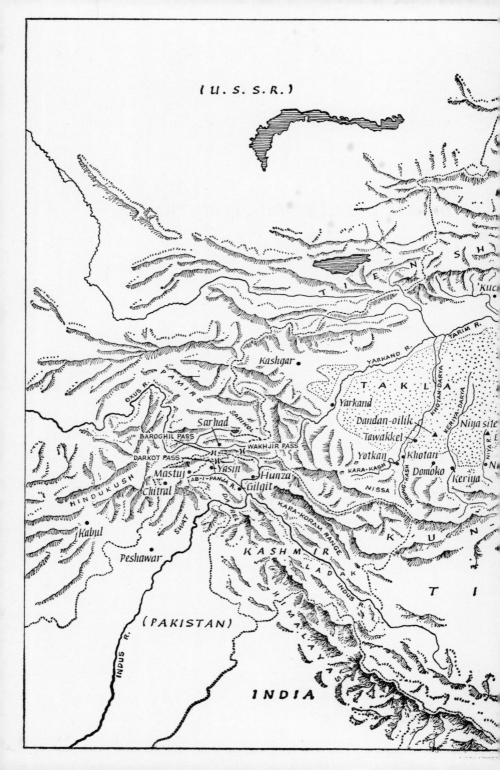

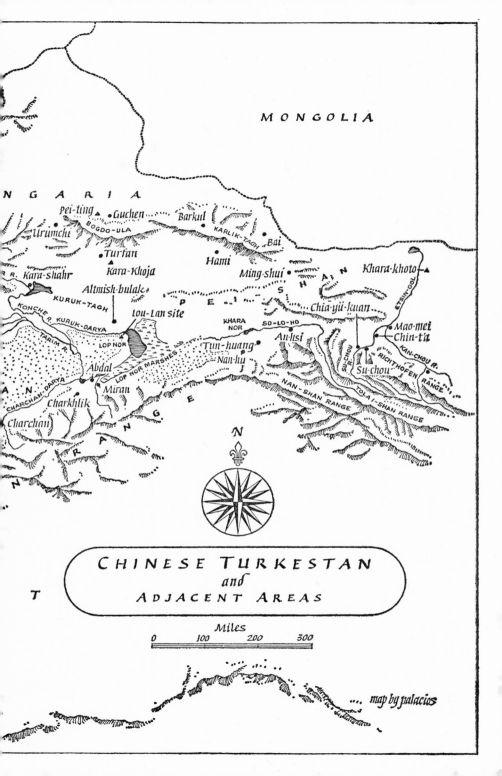

MONGOLIA

NGARIA

Pei-ting ▲ • Guchen • Barkul
Urumchi • BOGDO-ULA KARLIK-TAGH • Bai
• Turfan • Hami Khara-khoto ▲
R. Kara-shahr • Kara-Khoja Ming-shui PE-I SH AN ETSIN-GOL
KURUK-TAGH Altmish-bulak • Chia-yü-kuan
KONCHE R. KURUK-DARYA • lou-lan site Mao-mei
TARIM R. LOP NOR KHARA SO-LO-HO An-hsi Chin-t'a
Abdal NOR • Tun-huang SU-CHOU KAN-CHOU R.
LOP NOR MARSHES Nan-hu Su-chou RIGHT HOFEN RANGE
CHARCHAN-DARYA • Miran NAN-SHAN RANGE
Charkhlik RANGE TOLA-I-SHAN RANGE
Charchan

N

CHINESE TURKESTAN and ADJACENT AREAS

Miles
0   100   200   300

... map by palacios

ON ANCIENT
Central-Asian
TRACKS

Brief Narrative of
Three Expeditions in Innermost Asia
and Northwestern China

by SIR AUREL STEIN, K, C.I.E.

EDITED AND INTRODUCED BY
JEANNETTE MIRSKY

Pantheon Books
A DIVISION OF RANDOM HOUSE • NEW YORK

TO THE MEMORY OF

Sir Thomas Arnold

SCHOLAR, "SAINT," AND INCOMPARABLE FRIEND

WHOSE INSPIRING SYMPATHY
EVER FOLLOWED AND BRIGHTENED MY TRAVELS
THIS RECORD OF THEM IS INSCRIBED
IN UNCEASING AFFECTION AND GRATITUDE

———

INTRODUCTION

SIR MARK AUREL STEIN (he never seems to have used his first name) was born in Budapest in 1862 and studied Oriental languages and archeology there and in Tübingen and Oxford until 1887. He used his Hungarian military service interlude to complete courses in surveying and topography. When he had finished his studies, he accepted the position of Principal of Oriental College in Lahore and remained attached to the Indian Educational Service until 1910 when he joined the Indian Archaeological Survey.

While Stein was at Lahore the pattern of activity adhered to throughout his long life began: a voluminous outpouring of scholarly writing sandwiched in between continuous archeological field trips. Thus, his Sanskrit edition of the *Rajatarangini*, the chronicle of the ancient Kashmir kings composed by Kalhana, India's earliest historian, was published in 1892. Eight years later came his famous annotated translation of this work as well as an article on the Saki (Indo-Scythian) kings of Kabul. (The Scythians, but recently nomads from distant Chinese Turkistan, about 130 B.C. conquered the Greco-Bactrian kingdom established by a general of Alexander the Great and extended their power to the Indus valley.) No sooner had Stein finished his literary task than he started on an archeological trip (1898), making a quick survey of Buner, a little region of Kashmir, part of the former Udyana, whose great past had become familiar through his scholarly investigations.

The Northwest Frontier country was a region fallen from its former importance and centrality into a wild, backward, inaccessible land peopled by primitive tribes. Yet its mountain passes had once funneled cultural impulses in and out of India; its kings had maintained diplomatic relations with both the Roman and Han empires and, taking over the Hellenistic civilization they had conquered, hired Roman artisans to decorate their Buddhist stupas—stupas whose sculptured and frescoed beauty had welcomed weary Chinese pilgrims to the land where the Buddha lived and taught. India's Northwest Frontier Territory (now extending into Pakistan and Afghanistan) had been her ancient gateway to the other civilizations of the Old World.

When Stein began his work, the nature of Chinese Turkistan was being intermittently probed. (It took its name when Turkic peoples began settling in that corridor of migrations, the Tarim river basin, around the seventh century and became subject to the Chinese Empire that then exerted its authority over its oases. It is also called Serindia, as it lies between China, the Seres of the Greeks, and India.) Whichever it is called, it is a formidable and inhuman region. At its center lies the oval-shaped Taklamakan desert (250 miles from north to south and 1500 miles from east to west), rimmed on three sides by lofty mountain ranges. On its south stretches the long, bleak, serrated K'un-lun; on its north is the wild Altai; and on its west are the sky-piercing Pamirs, whose passes lie at 20,000 feet. As the geographical knowledge of Serindia was fragmentary, so was its history. But Stein did have useful clues. Research into European sources (made principally by Sir Henry Yule, the pioneer scholar of Marco Polo travels) had disclosed that during the centuries when the Mongol Empire covered all the land between the China Sea and the Danube, European ambassadors and Christian missionaries as well as commercial travelers like the great Venetian had safely crossed from Europe to Peking along patrolled caravan routes. Stein was also familiar with translations of the Chinese Annals, which related that between 138 and 115 B.C. agents of Wu-ti, the capable Early Han emperor, had opened up the Silk Road, the highway between East and West, and that subsequently, along with the traffic in luxuries, Buddhist missionaries and pilgrims had carried the Indian-born religion—its sacred statues as well as its scriptures—to the Far East. Stein had good reason to believe that in the six centuries between Polo's time and his own, no man of Western Europe had followed the entire length of the overland route from India to China.

He was superbly, almost uniquely, cast for the ambitious task he had chosen: deciphering Central Asia's history and surveying as much as he could of its vast terrain. As a scholar he had a command of and fluency in Oriental languages, his phenomenal memory held whatever he had seen or read; he had a scientific preoccupation with the importance of being accurate and a willingness—even an eagerness—to share his material with other scholars. As a field archeologist he could plan long, arduous expeditions; and as an explorer he was endowed with immense energy and endurance, with patience, ingenuity, and determination—the prerequisites for living, working and traveling in a terrain isolated and difficult. The idea of comfort never seemed very important; nor did the notion of rest; he seems to have been utterly without histrionics or heroics. In person he was "a little gnome of a man with apple cheeks and the eyes of youth": so Freya Stark described him when she met him in 1932. She added: "and with the gentle deceptive manner of those who always get their own way."

For forty-five years after his initial archeological reconnaissance into the Khyber Pass region until his death in 1943 (almost eighty-two, he was about to start a new dig near Kabul) Stein made a succession of expeditions. They were aimed at restoring the lost chapters in the history and prehistory (the word was newly coined then) of the Central-

Asian area and to read the geographical language of that region's mountain ranges and deserts, those awesome hurdles which in the past had not separated East from West. It is this unity of endeavor that gives unity to Stein's continuous, far-flung efforts. The areas in which he worked were chosen to resolve problems posed by his Central-Asian journeys and, as might be expected, in response to other contemporary archeological work. Thus in addition to his four extraordinary Central-Asian expeditions, 1900-01, 1906-08, 1913-16 and 1930, Stein's field trips fall into three categories.

First: it was inevitable that Stein would respond with action to the excitement and speculations raised by the discovery of the buried cities of the Indus valley, Mohenjo-daro and Harappa (1923-25). Had these heretofore unknown, pre-Aryan peoples who built and lived in large urban centers had contact with the high civilization of Mesopotamia? To verify archeologically such cultural contacts, Stein made a series of journeys (between 1927 and 1936) into the harsh country of Baluchistan and southwestern Iran. He was able to trace a continuous line of neolithic and chalcolithic settlements that tied the Indus-valley cities to the more ancient Mesopotamian culture. (Much of the mystery still remains—the origins of these Indus-valley dwellers as well as the deciphering of their written language.)

Having found where the Silk Road left China, and examined the effective military measures the Chinese had taken to safeguard this link to the West from the harassments of marauding nomads (the Huns were long a serious threat), Stein wanted to investigate its western terminus. This meant trying to find where the Roman Empire's eastern border had faced the Parthian Empire—for in their garrisoned commercial centers ended the Central-Asian caravans carrying goods for Rome. And as ideas and art styles also traveled along the Silk Road, Stein sought to locate the Greek colonies planted by Alexander the Great when he marched his army so far that it reached the Punjab, where his exhausted men refused to advance. (Alexander's camp has been called "a kind of moving capital city.") In some seventy new cities which the Macedonian planted so that Greeks would mix with Asians to create the basis of his One World empire, were the trained artisans who introduced Hellenistic art into Asia. On many short expeditions, Stein investigated some of the centers where Greco-Buddhist art had emerged, centers that exerted an influence thousands of miles away in an alien world across the heartland of Asia. (To locate these Alexandrias scattered in western Asia, Stein first had to determine the routes and battlefields of Alexander's campaigns during his momentous, victorious march from Arbela until his return to Babylon.)

Important as these archeological forays into western Asia were, Stein's main contribution was his Central-Asian expeditions, which Sir Leonard Woolley has called "the most daring and adventurous raid upon the ancient world that any archeologist has attempted."

Stein was the only European in these expeditions, acting at once as organizer and leader, interpreter and secretary, archeologist, geographer and cartographer (and, when necessary, the detective who found the Khotanese forger of antiquities and put him out of business). He was accompanied by two or three Muslims of the Indian Survey Department and a handful of key-caravan men; and he was assisted by a motley band of local recruits for digging. With such an unlikely group, Stein unearthed a host of oasis settlements abandoned to the sand, which, driven by fierce winds, had almost succeeded in obliterating their very existence. Nor was his task finished then: the immense amount of material salvaged under savage conditions was carefully packed and loaded onto camels to be brought out of Central Asia to the nearest railhead, where the collection was shipped to Delhi and London for display and study. In his four expeditions, Stein covered more than 25,000 miles on foot or pony-back. Each time he crossed the Pamirs he took a different route over another pass. He made the circuit of the Taklamakan desert, traversed it at its widest north-south part, and carried on his excavations when winter gripped the land. It was wisest to work there when the temperature was below zero, for even though the ink froze in his pen, water could best be transported as ice blocks loaded on camels.

Once Chinese Turkistan was fairly populous and much more prosperous. Ice-fed rivers rushing down from the snowy mountain ranges were skillfully led to nourish fields and orchards; the fertile oases were extended, making more towns, larger and more flourishing than those still left. Then the Tarim basin provided an easier highway for the transcontinental caravans. This story was repeated in site after site to which Stein was often guided by local treasure hunters. From long-dead temples Stein recovered stucco statues and reliefs and even their fresco paintings, while the abandoned houses yielded written records by the tens of thousands. He collected an assortment of languages and scripts written on wood slips, birch bark, palm leaves, paper and silk, documents in the ancient Indian Brahmi script used by the Kushana rulers of the Punjab; in Aramaic, once the state language of the Achaemenian Empire and one that is still written and spoken by Iranian people in distant Bukhara and Samarkand; in Kharoshthi, a script Stein knew from the coins and inscriptions of northwest India; in Tibetan, and in Chinese. Some of the unknown languages are still not deciphered. Fortunately, many others, especially the Chinese, were dated and so made it possible to restore the chronology of past events.

Stein's collections made it clear that Central Asia had been a meeting place for many nations. At first it was controlled by the Han emperors: their policy viewed the Tarim basin as their empire's vital avenue to the West to be protected by troops stationed at strategic places along the line of oases. Many of these military outposts were manned by men who belonged to Indo-Scythian tribes, those ancient enemies of the northern Huns who had decisively defeated them, driving them from their traditional home in Turkistan to Sogdiana, far to the west. Another tribe in the Indo-Scythian family established the Kushana dynasty, with Taxila in the Punjab as its capital; its greatest king, Kanishka (A.D. 144-73), was the powerful patron of Mahayana Buddhism. Through this tribal affiliation, Buddhism also became the religion of Turkistan: their documents with some of the earliest examples of Indian writing were found far to the east, and their Greco-Buddhist style of sculpture, created to beautify Punjab temples, also decorated stupas in distant Turkistan. But there was a subtle, unmistakable difference, for inevitably, as the western style moved further and further to the east, it was modified by contact with powerful art styles, the Iranian and the Chinese.

The collapse of the T'ang dynasty in the tenth century hastened the abandonment of a region so far from China. As the administrative officers charged with maintaining the irrigation works left, many oases were at the mercy of the capricious rivers that changed their courses and bypassed the irrigation ditches. Slowly the fields that had been won for crops and trees became non-productive; the population diminished. During these centuries of attrition the Silk Road continued to serve as the highway: Chinese pilgrims still crossed on it to India (though more and more used the sea route), and caravans still plodded along its length. It continued to serve when in Mongol times men like Marco Polo traveled to China. By the time of Europe's Age of Discovery even the memory of this ancient thoroughfare between East and West was lost.

Reading Stein's narrative of his four Central-Asian expeditions—leisurely in its pace, gentle and moderate in tone, learned about a little-known, fascinating, and increasingly significant period of history, and simply told by an explorer who felt at home in an unfamiliar and terrifying world—is both a delight and an education. Aurel Stein invites by the very nature of his achievement. This account organizes and interprets the prodigious amount of materials he collected, rich in content, varied in form. From the sand-buried ruins around Khotan—Niya, Keriya, Endere, and the other settlements where once men farmed and lived and worshiped, from other oases—

Dandan-oilik, Lou-lan, Miran, haunting names plucked from oblivion; from the nameless guard-tower stations spaced along the "Old Wall," the ancient Chinese *Limes,* whose refuse heaps, still vilely odorous, yielded masses of official documents, Stein was led to his most spectacular discovery: the Caves of the Thousand Buddhas at Tun-huang.

None of Stein's discoveries was accidental, because, as one of his colleagues said in characterizing Stein's linguistic, geographical and historical preparedness, "he knows what he is looking for." So he was led to that oasis in northwestern China by the enthusiastic report written by the Hungarian Geological Survey (1879), whose members were the first Westerners to see those marvelously decorated cave temples. But once there, it was Stein whose sharp ears caught a vague rumor of "a great mass of ancient manuscripts which had been discovered by chance." Not even this always moderate scholar-scientist could hide the emotions he felt when telling how, after patient, delicate negotiations, he finally held samples of that priceless hoard in his hands. "Joyful excitement" are the words he used.

In his Central-Asian expeditions Stein was principally guided by accounts left by two earlier travelers. There was, of course, that dictated by Marco Polo, the greatest traveler of medieval Europe, whom Stein followed across the "Roof of the World," as he called the Pamirs, and across the fearsome "Desert of Lop" into Kansu and China proper. Six centuries before the Venetian, another traveler, equally great, had written of his memorable journey from China to India. Hsüan-tsang, the pilgrim of pious memory whom Stein called his "patron saint," returned to China laden with Buddhist relics and sacred books after years of wandering and studying in the Western Regions, as he called the account he wrote upon his return. To these classic records left by two extraordinary way-farers and wanderers. Stein has added a third: *On Ancient Central-Asian Tracks.*

JEANNETTE MIRSKY

PREFACE

THIS BOOK IS MEANT to present a succinct account of the explorations, antiquarian and geographical, which I had the good fortune to carry out in Chinese Turkistan and adjacent parts of innermost Asia. The years spent on hard travel in those little-known regions, difficult of access and trying in their physical features, remain among the happiest memories of my life. But more strenuous still and longer were the years needed for the elaboration of the abundant scientific results which my three Central-Asian expeditions had yielded.

By the publication of personal narratives on the first two journeys and of eleven heavy quarto volumes of detailed reports on all three, I may well believe my duty done in the matter of record. But with the exception of *Ruins of Desert Cathay*, containing a full account of the personal experiences on my second expedition (1906-08), all the above publications have long ago passed out of print and are now difficult to secure.

Since the last of those labors were disposed of, fully twenty-seven years after my return from the first journey, I have been free to turn to new fields of archeological exploration farther south. But my recollections of those fruitful years spent in the deserts and mountains of innermost Asia are still as fresh and cherished as before. So when the President of Harvard University kindly invited me to deliver a course of lectures at the Lowell Institute, Boston, I gladly availed myself of the opportunity offered to describe the travels and discoveries of those years in a condensed form suited for a wider public.

Considering the great extent and varied character of the explorations, it would have been still more difficult to achieve the requisite condensation had I not been able adequately to illustrate my account of them on the screen. This need made itself felt also when presenting here these lectures in print with suitable additions and changes. Hence I must feel grateful for the discerning consideration of my publishers which has rendered it possible to provide sufficient illustrations both of the scenes of my explorations and of the funds that rewarded them at ancient sites.

Before taking the reader to the distant region of Asia over which those explorations extended, it seemed necessary to sketch in broad outlines its characteristic physical features. Equally helpful it appeared to give a summary account of the history of which that region had been the scene for the last 2,000 years, and for which it was destined mainly by its geography. For these introductory chapters I was able to avail myself largely of what I had occasion to set forth in my lecture on "Innermost Asia: Its Geography as a Factor in History," delivered in 1925 before the Royal Geographical Society.

In the course of three long expeditions carried over a vast area where practicable routes are limited by great natural obstacles, it was unavoidable that geographical considerations and archeological tasks should cause certain parts of it to be visited by me more than once. This circumstance has made it advisable to order my account of the chief phases in my exploratory work according to the localities which witnessed them, instead of adhering to strict chronological sequence.

The results of those expeditions, extending altogether over close on seven years, could not have been achieved had I not from their start, and all through the years which the study and record of the results claimed, enjoyed very willing and effective help from many sides. Preceding publications have afforded me welcome opportunities to acknowledge these manifold obligations in detail. Here I must be content with the briefest record of gratitude.

To the enlightened support of the Indian Government, which I was privileged to serve first in its Educational Service and later in its Archaeological Survey, I owe my largest debt for requisite freedom and means to carry out my chosen tasks. The authorities of the British Museum, besides providing a share in the cost of my second expedition, gave very valuable help by granting accommodation for the arrangement and study of the antiquities brought back from all my journeys and allowing expert scholars on their staff to aid in these tasks.

On the geographical side I feel greatly indebted to the Survey of India, which provided me in the field with well-trained and hard-working Indian Surveyors and at considerable expense published the results of the topographical surveys, carried out by them under my direction and with my assistance, in successive large series of maps. In the same direction the Council of the Royal Geographical Society has at all times accorded me generous help and encouragement, as attested by their grant in 1909 of the Founder's Gold Medal.

It would have been quite impossible for me to do justice to the varied interest and importance of the antiquities discovered, including abundant relics of ancient arts and crafts as well as early manuscript remains in a dozen or so of different languages, had not a large number of distinguished Orientalist scholars and students of Eastern art most readily offered their expert collaboration. The names of such valued helpers are far too many for individual mention in this place. So I must rest content with the references made in some chapters to those scholars to whom the elucidation of particularly important classes of documentary finds is due.

In connection with the present volume I have to record my special thanks to the Government of India in the Department of Education, Lands and Health for permission to use here a selection of photographs taken by me on my journeys, as well as to the High Commissioner for India in London who authorized the reproduction from my detailed reports (*Ancient Khotan; Serindia; Innermost Asia*) of plates illustrating certain antiques. For the accompanying map I am obliged to the Secretary of the Royal Geographical Society, who kindly allowed it to be reproduced from the one published with the above-quoted paper in the *Geographical Journal*. With regard to the arrangement of the illustrative materials it affords me special gratification to acknowledge the same valuable help which my artist friend and assistant, Mr. Fred H. Andrews, O.B.E., has kindly rendered me for all my previous publications. To Mr. George A. Macmillan I owe sincere gratitude for his kindness in looking over my text with special regard to the needs of the general reader. Nor ought I to omit mention of the excellent work of Messrs. Henry Stone and Son, Banbury, on the color plates, which affords a guarantee for the faithfulness of these reproductions.

For the last thirty years the tasks entailed by the results of my explorations have imposed upon me prolonged periods of desk work in civilization, more exacting to me in some ways than efforts in the field. That most of this work could be done under the sheltering care and with the constant encouragement of those kindest of friends under whose ever hospitable roof I now write is a boon for which I cannot feel too grateful.

AUREL STEIN

At the President's Lodgings,
Corpus Christi College, Oxford.
September 18, 1932.

CONTENTS

Contents

ON ANCIENT *Central-Asian* TRACKS

CHAPTER I

A Bird's-eye View of Innermost Asia

THESE PAGES ARE MEANT to revive characteristic phases of those explorations which I had the good fortune to carry out under the orders of the Indian Government on three successive expeditions to the innermost portions of Asia. Those expeditions were started as long ago as 1900-01 and were continued from 1906 to 1908 and again from 1913 to 1916. They lasted altogether for close on seven years and allowed me by marches on horseback and on foot to cover distances aggregating to a total of some 25,000 miles.

Journeys carried out by such quasi-archaic methods of locomotion and over so great distances, so protracted in time and accompanied by systematic surveys, provided the right means of acquiring familiarity with a region vast in extent and presenting exceptional interest alike by its physical features and by the remains of its human history. It comprises Chinese Turkistan with its border lands toward the Oxus in the west and China proper in the east. Though composed for the most part of desert ground, whether in the mountains or in its drainageless sand-covered plains, it has yet played a very important part in the records of the past. For centuries it served as the channel for that interchange of the early civilizations of India, China and the Hellenized west of Asia which forms such a fascinating chapter in cultural history. These civilizations have left behind there abundant traces in the shape of remains of all kinds, which the aridity of the land has helped to preserve for us. The search for these remains of ancient civilization, together with the problems raised by the present physical conditions of the region, provided the strongest incentive for my explorations.

But from the modern point of view the economic and political importance of those lands in the heart of Asia is small, and smaller still the call of their natural attractions and resources. This makes it necessary in the first place to acquaint the reader with the general character of the region and thus to make it easier for him to understand the reasons which account for its importance in the past. I therefore propose in the introductory chapters to give a summary survey, a bird's-eye view, as it were, of the whole of that region and then to sketch in broad outlines what we know of the history of which it has formed the scene.

That innermost portion of Asia with which my explorations were concerned may be roughly described as comprising those vast basins, elevated and drainageless, which extend from east to west almost halfway across the central belt of Asia. Their longitudinal rim is well defined in the north by the big rampart of the T'ien-shan, the "Celestial Mountains," and in the south by the snowy K'un-lun ranges which divide those basins from Tibet. The eastern border of the region may be placed where the Nan-shan, itself a continuation of the K'un-lun, forms the watershed toward the drainage area of the Pacific Ocean. In the west it abuts on the mighty mountain mass of the Pamirs, the *Imaos* of the ancients, which connects the T'ien-shan with the Hindukush and on its western flanks gives rise to the headwaters of the Oxus.

On looking at the map, it might well seem as if this vast region had been intended by Nature far more to serve as a barrier between the lands which have given to our globe its great civilizations than to facilitate the exchange of their cultural influences. For within this area, measuring some 1500 miles in a direct line from east to west and, at its widest, more than five hundred miles from north to south, the ground capable of settled life is strictly limited to strings of oases, all with a few exceptions comparatively small. The rest of this area is occupied by huge stretches of desert. Whether they extend over high mountain ranges, or wide barren belts of foothills with their gravel glacis, or over plains overrun by moving sands, these deserts are almost everywhere devoid of water.

It is this extreme deficiency of water which invests by far the greatest portion of the area we are considering with the character of what I may call "true desert." I lay stress on the epithet "true" in order to make it quite clear that the ground over which I shall have to ask the reader to follow me differs so largely from those deserts with which Biblical stories, descriptions of Arabian, American or South African scenery and the like have made many of us, in a certain sense, familiar. These "tame deserts," as I should venture to call them by way of distinction, may well impress the town dweller, especially if he comes from our centers of congested humanity, with their sense of solitude, emptiness and, let me add, peace. But deserts in which whole tribes can wander about for long periods sure of finding water and grazing for their flocks, at least at certain regular seasons, deserts in which populations driven out from their seats or harassed by foes can safely seek refuge for a time, are not such as face us in most parts of the huge basin between the Celestial Mountains and the K'un-lun.

By far the greater part of this basin is filled by the dune-covered Taklamakan and the wastes of hard salt crust or wind-eroded clay of the Lop desert which stretch almost unbroken for a total length of over eight hundred miles from west to east. In them the absence of moisture bans not only human existence but practically also all animal and plant life. Conditions are almost as forbidding in the high mountains and plateaux of the K'un-lun. There vegetation is to be found only at great elevations where the proximity of glaciers provides moisture and allows vegetation to grow for a few months in the year under semi-arctic conditions, or else in the extremely confined space which the streams fed by those glaciers leave at the bottom of deep-cut narrow gorges. It is solely to the water carried down by these streams that the oases scattered along the edges of this and the basins adjoining eastward owe their existence; for nowhere is cultivation of any kind possible unless irrigation is provided by canals. It is clear that the almost total absence of atmospheric moisture which such conditions imply directly results from the geographical position of the basins. A glance at the map is enough to show how vast are the distances which separate them on all sides from the seas and their life-giving vapors.

Where Nature has been so chary of the gifts which create the resources necessary for human existence and favor close occupation, it is obvious that the ground, however extensive, can offer but little variety of scenery. Nevertheless, there are broad geographical features which divide this ground into several well-marked zones, and our rapid survey must take these in succession.

We may start from the mountain barrier in the west, not merely because it was from that side that the earliest influence of the classical world, of India and of Persia passed into innermost Asia and thence into China, but also because the mountain barrier to be crossed there has attracted more interest than the rest of the encircling ranges. I mean the great meridional range which from the high open valleys adjoining it westward may conveniently be referred to as that of the Pamirs. It joins the T'ien-shan on the north to the ice-clad Hindukush on the south, and was known already to the ancients by the name of *Imaos*. Ptolemy in his "Geography" quite correctly describes it as the range dividing the two Scythias, *intra* and *extra Imaon*. These terms closely correspond to the Inner and Outer Tartary of our grandfathers' geography and find their equivalents in the Russian Turkistan and Chinese Turkistan of our own. On this range lies the watershed between the drainage areas of the Oxus and the Tarim rivers. But it is of interest to observe that the line of greatest elevations, culminating in peaks rising to over 25,000 feet, stretches to the east of the watershed.

To the high plateaulike valleys of the Pamirs which extend to the west of this line and for the most part are drained by the headwaters of the Oxus and its main tributaries, it is unnecessary to make more than passing reference. We shall visit them in later chapters and then have occasion to mention the routes which have served since ancient times as arteries for the trade and cultural relations which link China and the Tarim basin with the Oxus region and thence with India.

If we follow eastward the routes just referred to, we reach through tortuous arid gorges the western margin of the huge trough appropriately known as the Tarim basin. Before we proceed to visit the great drift-sand desert of the Taklamakan which fills most of it, we may pass in rapid strides along the big mountain chains enclosing this basin; for were it not for the water which their glaciers send down into it and which the Tarim river gathers before it gets dried up in the Lop-nor marshes, the whole of this vast area would be barren of life.

On the southern flank of the basin there extends in an unbroken line the mighty mountain rampart of the K'un-lun. Starting from the side of the Pamirs, we find its ranges buttressing, as it were, in several high parallel ranges the great glacier-clad watershed which the Kara-koram forms toward the drainage of the Indus. Through these ranges have cut their way the Yarkand river and its tributaries, the main feeders of the Tarim. What grazing is to be found high up at the heads of their valleys is of the scantiest kind and barely suffices for the flocks of a few scattered Kirghiz camps. The routes which lead up these valleys all converge upon the Kara-koram pass. At an elevation of some 18,200 feet above sea level, this pass is the only practicable line of communication to give access to Ladak and the uppermost Indus valley. But we have no record of its use in ancient times.

Farther to the east the K'un-lun raises a practically impenetrable barrier to traffic of any sort. The two rivers which water the Khotan oasis, the Kara-kash and Yurung-kash, break indeed through the northernmost main range, which maintains from here onward a crest line of close on 20,000 feet for a distance of at least three hundred miles, but their passage lies largely through extremely deep-cut and for the most part quite inaccessible gorges. Even where less confined ground can be gained at the head of their valleys, the extremely rugged character of the northern slopes of the glacier-clad range would suffice to close the way to any but expert mountaineers. But quite as great a barrier is represented by the utter want of resources on the drainageless Tibetan plateaux, 15,000 to 16,000 feet in height on the average, which adjoin and extend for many marches to the south. They are bare of grazing, fuel and, in many places, even of drinkable water.

Very different in character and yet almost as forbidding and barren is the aspect which the outer slopes of the K'un-lun present above the Khotan section of the basin. Here by the side of wide loess-covered peneplains we find areas where a perfect maze of steeply serrated ridges and deep-cut gorges has been produced by erosion. Such a condition can only be due to prolonged water action, and yet only on rare occasions do these barren slopes, unprotected by vegetation, receive any heavy fall of rain or snow.

To the east of the glacier-girt high ground where the sources of the Yurung-kash river take their rise, the chain which overlooks the Tarim basin takes for over four hundred miles a trend to the northeast. Throughout the whole length of the chain the foot of its northern slopes is formed by a glacis of piedmont gravel, attaining in parts a width of forty miles and more, and everywhere utterly barren.

To the south of the point where the terminal course of the Tarim turns and dies away in the marshes of Lop-nor, the mountain rampart which hedges in the great basin resumes an easterly bearing and sinks to a lower level. Lhasa is over seven hundred miles away from the little oasis of Charkhlik, which corresponds to the ancient Shan-shan of the Chinese and is now practically the only permanent settlement in this part of the Tarim basin. Yet there is reason to believe that routes descending here had at times served for Tibetan invasions from the south and also for nomadic inroads. Such life-giving moisture as the high valleys and plateaux toward Tibet and Tsaidam may receive, whether from monsoon currents passing across India or from the side of the Pacific Ocean, certainly does not penetrate to the extremity of the Tarim basin north of this part of the encircling range. A wide and utterly barren glacis, in parts of bare gravel, elsewhere overlain by big ridges of drift sand, stretches down at this point to that huge waste of hard salt crust which marks the dried-up bed of the ancient Lop sea. To this we shall have occasion to return later.

Beyond the eastern extremity of the Tarim basin the K'un-lun imperceptibly merges in the Nan-shan, the "Southern Mountains" of the Chinese. In its western portion, where the Nan-shan overlooks the Su-lo-ho trough for over two hundred miles, its northern slopes with their aridity and far-advanced erosion closely reproduce physical features already familiar to us from the K'un-lun.

But, on passing east of the Su-lo-ho trough into the central portion of the Nan-shan, evidence of a climate far moister manifests itself to an increasingly striking degree. This symptom indicates approach to the vicinity of the Pacific drainage area, which along the Huang-ho or Yellow river extends to the adjoining parts of the Kansu province and to the northeastern uplands of Tibet. Favored by the moisture which air currents from the Pacific Ocean carry up at different seasons of the year, abundant vegetation clothes the valleys from the westernmost limits of the drainage of the Su-chou river. To eyes accustomed to the barrenness of the K'un-lun it is an impressive experience to see the excellent summer grazing offered by the open valleys at the headwaters of the Su-chou and the Kan-chou rivers, notwithstanding the great elevation, in parts well over 11,000 feet. Still farther to the southeast increasing snow and rainfall permits of plentiful forest growth in the valleys drained by the Kan-chou river in the northernmost range of the Nan-shan.

We have now arrived close to the watershed of the region which the Huang-ho drains into the Pacific Ocean, and thus to the eastward border of that wide belt of innermost Asia with which we are dealing. This is strikingly brought home to us by the fact that from the edge of the Kan-chou oasis eastward climatic conditions along the fertile foot of the Nan-shan permit of cultivation being carried on without irrigation and dependent on rain and snowfall only. But none of this moisture reaches the ocean.

From here we must turn back in order to complete our circuit of the mountains. Westward of the Etsin-gol which carries the waters from the Nan-shan into a drainageless basin there extend the barren ranges and plateaux of the Pei-shan (the "Northern Mountains"). These merge into the equally arid hill chains known by the Turki name of Kuruk-tagh, the "Dry Mountains." These again continue the great belt of ground incapable of settled life or even nomadic occupation for another four hundred miles or so westward. Pei-shan and

Kuruk-tagh in conjunction form a barrier, nowhere from north to south less than two hundred miles wide, between the nearest places where cultivation is nowadays possible.

In the eastern and western portions of this "Gobi," brackish wells or springs can be found at rare intervals in the depressions between the greatly decayed ranges, and thus render a crossing there practicable for small parties at a time. Violent winds, mainly from the northeast and icy even late in the spring, blow across this whole region at frequent intervals and cause its crossing to be dreaded by wayfarers.

It is to the east of the Hami oasis that begins the great mountain chain of the T'ien-shan, the "Celestial Mountains," which extends unbroken westward far beyond the Tarim basin and throughout forms its northern rampart. It varies considerably in height and width, but everywhere constitutes a strongly marked dividing line, in climate and all that depends upon it, between that great basin and the regions which adjoin it northward. These comprise the wide plateaux of Dzungaria stretching north as far as southernmost Siberia as well as great fertile valleys. Owing to a distinctly moister climate, grazing is to be found there both in plains and valleys, and this has at all times attracted waves of nomadic nations, from the Huns to the Turks and Mongols.

Notwithstanding the continuity of its rampart, the T'ien-shan range offers opportunities to nomadic neighbors on the north for plundering inroads upon the oases and trade routes in the south. These opportunities are due to the mountain rampart being pierced at intervals by passes practicable during a considerable portion of the year for mounted men and transport.

Thus to the southwest of the Turfan depression there descends from the grazing plateaux of Yulduz the wide valley of Kara-shahr, which has at all times served as an open gate for nomadic inroads into the northeastern corner of the Tarim basin. Farther to the west, we note that under corresponding conditions the great oases of Kucha and Kashgar are equally liable to attack across the T'ien-shan.

From the mountain barriers which enclose the Tarim basin we may now turn to a summary survey of the basin itself. Of its vast dimensions an adequate idea may be gained from the fact that from west to east it stretches over a direct distance of some nine hundred miles. Its greatest width is fully 330 miles. Vast as these dimensions are, the uniformity of the prevailing conditions makes it easy to take a bird's-eye view of the several zones represented in this basin and to describe them briefly. By far the greatest among them comprises the huge central desert of bare sand dunes which is popularly known as the Taklamakan.

Not one of the numerous rivers descending from the snowy K'un-lun succeeds in making its way through the Taklamakan, except the Khotan river, and that too only during a few summer months. All the rest are lost in this "sea of sand" at a greater or lesser distance from the line occupied by the oases or the areas of desert vegetation which they adjoin. But within historical times a number of these terminal river courses carried their water considerably farther north. This is conclusively proved by the ancient sites which I explored in the Taklamakan.

These explorations have familiarized me with the uniformity which prevails in the character of this huge desert, probably the most formidable of all the dune-covered wastes of this globe. Whether the traveler enters it from the edge of cultivated ground in the oases or from jungle belts along the river beds, he first passes through a zone with desert vegetation, mostly in the shape of tamarisks, wild poplars, or reeds, surviving amidst low drift sand. A very peculiar and interesting feature of this zone consists of "tamarisk cones," hillocks of conical form and often closely packed together. The slow but constant accumulation of drift sand around tamarisk growth, at first quite low, has in the course of centuries built them up to heights reaching fifty feet or more. Farther out in the Taklamakan there emerge from the dunes only shriveled and bleached trunks of trees, dead for ages, or sand cones with tamarisk growth from which life has departed even at their top. These too finally disappear among utterly bare accumulations of sand, in places heaped up into ridges rising three hundred feet or more (Fig. 2).

It is erosion by the winds which produces the material composing these dunes, all fine disintegrated clay and in itself perfectly fertile. The winds which during a considerable portion of the year blow with great force across the desert basin, especially from the northeast, constantly abrade the surface of the soft clayey soil, wherever there is a bare surface of ground not actually covered by dunes or protected by desert vegetation. At ancient sites in the desert all ruins of dwellings or even the remains of ancient orchards and arbors often occupy islandlike terraces rising high above the wind-eroded bare ground close by. The debris of walls or the fallen trunks of trees had here protected the soil from erosion and thus preserved the original level, while the ground around was being scooped out around them lower and lower.

The possibility of permanent human occupation within the Tarim basin is confined to the small zone of oases left between the Taklamakan and the encircling mountain ranges. Owing to extreme aridity, cultivation here wholly depends on canal irrigation. The same deficiency of atmospheric moisture restricts grazing to the narrow belts of riverine jungle. This explains why the great migrating tribes of Wusun, Sakas, Yüeh-chih, Huns, Turks, Mongols and the rest, who during the last 2000 years were in successive possession of the northern slopes of the T'ien-shan, were always ready to raid or to make tributary the oases of the Tarim basin, but never crossed the range to occupy it permanently. To them the laborious and narrowly circumscribed life of the cultivator in these irrigated oases could offer but little attraction as long as there were big open grazing grounds to hold or to conquer.

The cultivated ground within the Tarim basin could

never have borne more than an extremely slight proportion to the extent of absolute desert it comprises. As the map shows, the green oases of the basin appear like mere specks and splashes on the big canvas of yellow and light brown which marks the desert. The aridity of the climate accounts for the striking uniformity in physical conditions which prevails throughout these oases. Whatever their position or size, the traveler sees everywhere the same fields of wheat, maize or cotton slightly terraced for irrigation; the same winding lanes lined with white poplars and willows; the same little arbors or orchards inviting him with their shade and their plentiful produce of European fruits.

Within the Tarim basin there still remains for us to visit the terminal depression of Lop at its eastern end. The central and geographically most striking feature of this depression is the great salt-encrusted sea bed which our surveys have proved to extend for fully 160 miles from southwest to northeast with a maximum width of some ninety miles. This marks the position of a prehistoric salt sea which was fed by the drainage of the Tarim basin when the climate of Central Asia was moister. It already showed the same forbidding aspects as at present when the Chinese first became acquainted with it more than 2000 years ago. But in the now equally lifeless ground which adjoins this dried-up sea on the northwest there can still be traced, in an area of bare clay overrun by light drift sand and now undergoing excessive wind erosion, a series of well-marked dry river beds. Our surveys have proved that they belong to an ancient delta formed by the dried-up Kuruk-darya, the "Dry River." This during the first centuries before and after Christ carried the waters of the Konche river, which drains the Kara-shahr valley, together with water from the Tarim, to the then partially occupied territory of ancient Lou-lan. A remarkable hydrographical change has, during the last few years, brought back these waters again to a considerable portion of the desolate waste.

Abundant archeological evidence brought to light at various ruined sites of Lou-lan since Dr. Hedin first discovered one of them makes it certain that the waters from the Kuruk-darya reached here an ancient terminal oasis up to the beginning of the fourth century A.D. Through this once habitable ground, and across the difficult salt-encrusted expanse of the dried-up sea beyond it (Fig. 3), there had passed the earliest Chinese route leading from the Su-lo-ho trough into the Tarim basin. In a later chapter I shall describe the truly forbidding aspect of this now utterly lifeless ground, and shall give some account of the difficult explorations by which I was able to track the vestiges of the ancient route across this formidable desert.

This ancient Chinese route crossed the salt-encrusted sea bed east of Lou-lan and then turned up a valleylike depression to the northeast. This takes us across a dry lake bed surrounded by a maze of fantastically eroded clay terraces to the lowest portion of the basin of the Su-lo-ho, which contains this river's delta and its present terminal marshes.

Uninhabited except for the oasis of Tun-huang and a few minor oases, the Su-lo-ho basin need not detain us long; for notwithstanding its extent of some 220 miles from east to west, its natural features are remarkably uniform, as was its role throughout history. It derives its importance from the fact that, flanked by high mountains in the south and desert wastes in the north, it forms a natural "corridor" leading from northwestern China into Central Asia. In a subsequent chapter I shall describe how I discovered and explored the ruins of the ancient Chinese *Limes* or fortified border line intended to protect this corridor.

Beyond the Su-lo-ho basin at the famous Chia-yü-kuan gate of the medieval "Great Wall" of China we reach the easternmost of the undrained areas with which we are concerned. It extends from the headwaters of the Kan-chou river and the Pacific watershed in the southeast to the marshy lake beds in which terminates the Etsin-gol, which carries the united waters of the rivers of Su-chou and Kan-chou.

As we descend through the northernmost Nan-shan range by valleys which moisture derived from the Pacific has clothed with plentiful forest, we come to a broad belt of fertile alluvial fans stretching along the foot of the range at an elevation of from about 5000 to 6500 feet. Owing to its favorable physical features, this belt was destined in history to become a very important "land of passage" between China and Central Asia.

CHAPTER II

Chinese Expansion into Central Asia and the Contact of Civilizations

WITH THE PASSAGE LAND north of the Nan-shan to which the preceding chapter has brought us, we have completed our survey of the vast region which for close on a thousand years served as the principal scene for that important historical process, the early interpenetration of Far Eastern, Indian and Western civilizations. It is from this side of the area surveyed that we may start the rapid review of the chief phases in the political history of the whole region which is needed for the proper appreciation of that great process. Fortunately we can gather our knowledge of the earliest of these phases from a very reliable and precise source, the Chinese dynastic Annals.

Efforts continued for centuries to protect the Empire from those ever threatening neighbors, the Huns, on the side of Mongolia, led to the conquest, under the great Emperor Wu-ti (140-87 B.C.) of the Han dynasty, of the northern slopes of the Nan-shan. The story may be said to start with the adventurous Central-Asian mission of Chang Ch'ien. About 138 B.C. the Emperor Wu-ti dispatched that young officer to the tribe of the Great Yüeh-chih who later became the Indo-Scythian rulers of northwestern India. The object was to gain their aid against those hereditary foes of China, the Hsiung-nu, destined to appear later as the Huns in European history. These powerful nomad tribes, united in a great confederacy, had for centuries from the side of Mongolia harried the northern marches of the Empire. The Yüeh-chih, whom they had ousted some twenty years earlier from their old seats along the northern foot of the Nan-shan, had migrated far away to the west and established a new kingdom on the Oxus in what until quite recently was Bukharan territory. When Chang Ch'ien, after many trials and difficulties, including a ten years' captivity among the Huns, at last reached the Yüeh-chih, they refused to turn back and seek revenge on the Huns. But although the mission entrusted to Chang Ch'ien thus failed in its direct aim, it was nevertheless destined to open a new epoch in the economical and political relations of China with the world outside its own civilization.

Chang Ch'ien, after a total absence of thirteen years, succeeded in regaining China by way of the Tarim basin, with only one companion surviving out of the hundred with whom he had started. He brought back definite information about the Central-Asian countries he had passed through, including in the west the rich territories corresponding to the present Farghana, Samarkand, Bukhara and Balkh, as well as about the still more distant regions of Persia and India. It was he who first revealed to the Chinese the existence of great civilized populations beyond the ring of barbarous tribes by whom all their land frontiers were hemmed in. The great importance of securing access to these populations for the sake of trade and military aid was quickly realized by the Emperor Wu-ti, and the state of internal consolidation which the reign of this capable and energetic monarch assured, singularly favored expansion.

The avowed aim of this policy at the outset was to open the road leading through the Tarim basin to the large territories in the Oxus region. The hold of the Huns on the northern slopes of the Nan-shan blocked access to this, Nature's true highway from China to the settled lands of Western Asia. So it was against them that the Chinese effort was turned. And here the fortune of war soon rewarded the Emperor Wu-ti's persistent endeavors. After a series of successful campaigns the territories which correspond to the present Liang-chou and Kan-chou were in 121 B.C. freed from Hun domination. Then the Huns were finally forced to retreat to the north of the desert, and by 115 B.C. control of the newly secured border was united in the command of Chiu-chuan or Su-chou.

This military advance along the great highway toward Central Asia was accompanied by a rapid organization of Chinese political missions to the different states both within the Tarim basin and beyond, even as far as Bactria and Persia. These were meant to impress the states with the power of China and its industrial wealth. There can be no doubt that among the Chinese industrial products carried by these missions there prominently figured those fine silk stuffs which then began to reach the Mediterranean through Parthia and Syria, and soon carried the fame of the "silk-weaving Seres," *i.e.* the Chinese, to the great centers of Greek and Roman civilization. It is easy to realize the economic importance of this silk trade for China, since for centuries the production of silk remained its jealously guarded monopoly.

The pioneer of China's expansion westward, fittingly honored by the Emperor with high rank as "the Great Traveler," died about a year after his return from the first of those missions in 115 B.C. But the intercourse of which he had been the pioneer rapidly developed and increased, until embassies attended by several hundred men, we are told, "followed upon one another's heels all along the route."

In the interest of the development of China's internal resources it was very important to use the newly opened route for direct access to fresh markets for China's industrial products, and in particular for the most valuable among them, its silk textiles. There is in fact ample evidence in the Chinese records to show that the great westward move initiated by the Emperor Wu-ti was meant to serve economic considerations connected with trade quite as much as political aims. But even if the wish to obtain allies against the dreaded Huns in warlike tribes like the Yüeh-chih and Wu-sun north of the T'ien-shan had been absent, troubles attending the newly established intercourse with the West would soon have forced upon the Chinese government political and military expansion in the same direction. It did not take many years before Chinese missions on their way through the Tarim basin experienced serious trouble from the chiefs and inhabitants of petty territories which cut off their food supplies, obviously with a view to blackmail, or else directly attacked them. Worse still, the power of the Huns to the north of the T'ien-shan remained unbroken, and small parties of these formidable horsemen would at times "intercept west-bound envoys," where they passed through Lou-lan or Lop.

Thus the need for military protection beyond the newly conquered territory along the northern foot of the Nan-shan very soon asserted itself. Nor did it find the Chinese unprepared. Immediately after the first conquest of that great natural "corridor," they had started to establish military colonies along it and to construct a wall extending to the west the defensive border line of the "Great Wall" which Shih Huang-ti, the predecessor of the Han dynasty, had created for protection against Hun inroads.

There can be no doubt that this western extension of the earlier "Great Wall" was primarily intended to protect the newly opened highway into Central Asia. But, while the "Great Wall" of Shih Huang-ti appears to have borne that purely defensive character which we are accustomed to asso-

ciate with the familiar "Chinese Wall" of late medieval construction, the Emperor Wu-ti's wall was meant to serve as
the instrument of a "forward policy" conceived on a big scale.
The analogy it thus offers to the earlier *Limes* systems on the
borders of the Roman Empire is most striking. In a later chapter I shall describe the very interesting remains of this ancient
Chinese *Limes* which I was able to trace and explore over a
total distance of not far from four hundred miles.

Events moved rapidly enough. As so often in history,
the aims of peaceful penetration in the interest of trade and
civilized intercourse called before long for support by political influence and military action. It was the not unusual case
of the flag having to protect the trade. From the outset the
Chinese policy of Central-Asian expansion appears to have
fixed its hopes for profitable trade far more upon the large
and fertile territories in what is now Russian Turkistan than
upon the scattered and comparatively small oases of the Tarim basin. But the distances separating these western territories of Central Asia from China were great. Relying upon the
protection thus afforded, the people of Farghana after a time
treated the Chinese missions with scant regard. In the end
they robbed and killed some imperial envoys who had been
sent to secure a far-famed local breed of horses for their master.

Chinese prestige required prompt punishment of such an
offense, so a punitive expedition was dispatched in 104 B.C.
against Farghana. It ended in complete failure. The large
force sent became exhausted by the difficulties of the route
followed across the "Salt Marsh," *i.e.* the dried-up salt sea bed
of Lop (Fig. 3), and by the want of supplies beyond, long
before its remnant reached Farghana. There it was utterly
routed while besieging a town. When in its retreat it regained
Tun-huang, we are told "only one or two out of every ten
soldiers were left." To repair so signal a defeat, all the resources of the Empire were strained. By 102 B.C. the Chinese

general Li Kuang-li was enabled to set out once more from Tun-huang with a fresh army of 60,000 men supported by a huge train and commissariat.

This time the Chinese power of intelligent organization triumphed over all the difficulties of Nature. The force of 30,000 men with which the Chinese general reached the capital of Farghana sufficed to secure victory and the submission of its people. The prestige of China was so strengthened by this great feat that all the small states of the Tarim basin accepted imperial sovereignty. Henceforth Chinese control of the great natural highways, provided by the strings of oases in the Tarim basin, remained practically unbroken for more than a century, until internal disorder in China brought about the downfall of the former Han dynasty soon after the commencement of our era.

This prolonged maintenance of Chinese control was due far more to the successful diplomacy of the Empire's political representatives in these territories, and to prestige based on China's superior civilization, than to the force of arms. From the references of classical authors to the famous "Seric fabrics," *i.e.* silks, we know that these products of Chinese industrial skill then traveled westward in an unbroken flow. In return, China must then have received, particularly from Eastern Iran, many of the articles of foreign origin, both natural and manufactured, the introduction of which from the West is distinctly traceable in Chinese literary records.

It is to the same period of the "open road" through Central Asia that we may safely attribute the initial stages of that close mingling of cultural influences from China, Persia and India which archeological explorations at ancient sites of the Tarim basin have so clearly revealed as the characteristic feature of the civilization which prevailed throughout that region during the pre-Mohammedan epoch. It is true that the earliest relics of that civilization as yet brought to light there do not reach back so far. But there is every reason to believe that the people who cultivated the oases of the Tarim basin at the time when that great highway between China and the West was first opened were of the same race and speech as those whose documents and literary remains, written chiefly in a variety of Indo-European languages, we have recovered from ruins abandoned from the third century A.D. onward.

In that exceptionally arid region, climatic conditions would allow comparatively large communities to exist only on the basis of a highly organized system of irrigation. Such a settled population dependent on an orderly regime was specially suited for the absorption and transmission of cultural influences coming both from the Far East and the West. Geography in other respects, too, seems to have singularly prepared the Tarim basin for this its chief historical role. By denying grazing grounds to the vast basin between K'un-lun and T'ien-shan, Nature had protected it against ever becoming the scene of great migratory movements and of such upheavals as are bound to accompany them.

The Huns in the north still remained dangerous neighbors, blocking the route along the northern foot of the T'ien-shan range. But by 60 B.C. the Chinese put themselves in possession also of the outlying small basin of Turfan, containing a well-cultivated tract south of the eastern T'ien-shan, and thereby secured an important flank protection for the great trade route leading through the oases north of the Taklamakan.

The alternative line of communication along the southern rim of the basin, past Charchan and Khotan, was effectively protected from the danger of nomadic aggression by the mighty barrier of the K'un-lun, and still more, perhaps, by the utter barrenness of the high Tibetan plateaux which adjoin it. Not until some eight centuries later, when Tibet had risen from a congeries of barbarous tribes into a centralized state of military power, did Eastern Turkistan experience invasion from that side.

It is necessary to keep well in view the exceptional importance and advantages which the Tarim basin possessed for the Chinese as a safe line of passage for trade intercourse and political expansion westward, if we are to understand the reasons which induced them to face and overcome the forbidding natural difficulties which beset access to it through the Lop desert. The explorations carried on during my winter campaigns of 1907 and 1914 enabled me to trace the route used for Wu-ti's enterprises over the formidable wastes of sand, bare gravel and salt which it crossed. In Chapters VIII, IX I shall give an account of these explorations and describe in some detail the interesting discoveries which attended them on that truly forbidding ground.

The intercourse thus established through Central Asia suffered its first interruption about the beginning of our era through the rapid decay of internal order which took place in China during the short-lived reigns of the last two emperors of the Former Han dynasty (6 B.C.-A.D. 5). With the consequent weakening of Chinese control in the Tarim basin, "the principalities of the Western countries," we are told in Later Han Annals, "broke up and formed fifty-five territories." For some sixty years the Tarim basin was abandoned to the Huns until at last the need of effective protection of its northwestern borders from Hun raids forced the Chinese Empire again to start upon a "forward policy" in Central Asia.

The first move made in A.D. 73 under the Emperor Ming was aimed directly at the Huns by the taking of Hami. This strategically very important oasis was the key to that "route of the north" which passed along the foot of the eastern T'ien-shan and through the Turfan depression. It was destined by Nature to serve as the easiest road into the Tarim basin, provided it could be protected against nomadic attacks from across the T'ien-shan. But the first Chinese effort failed, and it was not until thirteen years later that Hami was reoccupied by the Chinese.

But meanwhile the Tarim basin had become the scene of events which in the end placed the Empire once again in undisputed possession of that great passage land. By a series of remarkable exploits the famous Pan Ch'ao, the greatest of the soldier-statesmen who ever served China's Central-Asian policy, succeeded in re-establishing effective imperial authority throughout the Tarim basin. Starting by the old desert route from the side of Lop, he gradually gained mastery over the chiefs of Khotan, Yarkand and Kashgar, not so much by the force of arms as by bold bluff and skillful diplomacy. Pan Ch'ao's maxim, as stated by him in a very interesting memorial to the Emperor, "was to use the barbarians for attacking the barbarians."

Chinese political influence was, in consequence of Pan Ch'ao's triumphs, extended westward even beyond the Pamirs. Diplomatic relations were established with the Parthians and direct contact sought with distant Ta-ts'in, or Syria, by means of a mission which A.D. 97 appears to have reached the sea in the Persian Gulf. By A.D. 102, when Pan Ch'ao, grown old and laden with imperial honors, returned to the distant capital soon to end his days there, Chinese prestige and power in Central Asia may be said to have reached its culminating point. It is just about this time that we may assume *Scythia extra Imaon*, or the Tarim basin, to have been traversed by the trade agents of that Macedonian merchant, Maës Titianus, whose reports enabled Marinus of Tyre and through him Ptolemy, the Alexandrian geographer, to furnish us with information on the route followed by the caravans which brought to the West the silk of far-off Serikê, the land of the Seres, *i.e.* China.

But Hun inroads and local revolts soon began to change the conditions favorable to peaceful intercourse. Imperial prestige gradually decayed in the Western Regions during the century of increasing internal weakness which preceded the final downfall of the dynasty, A.D. 220, while the silk trade to the Roman Empire took more and more to the sea route, which by then had been opened through the Indian Ocean and the Red Sea.

The epoch of the "Three Kingdoms" which followed this event saw China divided between rival dynasties. Effective Chinese control over the whole of the Tarim basin was not likely to be maintained in these troubled times. Yet there is evidence that those territories still continued to be open to trade and cultural influences both from the East and the West. The evidence I allude to is fortunately supplied by the abundant remains of two very interesting ruined sites I have been able to explore. I mean the ancient settlement brought to light in the desert sands beyond the termination of the Niya river, and the ruins at and around the ancient Chinese station of Loulan. In Chapters v, vi, viii I shall have occasion to deal at some length with the manifold interesting aspects of the conditions of life and administration which the abundant discoveries made there have revealed. At both sites we have conclusive evidence that occupation continued until about the close of the third century of our era and then completely ceased.

At the Niya site it is particularly easy to reconstruct the conditions of life once led there. The careful construction of the houses once tenanted by local officials or landholders (Fig. 5), remains of well-made household furniture and implements, objects of decorative art in the shape of fine wood carvings, etc., all attest a highly developed state of civilization. The products of local industrial arts and crafts clearly show the prevalence of a strong Hellenistic influence as transmitted from Eastern Iran and the northwestern borders of India.

Finds of objects of Buddhist worship make it quite certain that Buddhism had by that time already acquired a predominant position in the religious and intellectual life of the indigenous population of the Tarim basin. This strong influence of Indian culture is very strikingly reflected also in the mass of written records recovered in the ruined dwellings and the refuse heaps adjoining. At the Niya site I found by the hundred wooden documents comprising correspondence, mainly official, contracts, accounts, miscellaneous memoranda and the like, all written in that Sanskritic language and Kharoshthi script which during the first centuries before and after Christ were used on the Indian northwest frontier and in the adjacent portions of Afghanistan.

We are able to reconstruct almost as clearly the physical aspects of the life once witnessed by these sites. Everything in the orchards and arbors dead for sixteen centuries but still clearly recognizable; in the fences; in the materials used for buildings, etc., distinctly point to conditions of cultivation and local climate having been essentially the same as those now observed in oases of the Tarim basin similarly situated and still occupied.

Just as in the present terminal oases of the Tarim basin, so cultivation at those sites must have been entirely dependent on irrigation. Had not conditions of extreme aridity already prevailed in ancient times, it would be impossible to account for the survival in almost perfect preservation of a multitude of objects, very perishable by nature, in places so exposed as mere refuse heaps outside houses. Exactly corresponding observations are furnished by what archeological explorations at other ancient sites of the Tarim basin have taught us. The climatic conditions of the periods immediately preceding abandonment must have been practically as arid as they have been since and are now.

This uniform and important fact has a direct bearing upon an important and much-discussed geographical question usually spoken of as that of "desiccation." It is too large to be more than touched upon here. If the climatic conditions were sixteen centuries ago quite as dry as they are now, how is it to be explained that cultivation at those two ancient sites and at others also has since their abandonment become wholly impossible?

I believe that the explanation as far as the Tarim basin is

concerned is supplied by the diminished volume of the rivers upon which cultivation is wholly dependent. The most likely cause of this diminution may be sought in the shrinkage of the glaciers on the high ranges which mainly feed those rivers. The shrinkage itself can well be accounted for by assuming, as has been suggested by Sir Sidney Burrard and Professor Von Ficker, that those glaciers comprise great reserves of ice which have been left behind by the last glacial period and have since been undergoing slow but more or less continuous reduction through milder climatic conditions. This process of using up what might be called "fossil ice" would suffice to explain shrinkage in the sources of irrigation during historical times without the climate of the basin as a whole having undergone any appreciable change.

But let us now resume, however rapidly, our survey of the part which the Tarim basin by its geographical function as a great "corridor" played in later phases of Central-Asian history. For more than three centuries our knowledge of this history is very meager indeed; for, with the disappearance of Chinese political control, our chief sources of trustworthy historical information about the "Western Regions" for the most part dry up. While China itself was divided between rival dynasties, several of them of foreign origin, the Huns in the course of the fourth century had started westward on the great move which ultimately led them to water their horses on the Danube, Rhine and Po. After an interval the whole of the Tarim basin, together with vast territories to the north and west, passed for about a century under the domination of a branch of the Huns known in Western Asia as the Hephthalites or White Huns.

Neither this domination from outside nor the period of contested sovereignty within, which preceded it, appears to have seriously affected the firm footing which Chinese civilization had acquired in the oases or to have interfered with the steady flow in the opposite direction of Buddhist doctrine and literary as well as art influences from easternmost Iran and India. The closeness of the religious and intellectual relations thus established is reflected in the accounts left to us of the journeys of Chinese Buddhist pilgrims, who at this period made their way right through Central Asia to the sacred places of Buddhism in distant India.

By the middle of the sixth century a fresh wave in the stream of nomadic migration which was moving westward along the T'ien-shan, slowly at one time, more rapidly at another, had put the great confederation of Turkish tribes, known to the Chinese as the Western Turks, in ascendancy over the vast Central-Asian region previously dominated by the White Huns. Like their allies, the Northern Turks, they were in the east troublesome neighbors to the Chinese Empire, which by A.D. 589 had after nearly three centuries of division become once more united.

The gradual consolidation of Chinese power which continued after the accession of the great T'ang dynasty by A.D. 618 was at first accompanied by a policy of rigid seclusion on the northwestern marches. But this was soon to give way to a "forward policy" on a grand scale which for over a century made Chinese imperial power under the T'ang dynasty expand over wider regions of Central Asia than it had ever before. The power of the Western Turks was already weakened by tribal dissensions which Chinese diplomacy skillfully fostered. First Hami and subsequently Turfan were wrested from Turkish supremacy. By A.D. 660 it was finally shattered by the Emperor Kao-tsung's forces. China thus succeeded to the Western Turks' claim over a vast dominion extending from the Altai Mountains to beyond the Hindukush.

But the fact of China now claiming succession to the wide dominions once held by the Western Turks was bound to prove in time a source of trouble and weakness. The Chinese forces stationed in what were called "the Four Garrisons" had to guard not merely the oases of the Tarim basin but also territories to the north of the T'ien-shan. These offered attractive grazing grounds to nomads, and were hence constantly subject to being disturbed by restless Turkish tribes, such as are still hovering now between the Altai and T'ienshan. More serious still was the danger presented by aggression on the part of the Tibetans who were then rapidly growing into a new military power.

Toward the middle of the eighth century there was added to the pressure from the Tibetans in the south fresh danger in the west from the steady advance of Arab conquest in the Oxus basin. The Tibetans were endeavoring to join hands with the Arabs as common foes of China's Central-Asian supremacy. By pushing down the Indus valley and thence across the Hindukush territories which correspond to the present Gilgit and Yasin, they actually reached the uppermost Oxus valley. This junction threatened the Chinese position in the Tarim basin with being outflanked simultaneously both on the east and the west. The endeavor to avert this serious strategic risk led to a remarkable military expedition conducted A.D. 747 by the Chinese general Kao Hsien-chih right across the "Roof of the World," the Pamirs, and the ice-crowned Hindukush pass of the Darkot. In Chapters III, xx I shall give some details about this memorable Chinese enterprise. It stands out as a striking proof of Chinese capacity for overcoming by organization formidable geographical obstacles.

The prestige accruing to the Chinese arms from Kao Hsien-chih's expedition was deservedly great. But it did not save them from being signally worsted two years later. In a battle near Tashkent, Kao Hsien-chih was completely defeated by the Arabs and the revolted Turkish tribes, their allies. About A.D. 750 the Tibetans from the south secured mastery over Tun-huang and the adjoining tracts at the foot of the Nan-shan, and thus cut off the Tarim basin from all direct communication with the Chinese Empire. Yet the Chinese administrators and garrisons within the Tarim basin, notwithstanding their isolation, succeeded in holding out for another forty years—a heroic but obscure chapter in history.

The period of about four hundred years following the disappearance of T'ang rule is for the most part a dark one in the history of the Tarim basin. We know that Tibetan domination in that region did not outlast a century and also that Islam was spreading under the Turkish chiefs who acquired control over Kashgar and other oases in the western portion of the Tarim basin. From about the middle of the tenth century onward this led to the gradual overthrow of Buddhist doctrine and culture by force as well as by propaganda.

In the northeastern portion, however, and in the outlying territory of Turfan, Buddhism continued to flourish much longer, side by side with Manicheism and Nestorian Christianity, under the protection of Uighur chiefs. To the predominance of those chiefs and to the capacity shown elsewhere, too, by Turkish tribes to digest other racial elements from conquered populations more advanced in civilization we must attribute the fact that throughout the Tarim basin, Eastern Turkish is now, and has been for centuries, the only language spoken. Yet the population there still retains in the main the *Homo Alpinus* type, preserved in purity by the Iranian-speaking hillmen of the Pamir region, and represented also in Western Europe, and shows but slight admixture of true Turkish blood.

It is difficult to believe that under the political conditions prevailing from the ninth to the twelfth century the Tarim basin could have played so important a part as a channel for the interchange of cultural influences between Western Asia and China as before. It was a time when China, under the weakening rule of the T'ang and then later under the Sung dynasty, was obliged to maintain toward Central Asia a policy of passive defense if not of rigid seclusion.

The phenomenal rise of the Mongols under the great Chingiz Khan, another Napoleon, in the first quarter of the

thirteenth century brought about vast changes in political
conditions throughout Asia. By the time he died in Kansu,
A.D. 1227, his astonishing conquests had brought all countries
from the Black Sea to the Yellow river under direct control
of the Mongol "Great Khan." The operations continued by
his immediate successors ended some thirty years later in uniting the whole of China under the same Mongol dynasty which
by its several branches held sway over all Central Asia as far
as Persia, and over a great part of Eastern Europe as well.
The establishment of one sovereignty across the whole of
Asia again cleared the way for direct intercourse and trade
between China, the Near East and Europe.

For more than a century the trade routes to the north and
south of the T'ien-shan saw an undisturbed flow of traffic. The
accounts perserved to us of envoys, traders and travelers from
Europe then seeking far-off Cathay tell us a good deal of
those routes and of the ground which they crossed. None of
these accounts, in accuracy of detail and human interest, approach the immortal record of Marco Polo, the greatest of
medieval travelers.

The Mongol dominion over China which Marco Polo still
saw in its full greatness under the Emperor Kublai came to an
end through internal decay within a century of Kublai's accession. The Chinese dynasty of the Ming which replaced it was
content with safeguarding the northwestern borders in Kansu
against fresh Mongol inroads by a policy of strict seclusion
which stifled trade.

The use of the sea route to China, greatly developed by
the Arabs and becoming still more important after the first
Portuguese voyages to India, had deprived that ancient Central-Asian highway of its former value for Western trade. But
toward the close of the seventeenth century the growing
power of the Oirats, or Dzungars, Mongolian tribes established north of the T'ien-shan, forced a fresh advance into innermost Asia upon China after it had passed under the Man-

chu dynasty, then young and vigorous. But it was not until 1755 that expeditions organized by the great Manchu Emperor Ch'ien-lung finally brought the whole of the Tarim basin as well as Dzungaria north of it under direct Chinese administration. Once again, as under the Han and T'ang, a policy purely defensive in its origin had resulted in Chinese expansion over vast Central-Asian regions right up to the Pamirs and the Altai Mountains.

Chinese control of these regions has continued to the present day, in spite of the growing internal weakness of the Empire and the great upheaval caused by the Tungan or Chinese Mohammedan rebellion in the third quarter of the last century. The explanation lies in the fact that for the first time in history China's Central-Asian frontiers had become contiguous with those of a great civilized power, such as the Russian Empire was, capable of dominating the border populations and gradually restraining nomadic migrations. It was Russia's temporary occupation of Kulja and of the fertile Ili valley which facilitated the reconquest of the New Dominion in 1877 after the great Mohammedan rebellion had flung the Tarim basin for a decennium first into anarchy and later on into oppressive misrule under Yakub Beg, a usurper from Western Turkistan.

The strings of oases between the T'ien-shan and the K'un-lun no longer serve a great trade route. The brave, patient camels that carry what traffic there is as efficiently as in the times of Chang Ch'ien or Marco Polo have not yet been replaced by the rushing motor car or the bustling railway. The traditions of China's great past as a Central-Asian power still protect the peace of the region. Only the future can show whether they will suffice also hereafter to ward off those troubles and sufferings of which its less secluded neighbor, Russian Turkistan, has had abundant experience during recent years.

CHAPTER III

Across the Hindukush to the Pamirs and K'un-lun

AMONG ALL THE MANIFOLD influences in culture, religion, race and language for which throughout historical times, but in particular during the Buddhist period, Chinese Turkistan had formed the meeting place, none have left their impress more clearly upon the remains of its ruined sites than those received from the side of India. There is good reason to believe that in almost all instances these influences had directly or indirectly emanated from that extreme northwest of India which in the centuries just before the time of Christ and for several centuries after had been a chief seat of Buddhist worship and propaganda. This border region between India and easternmost Iran, where the successive conquerors of India in old times had invariably secured their first foothold, has ever since my youth had the greatest fascination for me.

It was a special boon of my life that in the glorious alpine scenery of Kashmir, which forms the most attractive part of that border region, I have, from the beginning of my Indian career forty-five years ago, found the base for scholarly researches and labors which has proved best adapted to my personal tastes and qualifications. There I have spent happy vacations over antiquarian tours connected with work on the history of Kashmir as recorded in its old Sanskrit Chronicle. Still longer periods I have passed in later years while encamped on a high mountain top 11,000 feet above the sea, hard at work on the results of the explorations which had carried me to far more distant parts in the north. This life for many years in peaceful alpine seclusion has made me look upon my tents in Kashmir as my only real home.

It was a consequence quite as much of the geographical position of Kashmir as of my attachment to this mountain land that it served as the starting point for all my Central-Asian expeditions. Of course, I took care to choose on each occasion a new route through those high ranges of the Hindukush, the westernmost portion of the Himalayas, which divide the valley of the Indus from the Pamirs and the southwestern confines of Chinese Turkistan. On all three journeys my passage through that westernmost portion of the Himalaya, so barren and yet so attractive in its grandeur, has left behind most impressive memories.

On the first expedition in 1900 my route from Kashmir to Chinese territory lay through Gilgit and Hunza, the latter a mountain tract offering the grandest scenery. Since a good mule track was engineered in the late eighties to Gilgit for the sake of maintaining there a small garrison of Imperial Service troops, and since the hill chiefships of Hunza and Nagar were by 1891 brought under effective British control, those valleys have become fairly well known. For the third journey in 1913 I was able to follow a line of approach which allowed me to visit as the first European two hill territories, Darel and Tangir, never explored before, and then to gain the Taghdumbash Pamir on the Chinese side over a succession of difficult snowy passes. But the route that appealed to me perhaps most by its varied geographical and ethnographic interest as well as by its historical associations was the one followed in 1906 at the start of my second expedition. So I may choose this route as the one on which to conduct the reader to the scenes of my Central-Asian explorations.

This route, ordinarily closed to the European traveler from political considerations, was to take me from the Peshawar district, at the northwestern extremity of the Indian administrative border, through the tribal areas of Swat and Dir into the Dard territory of Chitral. Thence the uppermost Oxus valley and the Afghan Pamirs could be gained across the Baroghil saddle. My lamented late chief, Colonel Sir Harold Deane, then Chief Commissioner of the North-West Frontier Province, had readily agreed to my project, while an auspicious political constellation had caused the late Amir Habibullah, King of Afghanistan, to grant me permission to cross a portion of his territory, otherwise jealously guarded, with a promptness I had not ventured to hope for.

The end of April, the earliest time for a start northward across the snowy passes, saw my small party duly mobilized. As on all my three expeditions, it included only Indian assistants. The Survey of India Department, from first to last ever ready to help me with my topographical tasks, had once more deputed with me one of its excellent native surveyors, Rai Ram Singh, who had accompanied me on my first journey. Then there was Naik Ram Singh, a corporal of K.G.O. First Bengal Sappers and Miners, who, thanks to sound technical training in his corps, was to prove a very capable "handyman." Jasvant Singh, a wiry little Rajput from Kangra who has acted as the surveyor's cook on all my journeys, was included in the party. I wished I had ever myself been able to benefit by the services of an Indian follower so reliable and so gentlemanly in manners. But unfortunately his high caste precluded ministrations in such a capacity to a European, so the posi-

tion of cook to my own person had to be filled by a Mohammedan Indian, about whose qualities, professional and personal, the less said the better.

I just mention these details, as my modest staff remained
much the same on my other expeditions also. Of course,
Turki pony and camelmen had to be added after I had
reached on Chinese soil the proper field of work and there
had to organize my own transport for explorations in the
desert. Among those local men, too, I secured a nucleus of
faithful followers. Considering all that our equipment had to
include in the way of scientific instruments, photographic ap-
paratus and glass plates, and a minimum of indispensable stores
likely to last for two and a half years, there was reason to
feel satisfaction that fourteen mules at the start sufficed for
the whole baggage.

By April 27 we set out from the fort which guards the
Malakand pass and with it the approach to the great valley of
Swat. Since the important military route to Chitral had been
first opened in 1895 the Malakand and the valley beyond had
been the scene of much hard tribal fighting. It was appropriate ground for the start on a journey which was to take me
not only to distant regions but also far back in the ages. For
those first stages led through trans-border valleys which more
than twenty-two centuries before had seen Alexander and his
Macedonians pass by to the conquest of the Indian marches.
There were to be seen, too, ruins of Buddhist shrines attesting
an ancient civilization that had vanished since the last of the
rulers who used to mint coins with Greek legends had ceased
to hold sway in the land and to protect with its prosperity also
its Buddhist sacred sites.

May 3 found us at the foot of the dreaded Lowarai pass,
over 10,200 feet high, and our crossing effected before daybreak through gorges deeply choked with the snows of avalanches, some quite recent, showed that the difficulties that
had been locally urged against an earlier passage northward

had scarcely been exaggerated. Over fifty stout tribesmen, starting in several detachments to lessen risks, were needed for the transport of our belongings. With this obstacle once safely taken, I could rapidly push up the deep-cut valley of Chitral to Fort Drosh, the northernmost outpost of British military power in India. Thence a long double march by the river, with the huge icy mass of the Tirichmir peak (about 25,000 feet high) in full view, carried me to the Chitral capital, a charming little oasis in this maze of steep barren mountains.

A few days of busy halt there enabled me to gather an ample anthropological harvest. In its autochthonous population Chitral holds an important branch of that "Dard" race which by its antiquity and ethnic and linguistic affinities may well claim special interest. Already in the days of the Achaemenian Empire its seat in these mountains was known to Ktesias. But the mountain fastnesses of Chitral have again and again offered shelter also to broken remnants of tribes unable to hold their own elsewhere. Thus I was able to take exact anthropological measurements alike of Iranian-speaking hillmen from across the Hindukush and of wild-looking refugees from Kafiristan. They were the last heathen remnant of those Kafir tribes who in their mountain fastnesses had held out for centuries against Afghan conquest and forcible conversion to Islam.

The survival of much ancient lore in customs, traditions, crafts, and even in domestic architecture, makes Chitral and the adjacent valleys a fascinating field for the student of early Indian civilization. But a variety of cogent practical reasons urged me onward to the Oxus and the "Roof of the World." Rapid as my marches up the Yarkhun river and through Mastuj had to be, I was able to trace and survey here an interesting series of early Buddhist rock carvings, sites of pre-Mohammedan forts, etc. It was curious to note how often local tradition connected the latter remains with dimly remembered periods of Chinese overlordship. The tenacity of such local

tradition in a secluded mountain region is significant in view
of that temporary extension of imperial Chinese power across
the Pamirs and even south of the Hindukush under the T'ang
dynasty to which I have briefly referred in the preceding
chapter.

It was on far more interesting ground that I was soon able
to verify the accuracy of those Chinese annalists who are our
chief guides in the early history and geography of Central
Asia. Years before I had studied their record, of course in
translation, which relates to the Chinese expedition under Kao
Hsien-chih, which, as already mentioned, in A.D. 747 successfully invaded the territories of Yasin and Gilgit then occupied by the Tibetans. I had then been induced to assume that
the route taken by the Chinese general and his force of 10,-
000, after starting from Kashgar and crossing the Pamirs, had
led over the Baroghil and Darkot passes. The former has to be
crossed on the way from the uppermost Oxus valley to the
headwaters of the Mastuj river, while the difficult glacier
pass of the Darkot forms the only practicable approach from
them to the Yasin valley.

I was naturally very anxious to trace on the actual ground
the route of this remarkable exploit; for it is the only recorded
instance of an organized force of comparatively large size
having ever surmounted the formidable natural barrier which
the Pamirs and Hindukush present to military operations.
How such a force could be maintained in that elevated mountain region bare of all resources is by itself a problem that
might baffle any modern general staff.

The ascent of the Darkot pass, about 15,400 feet above sea
level, undertaken with that object on May 17, proved a very
trying affair; for the miles of magnificent glacier over which
the ascent led from the north were still covered by deep
masses of snow. Only after nine hours of toil in deep snow,
concealing ice full of crevasses, did we reach the top of the
pass. Even my hardy Mastuji and Wakhi guides had held it to

be inaccessible at this early season. The observations gathered there and subsequently on our marches across the Baroghil saddle to the Oxus, fully bore out the exactness of every topographical detail furnished by the official account of that remarkable Chinese expedition.

As I stood on the glittering expanse of snow which marks the top of the pass and looked down the precipitous slopes which lead some 6000 feet below to the head of the Yasin valley, I could realize also why Kao Hsien-chih's braves when they had struggled up to this height at first refused to move farther. Their resourceful general had foreseen this awkward predicament and prudently arranged a clever ruse which induced his men to advance into the deep valley below. There their mere appearance after surmounting such a formidable barrier created a panic among the occupants of Yasin and promptly assured complete victory. But that as well as the stratagem employed by Kao Hsien-chih is "another story." I felt sorry at the time that there was no likelihood of a monument ever rising on the Darkot to the brave Chinese general. For, judged by the difficulties encountered and vanquished, this crossing of the Darkot and the Pamirs may well be held to surpass the great Alpine feats of commanders famous in European history, from Hannibal to Napoleon and Suvorov.

Two days later we crossed the main Hindukush range over its lowest depression, the Baroghil, about 12,400 feet above the sea. The abnormally heavy snowfall of that year had caused this otherwise easy saddle to be still covered with great masses of snow. Their condition proved so bad that but for the assistance sent from the Afghan side it would have been quite impossible to get our loads across.

It was a delightful sensation to find myself at the headwaters of the Oxus and thus brought nearer to that fascinating region of ancient Bactria lower down its course toward which my eyes had been eagerly turned since my early youth. Access to them, however, was barred for me—and through adverse political circumstances has, alas, remained so to this day. But for my progress eastward to the Chinese border on the Pamirs, every help which the scanty resources of poor Wakhan could provide was forthcoming under the Amir's orders.

At Sarhad, the highest village on the Oxus and a place of ancient occupation, the kindest reception awaited me. Colonel Shirindil Khan, commanding the Afghan frontier garrisons on the Oxus, had been sent up there with an imposing escort. This delightful old warrior had fought through all the troubled times preceding and following the accession of that remarkable Afghan ruler Amir Abdurrahman. He proved a fountainhead of interesting information about Badakhshan, its people and ancient remains. Was it not like being wafted back many centuries to listen to this gentlemanly old soldier who, in his younger days, when Abdurrahman was still new in the saddle, had helped to build up pyramids of rebel heads just to establish order, after Isa Khan's great rising, in the time-honored fashion of Central Asia? Gladly should I have tarried by the Oxus to absorb more of this living historical record. But regard for the hardships already undergone by my military hosts—and touching appeals from the peaceful Wakhi villagers, whose scanty resources were threatened with exhaustion by the escort's prolonged stay—urged me onward.

The first two marches up the Oxus were made very trying by the fact that the winter route along the river bed was already closed by the flooded river, while the high summer track was still impracticable owing to heavy masses of snow. The agility with which our Badakhshi ponies scrambled up and down precipitous rock slopes was wonderful to behold. Again and again only the incessant watchfulness of our escort saved the baggage from bounding down into the tossing gray waters of the river.

A bitterly cold day spent in the Kirghiz camp of Bozaigumbaz made it possible for me to visit the Little Pamir Lake. It lies at a height of 13,000 feet on one of those bleak and wide upland valleys which form so characteristic a feature of the "Roof of the World." What looked from this flat expanse like a modest hill range, still snow-covered, separated us from the Great Pamir Lake. Past this, I knew, lay the route which Marco Polo had followed on his journey through the wilderness of the "Roof of the World" and which he so graphically described. Hsüan-tsang, too, the great Buddhist pilgrim, whom I have grown accustomed to claim as my Chinese patron saint, had passed there when, centuries before, he came back from his long pious wanderings in India. Not until nine years later could I follow their track there and that of Captain Wood, who in 1838 was the first European since Marco Polo to visit the great lake.

It was along the uppermost course of the Ab-i-Panja, the main feeder of the Oxus, and on an ancient route, that we reached the foot of the Wakhjir pass. It is flanked by the glaciers where Lord Curzon had rightly placed the true source of the Oxus. A long day of toil saw us across the pass and so across the Afghan-Chinese border. We started by 3 A.M. Our Afghan escort remained camped behind at the foot of the pass to make sure that our Wakhi and Kirghiz transport would not desert halfway. Enormous masses of snow still covered the Wakhjir. In spite of a minimum temperature of 25° F. in the morning, their surface soon grew so soft that the powerful yaks of the Kirghiz had to be relieved of loads and left behind. Only fear of our Afghan protectors induced the Wakhis and Kirghiz to persevere in their efforts to carry our baggage across. Even so, it was midnight before the first point on the Chinese side was reached, where fuel and a dry spot made it possible to lie down and rest.

Here, at the head of the Taghdum-bash Pamir, I found myself once more at the point where in 1900 I had first set foot on Chinese soil. Down this high valley where, according to the saying of the Sarikolis who occupy its lower end, winter lasts ten months and summer two, Hsüan-tsang, the great Chinese pilgrim, had traveled when about A.D. 642 he returned from his many years' travels in India. I had traced his footprints before to many sacred Buddhist sites, and was now setting out to follow them so much farther to the east.

So I felt particularly gratified when I was able on my way down definitely to locate the ruined rock fastness where a curious ancient legend related by the pilgrims supposed an imperial princess, on her way from China to Persia, to have been once placed for safety. The fortifications which I traced on the top of an almost completely isolated rock spur rising above a gloomy defile of the Taghdum-bash river and known as Kiz-kurghan, "the Princess's Tower," must have been long in ruins already in Hsüan-tsang's time. But owing to the dryness of the climate, the walls defending this ancient place of refuge were still clearly traceable. Yet their material was mere sun-dried bricks with regular layers of juniper twigs embedded between them. Far away to the east we shall meet with the same ancient Chinese method of construction in the border wall of the Han *Limes* built in the second century B.C.

At Tash-kurghan, the headquarters of Sarikol, I revisited the site of the old capital of the territory. It is marked by crumbling stone walls enclosing a wide area around a tumbledown Chinese fort and what has now dwindled to a mere little village. Then I moved on to Kashgar northeastward by the direct route across the high Chichiklik plateau, close on 15,000 feet high. It led past the flank of the great Muz-tagh-ata massif and over a succession of minor passes. Rapid as my marches had to be—I covered the distance of close on 180 miles in six days, in spite of difficulties caused by melting snows and flooded streams—I traced unmistakable topographical and archeological evidence which showed that the route was the same which Hsüan-tsang, my Chinese patron saint, had followed more than twelve centuries before.

At Kashgar, under the hospitable roof of my old friend Mr. (now Sir) George Macartney, the representative of the

Indian Government, I was kept exceedingly busy by a host of practical tasks connected with the organization of my caravan, purchase of ponies and camels, etc. Mr. Macartney's kind offices, supported by his great personal influence, secured the goodwill of the provincial Chinese government for my explorations. But it was a service of quite as great importance when he recommended to me a qualified Chinese secretary in the person of Chiang Ssŭ-yeh. It had not been very difficult for me before to acquire a fair colloquial knowledge of Eastern Turki, the language spoken by the people of Chinese Turkistan. But for a serious study of Chinese, the language of its rulers and administrators, I regret I never had had needful leisure.

It was a piece of real good fortune which gave me in Chiang Ssŭ-yeh not merely an excellent teacher and secretary but a devoted helpmate ever ready to face hardships for the sake of my scientific interests. Once I had mastered the rudiments of conversational practice in Chinese (I regret to say, only in that troublesome Hunanese variety of the Mandarin), his ever-cheerful companionship was a great resource during long months of hard travel and exertion. With the true historical sense innate in every educated Chinese, he took to archeological work like a young duck to the water. Slight and yet wiry of body, he bore the privations and discomforts of desert life with a cheerful indifference quite surprising in a *literatus* accustomed all his life to work near the fleshpots of the Ya-mêns. Yet whenever travel brought us in the oases to the hospitable board of Chinese Mandarins, he could show keen appreciation of the good things there provided. Excellent *causeur* as he was, he would keep the whole company in good spirits by his humorous talk. How often have I longed all these years for my ever-alert and devoted Chinese comrade, now, alas, long departed to his ancestors!

When on June 23 I started from Kashgar, my goal was Khotan, a fortnight's journey by the caravan route to the southeast. That oasis must have all through historical times been just as now by far the most important area of cultivation to the south of the Taklamakan. Ancient sites abandoned to the sandy desert far away to the northeast of the present oasis had been the first to yield plentiful relics of the Buddhist period when on my first expedition I began explorations in this region. I knew this field for interesting archeological work to be by no means exhausted, and was hence anxious to start fresh and more extensive explorations. But owing to the great summer heat of the plains, work at sand-buried ruins in the desert could not be thought of until September. In the meantime I was free to turn my attention to geographical and other tasks.

For a few days I halted at the great and flourishing oasis of Yarkand, to which the Tarim river, where it debouches from the mountains, assures plentiful irrigation, and then proceeded to the foothills of the K'un-lun range to the south. Proofs and other literary tasks connected with the completion of *Ancient Khotan,* the detailed report on my first expedition, had, alas, to be brought along so far. While busily at work on their final disposal in the peaceful small oasis of Kök-yar, I found my hands full, too, with collecting anthropological measurements and data about the little-known people of Pakhpo. At first they fought terribly shy of leaving their high valleys, just as if real heads were to be taken instead of mere measurements and photographs with perfectly harmless instruments. But the trouble was amply repaid. The evidence collected showed that this small tribe, though it now speaks only Turki like the rest of the population all through the Tarim basin, had yet in its alpine isolation preserved remarkably well the main physical features of that *Homo Alpinus* race which in ancient times appears to have extended right through to Khotan and farther east along the southern edge of the Taklamakan. There is reason to believe that its original speech was probably Eastern Iranian, like that which prevails

among the closely allied stock of the present Wakhis, Shugh-
nis, etc., on the uppermost Oxus. To this language branch belongs also the old tongue of Khotan, as proved by the documents which have been recovered at sand-buried sites of the
Khotan region.

After carrying my plane table survey by a little-known
route through the barren outer hills, I reached Khotan by the
close of July. It was a great satisfaction to find myself once
more in that flourishing great oasis which, since my successful
first explorations five years before, I had come to look upon
as my cherished Central-Asian base. Cheering, too, was the
welcome I received from old friends among the local Turki
gentry and the Afghan traders there settled as well as from
the amiable Chinese magistrate, or "Amban," to use the term
by which Mandarins are usually known to the Turki people.
His ready help enabled me quickly to set out for the task I
had in view within the next four weeks. This was to supplement our survey of 1900 in the high K'un-lun range south
of Khotan by ampler topographical details about the great
glaciers which feed the headwaters of the Yurung-kash river,
one of the two rivers of Khotan.

Pushing up by a route discovered in 1900 across rugged
outlying spurs, we reached the Nissa valley by the middle of
August, and were soon busily engaged in mapping the huge
ice streams which descend toward its head from the main
K'un-lun watershed. The effects of far-advanced disintegra-
tion of rocks, due evidently to great extremes of temperatures,
were everywhere most striking. The precipitous ridges we had
to climb for the sake of survey stations were composed on
their crests of nothing but enormous rock fragments heaped
up as by the hands of Titans, and quite bare of detritus from
about 14,000 feet upward. Enormous masses of rock debris
thrown down from these ridges almost smothered the ice
streams below. Covered by this debris and permeated by black
glacier grit, these ice streams looked for miles like huge dark

torrents suddenly petrified in their wild course. Big ice falls and gaping crevasses showed indeed that these accumulations of debris were being steadily if slowly carried onward. But even there the exposed ice surface looked almost black, and when at the Otrughul glacier I had under serious difficulties clambered up for some five miles from the snout to an elevation of about 16,000 feet, the reaches of clear ice and snow descending from the buttresses of a peak over 23,000 feet high seemed still as far away as ever.

Two years later, coming from explorations on the desolate high plateaux of northwestern Tibet, I was able to climb up to the flank of this snowy peak and to sight from the watershed, at an elevation of 20,000 feet, the névé beds which give rise to this great glacier. How I reached the snowy cornice of the crest after a long climb up a much-crevassed glacier and lost there the toes of my right foot is another story and need not be told again here.

The huge accumulations of debris which cover all glaciers of the K'un-lun probably help to account for the important part which the survival in those glaciers of "fossil" ice from the last glacial period and its gradual reduction during the last few thousand years may, according to the theory mentioned in the preceding chapter, be assumed to play as regards the volume of the rivers fed by those glaciers and hence as regards the extent of irrigation obtainable from these rivers within the oases.

Old moraines of huge size could be traced clearly at the head of the Nissa valley down for about three miles below the present foot of the Kashkul glacier, at an elevation of about 13,000 feet. Thick layers of fine loess dust deposited since ages by heavy clouds of dust, such as we saw again and again swept up by the north wind from the great desert plains to the north, had covered up these ancient terminal moraines. On them alone at an elevation between 12,500 and 13,000 feet, where moisture seems to be less deficient than elsewhere in these forbidding mountains, was the eye refreshed by the sight of real green grass and a few alpine flowers. The barrenness of the valleys lower down was great, and the bleak steep slopes of rock or detritus plainly told the story of rapidly progressing erosion. The perfect maze of steeply serrated ridges and deep-cut gorges between them which is to be found in parts of the outer slopes of the K'un-lun strikingly illustrates how far this process has advanced there.

I have described elsewhere the difficulties encountered in our search for an old route across the main K'un-lun range by which communication with Ladak on the Indian side of the high Tibetan plateaux was once maintained in times of emergency. These difficulties were not entirely those of Nature. They were caused quite as much also by obstruction on the part of the small settlement of semi-nomadic hillmen and select malefactors exiled from Khotan who, counting probably less than two hundred souls, form the only population in this desolate mountain region. There seemed significance in its general name Karanghu-tagh, "the mountains of blinding darkness."

●
———

CHAPTER IV

First Explorations
at a Sand-buried Site

AFTER STRENUOUS WEEKS of geographical work in those forbidding mountains south of Khotan where the utter barrenness of Nature had given no chance for history to leave its
traces, the time came when I could turn to the fascinating task
of exploring sand-buried ancient sites in the desert. I had gathered my earliest experience of such work in December 1900,
when on my first expedition I set out from the Khotan oasis
into the sandy wastes northward. The observations and encouraging discoveries then made were so instructive and have
remained so fresh in my memory that I feel induced to take a
step back in chronology and to ask the reader of these pages
to accompany me on that initial archeological venture.

The weeks immediately preceding it had been spent
within the Khotan oasis, then looking rather bare and bleak in
spite of all its fertility. The last dust storm of the year had
effaced all view of the K'un-lun, near as its outer range is to

the oasis where it extends by the Kara-kash and Yurung-kash rivers as they debouch from the mountains. It had brushed away all gay-colored leaves from the trees of the orchards and arbors and spread over the fertile plain the atmosphere of a foggy autumn day in England. I had succeeded in safely identifying all the sacred Buddhist sites which Hsüan-tsang, my Chinese pilgrim guide, had visited and described within the Khotan oasis. On ground continuously cultivated and irrigated for centuries, nothing of structures built with sun-dried bricks could of course survive except low shapeless mounds at the best. But there were still traditions which indicated survival of ancient local worship at places where Buddhist sanctuaries had been replaced by Ziarats, or tombs of supposed Mohammedan saints.

The site of the ancient capital of Khotan could indeed be definitely located at the little village of Yotkan, about halfway between the two rivers and some seven miles to the west of the present chief place of the district. The digging carried on there for some thirty-five years by "treasure-seeking" villagers had revealed a "culture stratum" of completely decayed matter buried under a very deep layer of alluvium. Curiously enough, this has been dug and washed mainly for the flakes of gold leaf which at one time were rather plentifully obtained from it. These were the relics of the rich gilding which, according to the testimony of an early Chinese pilgrim, had covered not only images but many parts of Buddhist religious structures at the capital. In recent years antiques such as ornamented fragments of pottery, terracotta figurines, chiefly of monkeys, engraved stones and coins had come to be counted as a kind of secondary by-products of a salable kind.

Interesting as it was to collect such small remains and to survey the strangely revealed site which they indicated, yet I felt glad when, after careful completion of all arrangements for supplies and transport, I was free to start by December 7, a misty and bitterly cold day, for my first winter campaign in the desert. Three dreary marches down the Yurung-kash river, winding between fairly high sand dunes, brought us to the outlying small oasis of Tawakkel. Turdi, an experienced old "treasure seeker" whom Badruddin Khan, the Aksakal or headman of the Indian traders at Khotan and an ever helpful friend, used to employ on the search for antiques, was to be our guide to the ruined site some sixty miles off in a straight line to the northeast. To him and others at Khotan belonging to the luckless little fraternity of venturesome seekers for "treasure," it was known by the name of Dandan-oilik, "the place of houses with ivory."

But I had engaged also two hardy Tawakkel hunters, Ahmad Merghen and Kasim Akhun, who had guided Dr. Hedin years before on his short visit to that site and then down the Keriya river, to help us on the desert journey. They were splendid men, inured to all hardships by their roving life. They proved very useful from the start when it came to collecting a party of thirty laborers for intended excavations. Owing to superstitious fears and in view of the expected rigors of the winter, the cultivators were naturally reluctant to venture so far into the desert. Notwithstanding the ample pay offered and stringent instructions issued by Pʻan Ta-jên, the scholarly Amban of Khotan who befriended me then as on all my subsequent journeys, it needed the confidence inspired by the two hunters to overcome this reluctance.

Seven camels of mine and a dozen locally hired donkeys had to suffice for the transport of the baggage of our whole party and of food supplies for four weeks. The donkeys offered the advantage of needing only a minimum of fodder. For the camels only a quantity of oil made of rape seed could be taken. Less than half a pint every second day of this evil-smelling liquid proved wonderfully effective in keeping up their stamina on desert marches when they had to go often for a number of days without water or grazing. Our riding ponies were sent back to Khotan, and, of course, all of us had to walk.

When at last by December 12 we could set out with a minimum of indispensable impedimenta and with my troop of laborers duly collected, half the population of Tawakkel seemed to be assembled to witness our departure. A small advance party had been sent ahead two days previously under the guidance of Kasim, the younger of the two hunters. He had orders to dig wells at all places suitable for camps. The footprints left by them served as our guide.

The dunes were low in the area crossed during the first two days after striking off from the river. Even beyond they did not rise to such heights as were subsequently encountered on my desert crossings. Yet marching in the drift sand proved slow work. Since the animals had to be saved all overexertion, progress of the heavily laden camels was reduced to about a mile and a quarter per hour.

The tamarisk and reed scrub, plentiful at first, grew rare in the course of our second march, while the wild poplars, the only other vegetation, disappeared altogether as living trees. Luckily at intervals there rose small conical hillocks of sand thickly covered with tamarisk scrub, the dead roots of which supplied excellent fuel. It was near such hillocks, in hollows scooped out of the soil by the erosive action of the wind, that Kasim's advance party had always dug their wells for us to camp at. The water, scanty enough for so large a party, was very bitter at the first two camps and scarcely fit for human consumption. Curiously enough, as we moved farther away from the river it became comparatively fresh.

The winter of the desert had now set in with full rigor. Fortunately in daytime while on the march there was little to complain of. Though the temperature in the shade never rose above freezing point, yet there was no wind, so that I could enjoy without discomfort the delightfully pure air of the desert. As always when I moved on true desert ground in the winter and the atmosphere kept calm, I felt thoroughly refreshed by its absolute repose, which nothing living disturbs, and by its cleanness.

But at night, when the thermometer would go down to minimum temperatures from zero to ten degrees below zero Fahrenheit, my little tent, notwithstanding its extra serge lining, was a terribly cold abode. When the temperature, in spite of the embers kept in a little "Arctic stove," had gone down to about six degrees below freezing point, writing became impossible. Then I had to retire among the heavy blankets and rugs of my camp bed. There "Yolchi Beg" ("Sir Traveler"), as Dash, my little fox terrier, was known by his Turki incognito name, had long before sought a refuge, though he too was provided with a good fur coat.

On the evening of the fourth day after entering the desert, two of the men sent ahead returned to report that Kasim's party had failed to trace the ruins. It was now the turn of old Turdi, my "treasure-seeking" guide, to prove his superior knowledge of this dreary region, though he had only once before approached Dandan-oilik from this side. On the march he had more than once before told me that he thought the route taken by Kasim was leading too far north; but apparently, from a feeling of professional etiquette or pride, he had refrained from pressing his advice. Now, on the hunters' plain avowal of their inability to trace our goal, a gleam of satisfaction passed over his wrinkled face. A short conversation with the returned men suffice for him to locate the point which Kasim's party had reached. So next morning the men were sent back with full instructions to guide Kasim back into the right direction.

Old Turdi, with the instinct bred by the roamings of some thirty years and perhaps also inherited—his father had been a "treasure seeker" before him—would find his bearings even where the dead uniformity of the sand dunes seemed to offer no possible guidance. So, skirting the foot of several higher ridges of sand, he brought us next evening to ground where dead trees were seen emerging from heavy sand. Shriveled and bleached as they were, Turdi and the men could recognize among them trunks of the white poplar, the willow and other planted trees, unmistakable proofs that we had reached the area of ancient cultivation.

In a steep-banked hollow, about a mile and a half farther to the southeast, we succeeded in digging a well to camp by. Next morning, guided by old Turdi, a couple of miles farther south I found myself amidst the ruined structures which mark the site of Dandan-oilik. Scattered in small isolated groups over an area which my subsequent survey showed to extend for about a mile and a half from north to south with a width of three quarters of a mile, there rose from among the low dunes the remains of buildings, modest in size, but of manifest antiquity. Where the sand had blown away, the walls constructed of wattle and plaster were exposed to view, broken down to within a few feet of the ground. Elsewhere the walls could be made out only by rows of wooden posts emerging above the drift sand. All structural remains left exposed showed signs of having been searched by "treasure seekers." The damage done by their operations was often only too evident.

Under the guidance of Turdi, thoroughly familiar with the site which we jokingly used to call his own village, I made a rapid survey of the ruins, which sufficed to furnish unmistakable proofs of their character and approximate date. On the much-injured walls of structures which had been dug into by Turdi and others of his fraternity, I easily recognized remnants of paintings representing Buddhas and Bodhisattvas. There could be no doubt that I stood amid the ruins of Buddhist places of worship. The style of these frescoes pointed to the last centuries preceding the advent of Islam as the probable date when these shrines and the settlement to which they belonged had been abandoned. Chinese copper coins bearing the date of the period A.D. 713-41 were picked up from the debris-strewn ground near them and confirmed the dating.

Old Turdi felt quite at home in these desolate surroundings. He had frequently visited the site since his boyhood, and his excellent memory allowed him quickly to recognize the places where he and others had been at work before. Fortunately their scanty resources as regards supplies and transport had never allowed them to stay long or to clear structures more deeply buried in the sand. So I could place my camp at a spot from which such ruins as had escaped unopened were all within easy reach. The camels were sent off eastward to graze by the Keriya river, while the donkeys were returned to Tawakkel. Then the men were set to work at excavations which kept us all busy for a fortnight. For me it was a happy time full of interesting finds and growing experience.

The first ruin cleared was a small square building which Turdi had once searched in his own fashion and knew as a "But-khana," or "temple of idols." The sand, though lying only two or three feet high, had not been removed. The clearing of this and other small shrines soon familiarized me with their typical arrangement. There was always an inner square cella enclosed on all sides by equidistant outer walls which formed a quadrangular passage. This was meant for the ceremonial circumambulation or *pradakshina* prescribed by Indian custom. The walls built with wattle and plaster were invariably decorated with tempera paintings. Judging from what remained of them on the lowest portions of the walls, these paintings often represented Buddhas above life-size, or else rows of small figures of Buddhist saints forming a kind of diaper. But occasionally there were left remnants, too, of legendary scenes or of representations of donors kneeling at the feet of the large Buddha figures. Needless to say, of the latter only the lowest parts could survive. Plenty of small stucco relievos showing Buddhas, Bodhisattvas, flying Gandharvis, a kind of Buddhist angels, etc., could often be picked as they had fallen from the walls higher up.

Wall paintings and stucco relievos alike showed a style unmistakably derived from that Greco-Buddhist art which had flourished during the early centuries after Christ in the extreme northwest of India. This art has been rendered familiar by a wealth of sculptures brought to light from ruined Buddhist sanctuaries in ancient Gandhara, the present Peshawar District, and the adjacent tracts of the Indo-Afghan Frontier. These remains of decorative art in Buddhist shrines of distant Khotan are far removed in time from the period when Greek art was first applied in the western borderlands of India to figures of Buddhist sacred lore. Yet they reflect quite as clearly the impress of Hellenistic style.

I cannot attempt here to give a detailed account of all the manifold interesting finds which rewarded the clearing of the less injured shrines. The briefest indications must suffice. In the center of the inner cellas there stood generally an elaborately stuccoed pedestal which had once borne a colossal Buddha image. The feet, which were all that survived, furnished an idea of its size. In a number of cases I found several painted panels of wood still resting against the foot of the pedestal just as pious hands had placed them as votive offerings.

Among the painted panels thus recovered there are fortunately several which, when they had been carefully cleaned at the British Museum, revealed very interesting representations of legendary scenes. Thus one of them shows a curious rat-headed divinity. This figure would have been difficult enough to interpret had not Hsüan-tsang's account of Khotan preserved for us the story how sacred rats and their king, by destroying the horses' harness, etc., of an invading Hun host, had caused its defeat and thus saved the land. The legend still lives, as I was able to prove, in a form modified to suit Mohammedan notions, at the same spot where old Hsüan-tsang heard it located, on the caravan track leading to Khotan from the west.

Still more curious, perhaps, was my later discovery that one of those painted tablets represents the Chinese princess who, according to a story also recorded by Hsüan-tsang, was believed to have first introduced sericulture at Khotan. There it was in the pilgrim's time a flourishing industry just as it still is at present. The princess was supposed to have brought hidden in her headdress the first silkworm seeds from China, which jealously prohibited their export. For this pious fraud the clever lady was subsequently deified in her adopted country, and a famous shrine which the pilgrim visited near the capital was dedicated to her memory.

The painted panel I have referred to remained very puzzling for a long time. It shows seated in the center a richly dressed lady with a high diadem on her head and girls kneeling on both sides of her. At one end of the oblong panel is seen a basket filled with what might be taken for fruits, at the other a much-effaced object difficult at first to interpret. The puzzle was solved when I recognized the meaning of the gesture by which the attendant figure on the left with her raised left hand points to the diadem of the lady. It was under this diadem that the princess had smuggled the silkworm seeds out of China. In the basket at one end of the panel are represented the cocoons produced from them, while the object at the other end reveals itself as a loom for weaving the silk spun from the cocoons.

Among the dozen or so of ruined structures which I could trace and carefully clear, several proved to have belonged to small Buddhist monastic establishments. In the sand filling their lowest apartments, which were all that survived, we first recovered long detached leaves of paper manuscripts, then whole little packages of folia. They could at once be recognized by me as written in early Indian Brahmi script, containing Buddhist texts partly in Sanskrit, the classical language of India in which the canonical literature of Northern Buddhism is composed, and partly in a previously unknown language which has proved to have been the indigenous tongue of the Khotan population.

The writing as well as the shape and arrangement of these manuscripts are, of course, derived from India, the original home of Buddhism. But the researches of competent scholars, working partly on materials which had been secured previously from Khotan as the result of local "treasure-seeking" operations, have proved that old Khotanese language to be Iranian. It appears to have been closely allied with that spoken in the early centuries of our era in ancient Bactria and elsewhere on the Middle Oxus. We know that Buddhist cult and doctrine had penetrated very early through the present Afghanistan into that part of Eastern Iran, and there can be no doubt that Buddhism and the Indian cultural influences associated with it had reached the Tarim basin first, if not solely, through the same region. Buddhist cult and iconography can be shown to have absorbed Iranian elements also on this passage.

Their impact is illustrated in a very striking fashion by a remarkable and fairly well-preserved painted panel (Fig. 4) which came to light as a votive deposit in one of the temple cellas cleared. On one side is seen the figure of a powerful male, wholly Persian in physical appearance and style of dress, yet obviously intended for a Buddhist divinity. The long, ruddy face, surrounded by a heavy black beard, is a feature never seen on any sacred Buddhist figure. The large, curling mustache and the bushy black eyebrows add to the martial look of the face. Over the head with its long black locks rises a high golden tiara closely resembling the headdress of the Sasanian "kings of kings" of Persia. The body, narrow-waisted in keeping with the traditional Persian type of manly beauty, is dressed in a brocaded coat. Below this are shown the feet and legs encased in high black topboots. From the waist is suspended a short curving sword. From the neck descends a curling scarf which winds around the arm just as usually seen on Bodhisattva figures of Central Asia. As so often among these figures, the divinity is shown with four arms. Of the emblems which three of them carry, two only can be clearly recognized, and both of these, a drinking cup and a spearhead, are unmistakably secular.

The picture on the opposite side of the panel in curious contrast shows a three-headed figure of demonic look and distinctly Indian type. The dark-blue flesh of the body, nude but for a tiger skin descending from the waist, the two bulls *couchant* below the crossed legs and the emblems carried in the four hands all suggest affinity to some Tantric divinity of India. Subject and style of this picture seemed so far removed from the "Persian Bodhisattva" on the other side of the panel that to find any connection between the two was very puzzling.

The clue to the interpretation of the two figures and their juxtaposition did not offer itself until fifteen years later when, toward the close of my third Central-Asian expedition, I came to explore an imposing ruined site on the hill of Koh-i-Khwaja, which rises above the Hamun marshes of Sistan by the southeastern border of Persia. There I discovered the remains, unfortunately much damaged, of a large mural painting hidden behind a later wall. Its lower frieze represents a scene of homage and offerings presented to a youthful male of martial bearing, seated in a dignified pose. The upraised right arm carried a curving mace surmounted by an ox head. This shape of the mace corresponds exactly to the famous ox-headed *gurz* carried by Rustam, the great hero of Persian epic legend, and his recognized attribute throughout Persian iconography of Mohammedan times.

There can be no possible doubt that the chief figure in this mural painting of Koh-i-Khwaja represents Rustam, whom the Persian national epos as preserved in Firdausi's *Shah-nama* distinctly associates with Sistan. A comparison of his figure with that of the "Persian Bodhisattva" of the Dandan-oilik panel enables us now to recognize the head of Rustam's mace in the object, for the most part effaced, which crowns the top of the curving handle held in the upper right arm of that strange Bodhisattva.

But the comparison with the Koh-i-Khwaja fresco helps

us also to understand the significance of the three-headed demonic figure shown on the opposite side of the Dandan-oilik panel. For in the fresco we see Rustam faced by a closely corresponding three-headed personage offering homage with raised hands. In all probability it is meant for one of those demonic adversaries whom Rustam in popular legends of Persian epic tradition is represented as having overcome in hard struggles and triumphantly forced into loyal submission to his king. Thus the connection between the two figures of the Dandan-oilik panel is accounted for.

The wall painting of Koh-i-Khwaja belongs to the late Sasanian period ending in the seventh century A.D. This close contact in time with the remains of the Dandan-oilik shrines adds to the interest which the introduction of the deified Iranian hero into the local Pantheon of Khotan affords as an illustration of the accretions undergone by Buddhist cult on its passage into Central Asia.

The time when the site of Dandan-oilik was abandoned to the desert can fortunately be determined by converging chronological evidence from manuscript remains of a secular character. There were found in some ruined dwelling places, probably monastic, small sheets of thin paper with Brahmi script. On subsequent examination these have proved to be documents drawn up in Khotanese language and relating to petty local transactions, such as deeds of loan, requisition orders, etc. The paleographic character of these writings as well as of the canonical Buddhist manuscripts pointed to the eighth century as their probable date. The correctness of this approximate dating, due mainly to the scholarship of the late Dr. Hoernle, one of my oldest and most helpful collaborators, has been established by a series of Chinese documents brought to light from more than one of the ruined monastic quarters.

When examined by the late Professor Chavannes, the lamented great Sinologue of Paris and my unfailing guide in all that related to Chinese records, they proved to contain petitions for the recovery of debts, bonds for small loans, reports from a small local officer and the like. As was to be expected in documents drafted by people so strongly imbued with chronological sense as the Chinese are, these finds supply us with exact dates ranging from A.D. 781 to 790. They have given us also the Chinese name *Li-sieh* of the locality and that of one of its convents called *Hu-kuo,* "the country-protecting." Curiously enough, several monks there seem to have combined business as money-lenders with their religious occupations. The names given in one of the documents of the superintending priests of this monastic establishment are Chinese; but that the population which supported it was not Chinese is plainly indicated by the transcribed names of the borrowers and sureties.

But the essential value of these documents lies in their chronological evidence. From their very character and the condition in which they were found, scattered amidst rubbish in ground-floor rooms used as quarters or kitchens, it is quite safe to conclude that they were penned during the closing years of the occupation of the site and left behind when it was finally abandoned. This inference is completely borne out by the Chinese copper coins found on the site, which bear dates reaching down only to A.D. 760.

The time of abandonment thus established is in remarkable agreement with what the Chinese historical Annals tell us of Chinese control over the Tarim basin under the T'ang dynasty having finally come to its end about 791. The collapse of Chinese authority and the successful Tibetan invasion must have meant for Khotan a period of exceptional trouble. The effects of a great political upheaval in that part of the world are always felt most seriously in small outlying oases; for these are wholly dependent on a system of irrigation which only a firm and watchful administration can maintain. Considered in this light, the evidence furnished by the finds at Dandan-oilik may well help us in tracing the true relation between the abandonment of other ancient sites in this region and the cause or causes which, as briefly suggested in a previous chapter, have since rendered their reoccupation impossible.

Quite apart from the finds which my excavations yielded, there were also other interesting antiquarian observations to be gathered bearing on the general aspects and conditions of life. Thus I traced the remains of ancient orchards and avenues, lines of irrigation channels, debris-covered patches of ground marking the position of humble dwellings, etc., amidst the low dunes. But with such silent witnesses of the past we shall become still better acquainted at the fascinating old site to which the next chapter will take us.

Only one general observation may find room here. Everything at the site pointed to its abandonment having been a gradual one, and in no way connected with any sudden physical catastrophe such as popular legends current about the so-called "sand-buried cities" of the Taklamakan have induced some European travelers to assume. The Sodom and Gomorrha stories related all over the Tarim basin about "old towns" suddenly overwhelmed by sand dunes are more ancient than the ruins of Dandan-oilik. Hsüan-tsang had already heard them more or less in the same form in which they are now current. These legends are interesting as folklore, but in the face of plain archeological evidence to the contrary, such as the examination of Dandan-oilik and every other ancient site in this region has supplied, scientific inquiry need have no concern with them.

Detailed surveys, topographical as well as antiquarian, on successive expeditions have convinced me that the lands of Dandan-oilik were irrigated from an extension of the canals which for at least five centuries later brought the water of the streams of Chira, Domoko and Gulakhma to the extensive debris-covered site of Uzun-tati traced by me in the desert some forty miles farther south and identical with the *Pi-mo* of Hsüan-tsang, Marco Polo's *Pein*. A variety of relevant consid-

erations set forth in my detailed reports points to the conclusion that the successive abandonment of both Dandan-oilik
and "Pi-mo" was due to the same cause, the difficulty of maintaining effective irrigation for these outlying settlements.

CHAPTER V

●
————

Discoveries at the Niya Site

IN THE DESERT due south of Dandan-oilik but far nearer to the still cultivated ground of the village tracts of Gulakhma and Domoko were other old sites awaiting exploration. They were all duly visited by me in the course of my first and second expeditions and proved to have been abandoned to the sands about the same period as Dandan-oilik or some centuries later. But none of them proved so ancient, so interesting and so important in every way as the extensive sand-buried settlement which I discovered in the desert well beyond the present termination of the Niya river. So I propose to take my readers there straight, just as good fortune guided me there in January 1901 directly after I had said farewell to Dandan-oilik and the scene of my first excavations.

Three days of tramping across the dunes to the east had brought me to the Keriya-darya, hard frozen at the time. It is the only river among those descending from the K'un-lun east of Khotan which, being fed by considerable glaciers, manages to penetrate far into the Taklamakan before it, too, dies away among high ridges of sand. Marching up its course for four more days, no longer on foot now but thanks to a successfully arranged concentration on horseback, I reached the oasis and town of Keriya. The latter is a fairly large place and the head-quarters of a district which extended at that time over nearly five degrees of longitude, needless to say almost all desert. Its jovial Chinese magistrate gave me a very kindly reception.

Keriya is not an old place, and the "treasure-seeking" profession does not flourish there as in Khotan. But on the first day after my arrival an old and respectable villager came to tell me of ancient houses half buried in sand which he had seen ten years earlier well beyond the famous pilgrimage place of Imam Ja'far Sadik in the desert north of Niya. Others, too, had heard stories of this "old town" (*kōna-shahr*), to use the term which the people of the Tarim basin are accustomed to apply to every kind of ruin, even the smallest. So I set out for Niya on January 18 and, after a four days' journey along the line where the bare gravel glacis of the K'un-lun skirts the Taklamakan, reached the small oasis.

During the day's halt which regard for the due celebration of the Ramadan, the end of the Mohammedan month of fasting, obliged me to make there, I was greatly cheered by receiving unexpected proof of the great age of the ruined site I was bound for. Hassan Akhun, my sharp-witted young camelman, who was subsequently to share every one of my expeditions, had come across a villager possessing two inscribed tablets brought away from the site. When they were produced before me, I discovered to my joyful surprise that they contained writing in that ancient script of the extreme northwest of India known as Kharoshthi, and of a type which closely agreed with that prevailing during the first centuries of our era.

The man who brought me the tablets had picked them up

on the road to Imam Ja'far Sadik; but I soon ascertained the original finder in the person of Ibrahim, an enterprising young miller of the village who had dug them out a year before when searching a "house of the old town," beyond that pilgrimage place, in the hope of "treasure." He had found no "treasure," only a number of these, to him, useless tablets. He had brought away six, only to throw away some on the road and to give the rest to his children to play with. These, of course, were soon destroyed, and Ibrahim now greatly regretted their loss when he saw how well I rewarded the more sensible man who had picked up the others.

I lost no time in securing Ibrahim as a guide for my party. It was a happy evening when I examined these most promising finds. The very cursive form of writing and the faded ink prevented any attempt at immediate decipherment, but there could be no doubt that I held in my hands documents written in an early Indian script and older than any which have come to light in India apart from inscriptions. The writing alone was enough to assure me of the antiquity of the site for which I was bent; yet I little anticipated at the time what a rich harvest awaited me there.

The three days' march along the dying Niya river was brightened by this cheering prospect quite as much as by a delightfully clear sky. But the cold was still severe, the temperature at night falling to somewhere about eight degrees below zero Fahrenheit. The Mazar of Imam Ja'far Sadik is a famous pilgrimage place marking the spot where popular legend assumes the holy Muslim leader of that name to have fallen with many hundreds of the Faithful in fighting the infidels of "Chin and Ma-chin," *i.e.* Khotan.

There was nothing to detain me at the place. Apart from some pilgrim shelters, a tumble-down Madrasah or *soi-disant* college and trees decked with thousands of rags, votive offerings of pilgrims, there was to be seen there only a curious hillock composed of stony detritus overlying an outcrop of rock salt. From a little lake into which the water of the small terminal channel of the river is dammed up before it finally disappears, we filled two galvanized iron tanks brought from Calcutta as well as improvised sacks and nets with ice. This was to provide the indispensable minimum of water while my camp, counting from forty to fifty people, was pitched far out in the desert.

I cannot stop to describe how the belt of luxuriant jungle of wild poplar trees and tamarisks passed below the Mazar gradually changed into a wide expanse of low sand cones overgrown with scrub, groups of dead trees, gaunt and twisted by age, rising between them. Toward the end of a second easy march we passed a belt of more open ground where remains of broken pottery, an enclosure made of thickly packed rushes, a line of trunks of dead fruit trees and planted poplars, suggested the site of some ancient farm. Soon we arrived at the first two "houses" our guides had spoken of (Fig. 5).

They stood on what at first sight looked like small elevated terraces. But subsequent observation proved these to be merely portions of the original loess soil that had escaped the erosion which was proceeding all around. The mode of construction was materially the same as at the dwellings of Dandan-oilik, but the dimensions were much greater and the timber framework of the walls, rising above the sand which filled the rooms, far more elaborate and solid. The greater antiquity of these ruins became at once evident when in one of the rooms I found some finely carved pieces of wood, with ornaments common in Greco-Buddhist sculpture, lying practically on the surface.

Marching about two miles farther north across fairly high dunes, we arrived at a ruined structure of sun-dried bricks, half buried under a high conical sandhill. It proved to be a small stupa, or Buddhist relic tower, dug into long ago. There our camp was pitched in a position conveniently central for the exploration of the scattered ruins and near also, so Ibrahim assured me, to the dwelling in which he declared he had come upon those inscribed tablets. As I retired to my first night's rest among these silent habitations of a distant past, I wondered with some apprehension whether Ibrahim's story would prove true, and how much of the other precious documents on wood which he declared he had left behind were still waiting to be recovered by me.

Next morning I hastened off with Ibrahim and my diggers to this ruined dwelling. The mingled feelings of expectation and distrust with which I now approached it soon changed to joyful assurance. About a mile from camp I sighted the ruin toward which Ibrahim was guiding us. It also occupied the top of a little terrace rising high above the depressions of the ground eroded by the wind. On ascending the slope, I picked up at once three inscribed tablets lying amidst the debris of massive timber that marked wholly eroded parts of the structure.

On reaching the top, I found to my delight many more scattered within one of the rooms. Only a year had passed since Ibrahim had thrown them down there. The layer of drift sand was so thin as scarcely to afford the topmost ones adequate protection from the snow which a very slight fall, experienced also by us after leaving Keriya, had deposited. Owing to the bitter cold, it still lay in patches on shaded slopes. As it was, the sun of one year had bleached and partly effaced the writing of the topmost tablets where fully exposed. So I had a special reason to bless the good luck which had brought me to the site so soon after Ibrahim's discovery.

He at once showed me the spot where he had unearthed the tablets. It proved to be the corner of a small room situated in the northern wing of the building between other apartments. There, in a little recess between a large brick-built fireplace and the west wall of the room, he had come upon a heap of tablets by scooping out the sand with his hands. The "treasure" he looked for was not there. So the ancient documents which he had found stored there, apparently with some sort of arrangement, were just thrown away into an adjoining room.

My first task was to get the men to clear the room where Ibrahim had come upon those precious tablets. It was an easy matter, as the room was not large and the sand covering its floor nowhere more than four feet deep. In the course of this operation two dozen wooden documents were recovered on the original earthen floor and on a raised sitting platform by the side of the fireplace. When I next made a careful search myself for the scattered remains of Ibrahim's haul, no less than eighty-five more tablets were recovered. The subsequent clearing of the adjoining rooms in the north wing of the ruined house added still further to their number. So I found myself before the day's work was ended in the possession of truly abundant materials.

The remarkable state of preservation in which many of the wooden tablets were found made it easy for me even on the spot to recognize the main features of their use and outward arrangement. With the exception of a few oblong pieces, all the tablets found that day were wedge-shaped, from seven to fifteen inches long, and showed evidence of having originally been fastened together in pairs. I shall presently describe the ingenious method used for this fastening. The text, which was invariably in cursive Kharoshthi writing, running from right to left and parallel to the longer side, occupied the inner sides of the tablets. Other tablets bore on their outside surface a sunk socket for a clay seal and soon proved to have served the purposes of a kind of envelope. By the side of the socket there usually appeared brief entries forming a single line. These at once suggested the address or name of the sender. Where double tablets had remained together, and thus protected each other, the black ink of the writing on the inner surfaces looked as fresh as if penned yesterday.

Thus it was easy to recognize that the tablets, though written by many different hands, showed throughout the characteristic peculiarities of that type of Kharoshthi writing which in India is invariably exhibited by the stone inscriptions of the Kushana or Indo-Scythian dynasty. Its kings ruled over the Punjab and the regions to the west of the Indus during the first three centuries of our era. Thus even before any careful examination became possible I felt assured as to the high antiquity and exceptional value of the materials I was busy gathering.

And yet during that day's animating labors there remained a thought that did not allow my archeological conscience to become unduly triumphant. It was true that the collected text of the hundred-odd tablets I was carrying away as the result of my first day's work could not fall short of, if it did not exceed, the aggregate of all previously available Kharoshthi writings. But might not these strange records prove to be mere replicas of the same text, perhaps a prayer or an extract from some sacred Buddhist text?

Once in the comparative shelter of my tent, I began with impatience to examine the best preserved of these tablets. I was prepared from previous experience of Kharoshthi epigraphy for the exceptional difficulties likely to be presented by the cursive character of the writing and by all the uncertainties as to language, etc. Yet, sitting up in the cold of that evening wrapped in my furs—the thermometer showed next morning a minimum of forty-one degrees of frost—I gained assurance on two important points. A series of philological observations convinced me that the language was an early Indian Prakrit. It became equally certain that the text varied greatly, notwithstanding the same brief initial formula with which most of them opened. When later on I had definitely deciphered this formula as reading *mahanuava maharaya lihati*, "His Highness the Maharaja orders in writing," there remained no doubt that these particular documents conveyed official orders. The conclusion seemed thus justified that with the Kharoshthi script an early form of Indian speech had also been transplanted into this distant Central-Asian region, in any case for administrative use. Such a fact might well open fresh and wholly unexpected historical vistas over ground so far shrouded in darkness.

My eager hope for more finds of records proved well founded when I proceeded to clear the southern wing of the ruined building. Beyond a small room which seemed to have served as an antechamber for attendants, there adjoined a large apartment. It was a room twenty-six feet square with a raised platform of plaster running around three of its sides, very much as in the "Aiwan" or hall of any modern Turkistan house of some pretension. Remains of eight posts placed in a square indicated a central area over which a raised roof had been arranged to admit light and air just as in large modern houses. Elsewhere, too, the disposition and construction of the ancient dwellings with which I soon became so familiar at this site showed a striking similarity to the domestic arrangements still prevailing in the present oases.

Time and the erosive force of the winds had left little more of the timber-and-wattle walls than broken posts, and the protecting layer of sand was only about two feet deep. All the more delighted was I to find that even this had sufficed to preserve in a more or less legible condition the three score of tablets that were found covering the platform along the southern side of the hall. In some places they were rising in small, closely packed heaps, evidently just as left by the last occupants. But a considerable number of other wooden documents showed plainly by their position that they had been disturbed, apparently not long after the building had been deserted. Thus some were found resting on a large piece of strongly woven matting which must have formed part of a roof over the central area. Others turned up near a small open fireplace found beneath the fallen matting. They owed their excellent preservation obviously to this safe covering.

The great number of the wooden documents and the

condition in which those left undisturbed by later "treasure-seeking" visitors were found left no doubt as to this large apartment having served as an office. That it was that of some local official became clear later on from an examination of the tablets. Their variety in respect of size and shape was remarkable. The wedge-shaped tablets reappeared again, but in numbers they were far surpassed by inscribed boards of wood, all of oblong form but showing great variations in detail and arrangement. Some of them were of considerable dimensions, up to thirty inches in length. The great majority showed plainly, by the irregular arrangement of their writing, in small columns often ending with numerical figures; by the appearance of various handwritings, erasures, etc., that they did not contain texts or even connected communications, but in all probability memoranda, accounts, drafts and other casual records.

Two series of oblong tablets largely represented among the finds of this room showed far greater regularity and care in writing but were none the less puzzling at the time of their discovery. One series consisted of tablets of rectangular shape, from four to sixteen inches in length, with a raised rim resembling a margin at the narrower sides of their single inscribed surface. The initial line of writing ordinarily contained figures preceded by Prakrit words which I soon made out to mean "in the year . . . month . . . day." Obviously I held in my hands regularly dated documents. The other series consisted of rectangular tablets, smaller in size, with rarely any writing on their flat reverse, while the obverse, in its raised center, invariably showed a square or oblong socket, obviously intended for the insertion of a seal, together with a transversely written line or two. It was only later, after the remarkable rubbish heap to be mentioned presently had yielded up its antiquarian treasures, that the explanation, as definite as it was simple, revealed itself. Those curious seal-bearing tablets were meant to serve as a kind of wooden cover or envelope fitting between the raised rims of the wooden tablets which bore on their protected upper surface the text of a letter or legal document.

The sand covering the remains of this structure which had proved so rich a mine of inscribed tablets was not deep enough to protect relics of larger size, but the ruin itself served well to illustrate the extent to which this and other structures of the site had suffered from wind erosion. The small plateau which the ruin is seen to occupy, raised some fifteen feet above the surrounding ground, is unmistakably due to this destructive force. While the strip of ground actually covered by the debris, foundation beams of walls, etc., has retained the original level, the open surface near has been lowered more and more by the eroding action of the wind. That part of the ground, too, which is still occupied by remains of ancient structures is slowly being cut into and undermined. The photograph taken of the ruin aptly illustrates this slow process of destruction; for the heavy timber debris seen on the slope of the foreground marks a portion of the original building which has completely fallen.

The danger to ruins which is involved in this slow but incessant action of wind-driven sand was strikingly brought home to me by the condition of more than one group of ancient dwellings explored at this site. Thus half a mile to the northwest of the building first cleared, an area measuring fully five hundred feet square proved to be closely occupied by the timber debris of ancient houses. But as the dunes were only a few feet high and the ground everywhere greatly eroded, very little remained of the walls and still less of the contents of the rooms. Even thus, careful search had its rewards here.

Thus in a detached room of which the floor was covered by sand only half a foot to one foot deep, there came to light some fifty tablets of wood besides a variety of household implements of wood including a mouse trap, boot last, etc. Unfortunately, owing to the inadequate protection, the majority of these tablets had become withered and bleached until all trace of writing was lost. Others, though much warped, still showed their Kharoshthi writing. Lists of names and account items, which appear on most of these, pointed to records kept in some office. The extent of clerical labor once carried on here—and the occasional inconvenience of the wooden writing material—could be estimated by the size of these tablets, one much effaced piece attaining the inconvenient length of seven and a half feet!

The slight depth of the sand covering this area permitted me rapidly to clear here a considerable number of small houses. These served to acquaint me with the typical arrangement of the rooms, cattle sheds, etc., composing these homesteads. Finds of interest were here scarce, but I mention in passing that in an outhouse we came upon an unmistakable ice pit. A thick bed of ancient poplar leaves, once used to cover the ice, still survived.

More varied in character and more interesting, too, were the relics yielded by the excavation of the two large ruined houses passed on our first approach to the site. The one to the east (Fig. 5), judging from the size and number of the apartments, must have been the residence of a man of position. Its rooms held a far greater depth of sand, and hence its structural remains were better preserved. A very striking feature of this building was a large central hall measuring forty by twenty-six feet. The massive beams of poplar wood supporting the roof were forty feet long and, like the corbel on which the central beams rested, fine specimens of carving. The stuccoed walls still standing to a good height were decorated with a carefully colored design of large floral scrolls and festoons executed in tempera.

The hall had been completely cleared by its last dwellers or visitors, but from the smaller rooms adjoining to the north we recovered interesting relics illustrating the manu-

factures and arts of the period. Among other small specimens of local textile industry, there turned up portions of a
delicately worked woolen rug showing elaborate geometrical
patterns and harmoniously blended colors which only needed
a little brushing to reappear in their original brilliancy. Only
passing reference can be made to the remains of wooden implements found in the kitchen and of arms, such as a bow and
wooden shield, left behind in a storage place. Among articles
of ornamental woodcarving found here, none can compare
with that on an ancient chair. Its pieces, though disjointed,
lay together on the floor of one of the outer rooms. All the
decorative motifs of the carvings are familiar to us from the
Greco-Buddhist relievos of the Indian Northwest Frontier. I
was glad to note at the time how closely the date thus indicated agreed with the chronological evidence of the Kharoshthi writing.

The other large residence farther to the southwest also
yielded plenty of curious relics. In a room which seems to
have served as an office, there were found besides inscribed
tablets of varying shape blank wooden stationery, writing
pens of tamarisk wood and eating sticks such as are still used
by the Chinese. More interesting still were the well-preserved
upper portion of a guitar found in a passage and the remains
of an elaborately carved armchair. Its legs represent standing
lions and the arm-rests composite monsters of a Hellenistic
type, all retaining their original vivid coloring.

The arrangement of an arbor close by could be traced
with great clearness. The trunks of the poplars still rising
eight to ten feet above the ground were seen grouped in small
squares and enclosing avenues, just as they can be found now
in every "Bostan" or arbor from Kashgar to Keriya. It was
with a strange feeling, obliterating almost all sense of time,
that I walked between two parallel rush fences that still
form a little country lane just as they did nearly seventeen
centuries ago. Searching in the sand at the bottom of the

fences, my stick disclosed the rustling dead leaves of poplars and fruit trees. Among the fallen trunks of ancient trees such as I saw here and at other points of the site, my diggers easily distinguished white poplars once planted along lanes, as well as various fruit trees, such as peach, apple, plum, apricot, mulberry, the wood of which they knew from their own homes.

It was clear from the excavations just described that the ancient dwellings of the site had been cleared by their last inhabitants, or soon after their departure, of everything possessing intrinsic value or still fit for practical use. Thus my hopes of further archeological finds had to be based mainly on any rubbish remains. These hopes were soon confirmed in a very gratifying way.

In the course of a reconnaissance to the north I had sighted about half a dozen more groups of ruined structures scattered over an area of about three and a half miles from south to north and more than two miles across. In one ruin, greatly decayed and in no way attracting special attention, I had come upon a number of bleached tablets lying exposed, and a little digging had within half an hour brought to light more than two dozen inscribed pieces. Among them were two novelties: a narrow slip of wood with Chinese characters and a small fragment of leather with a line of Kharoshthi recording a date.

These finds were indeed promising. Yet I little anticipated how rich a mine of ancient relics I had struck within the half-broken walls of this room which once formed the western end of a modest dwelling place. When systematic excavation had begun, it revealed layer upon layer of wooden tablets mixed up with refuse of all sorts. It soon proved to be an ancient rubbish heap formed by the accumulations of many years and containing also what, by an anachronism, may fitly be called the "waste-paper" deposits of that early time.

From that consolidated mass of refuse rising fully four

feet above the original level, I recovered in the end more than two hundred documents on wood. They were all embedded among solid layers of broken pottery, straw, rags of felt and various woven fabrics, pieces of leather, and other less savory refuse. It was not an easy task with fingers half benumbed by cold, and in the dust which a fresh northeast breeze raised from the dug-up rubbish heap, to mark and carefully tabulate every inscribed piece. Yet it was obviously necessary to keep accurate record of the relative position in which each object was found; for this might help to establish the chronological order and possibly the internal connection of the dispersed documents. For three long working days I had to inhale the odors of this antique dirt and litter, still pungent after so many centuries.

The diversity in form and material of the documents was quite as remarkable as their good preservation. The first few hours' work brought to light complete Kharoshthi documents on leather. The oblong sheets of carefully prepared sheepskin, of which altogether two dozen were recovered, showed different sizes but were always folded up in the same way into neat little rolls. The Kharoshthi text covering the inner surface is usually written in a clear clerical hand and the black ink has remained very fresh. At the head of each document I could read with certainty the same introductory formula already referred to as indicating official origin. The dating is given separately below, usually only by month and day.

Still more interesting information as to clerical practice was yielded by the abundant finds of Kharoshthi tablets. Many of those unearthed here still retained intact the original clay seals and strings with which they had been fastened. There could be no doubt that wood was the general stationery. It was hence particularly fortunate that I could now definitely ascertain all technicalities connected with its use.

The wedge-shaped tablets which were in favor for short communications, especially those of a quasi demi-official character, invariably consisted of pairs of pieces fitted exactly to match each other in size. One end of the double tablet thus formed was cut square; the other runs out into a point near which a string hole is drilled through both pieces. The text occupies the smooth obverse of the under tablet and is protected by an upper or covering tablet which serves as a kind of envelope. On the reverse of this the writing was continued if the length of the communication required it. The wood of the upper tablet shows greater thickness toward the square end, and in this raised portion of the outside surface a square socket was neatly cut, intended for the reception of a square seal.

A double-stranded string of hemp was in a cleverly designed fashion first passed through the string hole and then drawn tightly over both tablets near the square or right-hand end. There grooves communicating with the seal socket held the string in regular cross-folds. The socket was then filled with clay, covering these folds of the string. When once the seal of the sender had been impressed into the clay, it became impossible to separate the under tablet from the upper tablet and to read the writing on the inner surfaces without either breaking the seal impression or cutting the string. Thus unauthorized inspection of the communication was absolutely guarded against.

Scarcely less ingenious was the method of fastening which the finds in that precious refuse heap proved to have been used for the rectangular tablets. From a number of double tablets which I recovered here practically intact, it became clear that in this case the under tablet was provided with a raised rim on either of the shorter sides. Between these rims fitted exactly a covering tablet the obverse of which, in its raised center, had a square or oblong socket for the reception of a clay seal. Here, too, a string passed transversely over both tablets and, being secured below, a clay seal effectually prevented any unauthorized opening and reading of what was written on the inner sides of the two tablets. Such a double tablet was found with the string broken but otherwise intact, both before and after the opening. More frequently the "envelopes" had become separated from their under tablets either before or when they were thrown away into this dust-bin, an ancient substitute, I might call it, of the waste-paper basket. But in the course of the careful examination which all these finds underwent at the hands of Professor E. J. Rapson, my distinguished scholar collaborator, first at the British Museum and subsequently outside it, most of the pairs could be be reunited.

I cannot detail here all the curious observations made in connection with this ancient stationery in wood. But mention should be made of the fact that subsequent discoveries at ruined sites far away to the east have proved all those ingenious devices to have originated in China and at a far earlier period. There, I may add, the invention of paper, dating from A.D. 105, was causing the use of wooden stationery gradually to become obsolete during the centuries following. But the new writing material, more convenient as it was, evidently made its way but slowly into distant Central Asia. For though the Niya site can be proved not to have been abandoned until the second half of the third century A.D., yet not a single scrap of paper ever turned up there in the course of my explorations.

On the other hand, the remarkable series of clay seal impressions which were found still intact on a number of tablets furnished from the start striking evidence of the way in which the influence of the West, through products of classical art, asserted itself so far away as the Tarim basin. It was a delightful surprise when, on cleaning the first intact seal impression that turned up, I recognized in it the figure of Pallas Athene, with aegis and thunderbolt, treated in an archaic fashion. Other clay sealings also showed Greek figures, such as a standing and a seated Eros, Heracles and another Athene. The engraved stones from which these impressions had been made very closely resemble in their style Hellenistic or Roman work of the first centuries of our era.

As if to symbolize this strange mixture of influences

from the Far West and the Far East, a covering tablet found here has two seals impressed side by side. One by its Chinese lapidary characters is shown to be the seal of the Chinese political officer in charge of Shan-shan, the present Lop district in the East; while the other presents a portrait head unmistakably cut after Western models.

Owing to the excellent preservation of many documents thus brought to light in the course of my first visit to this fascinating site, it proved comparatively easy almost from the start to clear up the essential antiquarian details relating to their character and use. But, as I soon recognized, the detailed decipherment of all these epigraphical finds in Kharoshthi was bound to prove a very difficult task. Owing to the very cursive character of the Kharoshthi script and the puzzling phonetic and other peculiarities of the early Indian dialect employed, this task has indeed taxed the scholarly zeal and acumen of that learned triumvirate of expert collaborators, Professor E. J. Rapson of Cambridge, M. E. Senart and Père Boyer, S.J., of Paris, who kindly undertook in 1902 the publication of these records.

The number of our Kharoshthi documents was greatly increased by the finds made here and at sites farther east on my subsequent expeditions. This will help to explain, together with delays consequent on the war, why their publication in several fasciculi could not be completed until 1928. The full interpretation of the texts thus rendered accessible to other Indologist students will still need labors extending over many years.

Not until these exegetical labors have been carried much further will it be possible to bring into focus all the light those records throw upon the economic and administrative conditions, the ethnic and cultural relations of the people, etc., prevailing in that region. But enough has become clear to permit of some definite glimpses being offered here. Of the great mass of the documents it is certain that they contain, as surmised by me from the first, official correspondence of various kinds. The bulk of this is made up of reports and orders to local officials on matters of local administration and police; complaints; summonses; orders for safe conduct or arrests, and similar communications. Records of payments or requisitions, accounts, lists of laborers, etc., form the usual contents of the mass of miscellaneous "papers" written on single tablets of irregular shapes and often in columns ending with numerical signs.

That a considerable proportion of the double rectangular tablets contains formal agreements and bonds was conclusively proved by the number of carefully sealed documents of this kind found unopened in a remarkable cache which, as described in the next chapter, came to light on my second visit to the site. Other rectangular double tablets have proved to contain letters dealing with private affairs which their writers obviously wished to keep between themselves and their correspondents. Of considerable philological interest are some tablets containing passages from Buddhist texts in Sanskrit.

The language used throughout all these Kharoshthi documents is an early Indian Prakrit with a large admixture of Sanskrit terms. We have good reason to suppose that not only the script but also this language was derived from the extreme northwest of the Punjab and the adjacent trans-Indus tracts. In India no writings of such early date, concerned with everyday life and administration, have survived. This fact invests these records found so far away to the north of the Himalayas with still greater interest. Their discovery in this region seems curiously bound up with the old local tradition, recorded by Hsüan-tsang and also in old Tibetan texts, that the territory of Khotan was conquered and colonized about two centuries before our era by Indian immigrants from Takshasila, the Taxila of the Greeks, in the extreme northwestern corner of the Punjab.

The titles given to the rulers in whose name orders are issued and with reference to whose reigns the more elaborate documents are dated (*Maharaja, devaputra*, "son of the gods," etc.) are purely Indian. They agree strikingly with the official nomenclature observed under the Kushana or Indo-Scythian princes who ruled over the extreme northwest of India and Afghanistan in the first centuries of our era. The names of the persons which occur in the documents are almost all Indian, and some of them point to a connection with the Indo-Scythian dominion. But by the side of official designations familiar from ancient Indian usage there appear titles which are distinctly non-Indian and still await explanation.

We often meet with the name of Khotan, in a form almost identical with that now in use, but also in the form *Kustana*, "breast of the earth." This, probably a product of "learned popular etymology," is recorded also by Hsüan-tsang. But, as might be expected in correspondence, we find other localities also, like the Niya oasis and Charchan, mentioned by their ancient names. Among the local names occurring in these documents I was later on able to identify *Chadota* as that of the ancient site itself. It figures under the Chinese transcription of *Ching-chüeh* as the designation of a small territory mentioned in the Han Annals to the east of Khotan and approximately in the right position.

Among the many curious facts revealed already by Professor Rapson's first decipherment, I may mention in passing that there existed a recognized official terminology for the various classes of wooden stationery. Thus, *e.g.*, the wedge-shaped tablets are always designated in their context as *kila-mudra*, literally "sealed wedges." But far more important is is that the painstaking research of the same distinguished scholar has recently succeeded in determining the chronological order of the successive rulers whose years of reign are indicated in the dated documents, and in proving that their seat was not Khotan but the territory of Shan-shan corresponding to the present Lop tract.

It seemed strange that these ruins far away in the north, overrun by what Hindu legends vaguely knew as the great "sand ocean," should have preserved for us in an Indian language records of everyday life far older than any written documents that have as yet come to light in India proper. From the first there was ample antiquarian evidence of the paleographic sort pointing to this conclusion; for, as already stated, the Kharoshthi writing of the documents showed close agreement with the Kharoshthi inscriptions of the Kushana kings whose rule over northwestern India falls mainly within the second and third centuries of our era. Their testimony was fully supported by the fortunate discovery in another ruin of a unique tablet showing by the side of Kharoshthi some lines written in Indian Brahmi characters of the Kushana or Indo-Scythian period. The evidence of the coins was equally eloquent, since the numerous Chinese copper pieces found during my stay at the site all belonged to issues of the Later Han dynasty, which came to a close in A.D. 220.

But the incontrovertible chronological evidence I had longed for came from one of the small pieces of wood inscribed with single lines of Chinese characters of which the ancient refuse heap had yielded up over two score. As was to be expected in the case of documents penned by precise official hands, they yielded to M. Chavannes' expert examination a series of very useful data. Most of them contain brief references to orders issued by specified Chinese authorities or relate to the movements of certain individuals who were to be arrested or allowed to pass. References to ancient localities both in the Tarim basin and in China offer points of distinct historical interest.

But what gratified me most was the discovery, first made in London by a lamented Sinologue friend, Dr. Bushell, that one of these little tablets was fully and precisely dated in a year of the Emperor Wu-ti corresponding to A.D. 269. Of him it is distinctly recorded that he re-established Chinese authority in the "Western Countries" and maintained it during his reign (A.D. 265-89). It is difficult to believe that the ruined site continued to be inhabited many years after Wu-ti's time. Great political and economic disturbances must have accompanied the withdrawal of Chinese authority from these parts, and with them one feels tempted to connect directly or indirectly the final abandonment of the site.

The clearing of some other ruined dwellings to the north did not yield many novel finds, apart from a few fine specimens of architectural wood carvings. This in a way made it less hard for me to tear myself away from this fascinating dead settlement than it would have been otherwise. Sixteen days of incessant hard work, together with the hardships implied by bitterly cold nights and mornings, had worn out all the diggers and my own men too. I fully realized that other structures were likely to have remained hidden behind dunes, though the men whom I sent out on reconnaissances failed to report any—for obvious reasons of their own. But then I had to think of other old sites both to the east and west about which I had received information, and of the comparatively short time still remaining at my disposal for their exploration before the season of sandstorms would set in and put an end to excavations at distant sites in the desert.

So I resigned myself with a heavy heart to take my leave by February 13 of this scene of fruitful and stimulating labors. When marching back to the end of the Niya river by a different route, we stumbled, as it were, on a group of houses not previously noticed owing to the height of the surrounding sands. And this helped to confirm me still more in the resolve that my farewell at the time should not be final.

CHAPTER VI

The Niya Site Revisited and the Remains of Endere

WHEN I LEFT in February 1901 that fascinating ruined site beyond where the Niya river is now lost in the sand, it was
with a firm wish and hope for its further exploration. So a
fresh visit to it was duly planned and prepared by the time
when my second expedition had, at the close of the summer
1906, brought me back once more to Khotan, as related
above in Chapter III. I had often thought in the interval how
great a help it might be if a search could be made from the air
for more ancient dwellings hidden away amidst the dunes.
But neither the use of a man-carrying kite nor of a balloon
could be thought of for obvious practical reasons, which
would equally have applied to the airplane if it had then been
invented. So I had arranged for my former "treasure-seeking"
guide Ibrahim to go out to the site as soon as the summer heat
had passed and to try tracing ruins that had before escaped us.

When, after prolonged excavation work in the vicinity of

Domoko between Khotan and Keriya, I had reached the Niya oasis again by October 15, 1906, it was encouraging to learn from Ibrahim that his search had been fruitful. Equally pleasing it was to see how readily my old Niya diggers rejoined me. I was resolved this time to take out as many laborers as I could possibly keep supplied with water. Thus, what with the example set by my "old guard" and the helpful local influence still possessed by my energetic old factotum, Ibrahim Beg of Keriya, a column of fifty diggers, with supplies for four weeks and additional camels for transport, could be raised within a single day's halt.

Once again three rapid marches lay through the luxuriant jungle belt which lines the dying course of the Niya river. At this season the glowing autumn tints of wild poplars and reed beds made a delightful treat for the eye. Picturesque parties of pilgrims returning from the lonely shrine of Imam Ja'far Sadik added a touch of human interest to this silent sylvan scenery. A few miles beyond the supposed resting place of that holy warrior and martyr, we filled all available water tanks and goatskins with water. There we left behind the last abode of the living and also the present limit of life-giving water. Two days later I had the satisfaction of camping once more amidst bare dunes not far from the center of that long stretch of sand-buried settlement. Subsequent surveys have proved its scattered remains to extend over an area of over fourteen miles from south to north with a maximum width of some four miles.

Already that day's route, slightly diverging from that followed on my first discovery of the site, had taken me past spots of ancient occupation, marked by the debris of completely decayed dwellings and remains of fences enclosing ancient orchards. It was a joyful sensation to find myself once more among the shriveled trunks of dead fruit trees and poplars that had flourished when there were still emperors ruling Rome. A little experimental scraping in the corner of a modest much-eroded dwelling had revealed some well-preserved wooden tablets bearing Kharoshthi script. They held out an encouraging promise at the outset, and also furnished conclusive proof that this area fully four miles to the south of the first ruins explored in 1901 held remains belonging to the same early period.

When in the twilight of that first evening I strolled across the high sands to a ruin sighted in 1901 but reluctantly "left over" for unavoidable reasons and lighted upon a fine carved cantilever since laid bare by the slight shift of a dune, I felt almost as if I had never been away, and yet grateful for the kindly Fate which had allowed me to return. But I little dreamt then how rich an archeological haul was awaiting for me close by.

Next morning, after tramping some four miles over absolutely bare dunes, I started our fresh excavations at the northernmost of the ruined dwellings which Ibrahim had discovered scattered in a line some two miles to the west of the area previously explored. These structures, then hidden from our view by high dunes, evidently marked what must have been the extreme northwestern extension of the area once reached by a canal from the terminal course of the Niya river.

The ruin we first cleared was a relatively small dwelling, covered only by three or four feet of sand, and just of the right type to offer an instructive lesson to my Indian "handyman," brave Naik Ram Singh, and the men. It occupied a narrow tongue of what, owing to the depression produced around by wind erosion, looked like high ground, extending in continuation of the line of a small irrigation canal still marked by fallen rows of dead poplars. As soon as the floor was being reached in the western end room Kharoshthi documents on wood began to crop up in numbers. After the first discovery of a "Takhta," or tablet, had been duly rewarded with some Chinese silver, I had the satisfaction in each of the three living rooms of the house of seeing specimen after specimen of this ancient record and correspondence in Indian language and script emerge from where the last dweller, probably a petty official, about the middle of the third century A.D., had left behind his "waste paper."

It added to my gratification to see that a number of the rectangular and wedge-shaped letter tablets still retained intact their original string fastenings, and a few even their clay seal impressions. How cheering it was to discover on them representations of Heracles and what appears to be a representation of the Genius Populi Romani, left by the impact of classical intaglios! To be greeted once more at these desolate ruins far away in the heart of Asia by tangible links with the art of Greece and Rome seemed to efface all distance in time and space.

Just as familiar to me were the household and agricultural implements, all of wood, which this ruin yielded. Remains of a wooden chair decorated with carvings of Greco-Buddhist style, weaving instruments, a boot last, a large eating tray, mouse trap, etc., were all objects I could with my former experience recognize at the first glance, and so also the various methods employed in constructing the wattled walls, with well-wrought timber posts and skillful wickerwork between the plaster.

Our next task was the clearing of the remains of a far larger structure close to camp. Here the walls and any objects which may have been left between them proved completely eroded, though the massive posts, bleached and splintered, still rose high, marking the position of the timber framework. But when I examined the ground underneath what appeared to have been an outhouse or stables, I realized quickly that it was made up of layers of a huge refuse heap. Of course, previous experience supplied sufficient reason for digging into this unsavory quarry, though the pungent smells which its contents emitted, even after seventeen centuries of burial, were doubly trying in the fresh eastern breeze which drove fine dust, dead microbes and all into one's eyes, throat and nose. Our perseverance in cutting through layer upon layer of stable refuse was rewarded, however, at last by striking, on a level fully seven feet below the surface, a small wooden enclosure which had probably served as a dustbin for some earlier habitation. There were curious sweepings of all sorts—rags of manifold fabrics in silk, cotton, felt; seals of bronze and bone; embroidered leather; wooden pens; fragments of lacquer ware; broken implements in wood; etc.

But more gratifying still was a find of over a dozen small tablets inscribed with Chinese characters of exquisite penmanship. Most of them, when examined by M. Chavannes, have proved to be labels originally fastened to presents made to members of the local chief's family. The reference which one of them makes to the home of one of the ruler's wives has rendered it possible to prove that the ancient site was included in the territory of Ching-chüeh, which the Annals of the Han dynasty mention as situated between Charchan and Keriya. Quite at the bottom of the enclosure we found a small heap of wheat, still in sheaves and in perfect preservation, and close to it the mummified bodies of two mice.

It seems probable that this large but unfortunately badly eroded structure marks the position of a residence at least temporarily occupied by a person of consequence. To this points the great size of a hall, measuring forty-one by thirty-five feet, and the discovery made on a subsequent visit to the site that to the southwest of the ruin there extends for over half a mile an area where the ground not hidden by dunes is thickly covered with fragments of pottery and other hard debris. It is obviously ground once closely occupied by houses which, being built only with walls of sun-dried bricks or stamped clay (the material used also nowadays for ordinary dwellings in towns and villages of this region), could not hold out so long against wind erosion as the superior timber-and-wattle-built structures of the well-to-do.

I cannot attempt to give details of the busy days spent in searching the chain of dwellings stretching southward. Some had suffered badly from erosion; others had been better protected, and the clearing of the high sand which filled their rooms cost great efforts. Kharoshthi records on wood, whether letters, accounts, drafts or memos, turned up in almost every one of these dwellings. Besides, there were found architectural wood carvings, household objects and implements illustrative of everyday life and the prevailing industries. Though nothing of intrinsic value had been left behind by the last dwellers of this modest Pompeii, there was sufficient evidence of the ease in which they had lived in the large number of individual rooms provided with fireplaces, comfortable sitting platforms, wooden cupboards, etc. Remains of fenced gardens and of avenues of poplars or fruit trees could be traced almost invariably near these houses. Where dunes had afforded protection, the gaunt, bleached trunks in these orchards, chiefly mulberry trees, still rose as high as ten to twelve feet.

But what at first fascinated me most was the absolute barrenness and the wide vistas of the desert around me. The ruins at this end of the site lie beyond the zone of living tamarisk scrub. Like the open sea, the expanse of yellow dunes lay before me, with nothing to break their wavy monotony but the bleached trunks of trees or rows of splintered posts marking houses which rose here and there above the sandy crests. They often curiously suggested the picture of a wreck reduced to the mere ribs of its timber. There was the fresh breeze, too, and the great silence of the ocean.

I must forgo any attempt at detailed description of the results here yielded by a fortnight of exacting but fruitful work. Yet a particularly rich haul of ancient documents may claim mention were it only on account of the characteristic conditions under which it was discovered. I was clearing a large residence in a group of ruins on the extreme west of the site. It had on my previous visit been traced too late for complete exploration, and I had ever since kept it, as it were, faithfully *in petto*. Fine pieces of architectural wood carving brought to light near a large central hall soon proved that the dwelling must have been that of a well-to-do person. Finds of Kharoshthi records of respectable size, including a wooden tablet fully three feet long, in what appeared to have been an anteroom, suggested his having been an official of some consequence.

The hope of finding more in his office was soon justified when the first strokes of the "Ketman" laid bare regular files of documents near the floor of a narrow room adjoining the central hall. Their number soon rose to over a hundred. Most of them were "wedges" as used for the conveyance of executive orders; others, on oblong tablets, accounts, lists and miscellaneous "office papers," to use once more an anachronism. Evidently we had hit upon office files thrown down here and excellently preserved, under the cover of five to six feet of sand. The scraping of the mud flooring for detached pieces was still proceeding when a strange discovery rewarded honest Rustam, the most experienced digger of my "old guard."

Already during the first clearing I had noticed a large lump of clay or plaster near the wall where the packets of tablets lay closest. I had ordered it to be left undisturbed, though I thought little of its having come to that place by more than accident. Rustam had just extracted between it and the wall a well-preserved double-wedge tablet, when I saw him eagerly burrow with his hands into the floor just as when my fox terrier Dash was at work opening rat holes. Before I could put any questions I saw Rustam triumphantly draw forth from about six inches below the floor a complete rectangular document with its double clay seal intact and its envelope still unopened. When the hole was enlarged we saw that the space toward the wall and below its foundation beam was full of closely packed layers of similar documents.

It was clear that we had struck a small hidden archive, and my joy at this novel experience was great; for apart from the interest of the documents themselves and their splendid preservation, the condition in which they were found furnished very valuable indications. With a few exceptions, all the rectangular documents, of which fully three dozen were cleared in the end, had their elaborate string fastenings unopened and sealed down on the envelope. This manifestly confirmed the conjectural explanation I had arrived at in the case of a few previous finds of this kind. These were agreements or bonds which had to be kept under their original fastenings and seals in order that in case of need their validity might be safely established.

Characteristically enough, the only two open records proved to be letters addressed in due form to the "Honorable Cojhbo Sojaka, whose sight is dear to gods and men," whose name and title I had previously read on many of the official notes dug up in the scattered files. The care which had been taken to hide the deposit and at the same time to mark its position—for that, no doubt was the purpose of the clay lump, as Rustam had quite rightly guessed—showed that the owner had been obliged to leave the place in an emergency, but with a hope of returning.

Great care had to be taken in the removal to save the clay sealings from any risk of damage. A number of them held impressions from two or three intaglios. My care was amply rewarded when I discovered on clearing them at night in my tent that almost all had remained as fresh as when first impressed, and that most of them were from seals of classical workmanship representing an archaic Zeus, Heracles with club and lion skin, Eros, Pallas Promachos, helmeted busts, etc. It was strange how victoriously the art of the Greek die-cutter had left its marks in this distant region, and strange, too, to know myself the *de facto* possessor of Sojaka's deeds probably referring to lands and other real property buried long centuries since under the silent dunes. Where was the law court that might help me to claim them?

As our work proceeded to the south of the site the surroundings grew, if anything, more somber and almost lugubrious, in spite of the appearance of still living scrub. The ruins had to be searched for amidst closely set sand cones raising their heads covered with tangled masses of tamarisk, dead or living, to forty or fifty feet. Ruins just emerging from the foot of sand hills with deeply eroded ground on the other side made up weird pictures of solitude. The dust haze raised by a cold northeast wind added an appropriately colored atmosphere. It was almost with a feeling of relief that we emerged at last upon somewhat more open ground toward the southern end of the site. The ruined dwellings were small there; but an inspection of the ground near by revealed features of interest.

Only some sixty yards off the ruin that on my renewed visit had yielded the first tablets there stood a square of dead mulberry trees raising their trunks up to ten feet or more, which had once cast their shade over a tank still marked by a depression. The stream from which the canal which once fed the tank must have taken its rise was not far to seek; for behind the nearest ridge of high tamarisk-crowned sand cones to the west there still lay a foot bridge about ninety feet long stretched across an unmistakable dry river bed. Of the trestles which had carried the bridge two still stood upright. Beyond the left bank stretched shriveled remains of arbors for upwards of 200 yards. For over two miles to the northwest I could follow the traces of the ancient river bed, in places completely covered by drift sand, but emerging again among low dunes and patches of dead forest. Over all this strange ground, desiccation was written most plainly.

Particularly impressive evidence offered of the great change which had come over this ground when, beyond a curious deep depression probably wind-eroded and flanked by high tamarisk cones and not far from that foot bridge, we found the remains of a large and remarkably well-preserved orchard. The carefully arranged rows of various fruit trees and the trellis-carried vines, though dead for more than sixteen centuries, could be examined here in almost uncanny clearness.

The four-hundred-odd miles of desert through which my marches took me in November 1906 from the Niya site northeastward past Charchan to Charkhlik offered opportunities for interesting observations both geographical and archeological at more than one point. Here it must suffice to mention the solution which some fortunate finds at an ancient site to the east of the Endere river afforded for a problem of distinct antiquarian interest. Starting from Imam Ja'far Sadik, we reached this site after a succession of trying marches across the forbiddingly high ridges of dunes which separate the dying courses of the Niya and Yartungaz rivers from the bed of the Endere river before this too loses itself in the sands of the Taklamakan.

I had first visited that ruined site of Endere in 1901, when excavations carried out within a small fort protected by a circular rampart had allowed me to clear a small Buddhist shrine closely corresponding in type to those found at Dandan-oilik. Among the interesting finds made there were remains of Tibetan Buddhist manuscripts, the oldest so far known specimens of that script and language. A Chinese inscription scratched into the wall of the temple cella recorded the visit of a Chinese administrator and gave a date corresponding to A.D. 719. This together with the deposit of Tibetan texts made it quite certain that the fort must have been occupied in the eighth century A.D., toward the close of which the Tarim basin passed for a time under Tibetan domination.

Now, it was curious that Hsüan-tsang, the great Chinese pilgrim who had passed by the same route from Niya to Charchan about A.D. 645, found no inhabited place on his ten days' desert march. But he distinctly mentions in a position exactly corresponding to the Endere site ruins of abandoned settlements which were described to him as "old seats of the Tukhara" famous in Central-Asian history.

Discoveries made on my second visit conclusively proved that we have here a definite historical instance of an old site at one time abandoned to the desert having been reoccupied after the lapse of centuries. A shifting of the low dunes near the fort had exposed much-eroded remains of some ancient dwellings which I had not previously noticed. When I had the consolidated refuse heaps which had saved them from complete destruction carefully cleared, there came to light some wooden documents in Kharoshthi script which clearly belonged to the early centuries of our era—and thus to the very period of Tukhara, *i.e.* Indo-Scythian ascendancy.

Further striking evidence of the often proved accuracy of my old pilgrim guide came to light when I discovered that the rampart of the circular fort, obviously built after his passage, was in one place actually raised over a bank of refuse which belonged to the first centuries of our era. This was proved by a Kharoshthi document on wood found there. It is significant that the time which saw the fort built and life brought back again to Hsüan-tsang's ruined site coincides with the re-establishment of Chinese power in the Tarim basin which assured its peace and security. I may add that on a later visit to the Endere site I was able to trace more remains of that earlier settlement which Hsüan-tsang on his passage had found abandoned to the desert.

CHAPTER VII

The Ruins of Miran

BY THE BEGINNING of December 1906 I found myself at the small oasis of Charkhlik. Though now merely a modest village, it represents the chief place and official headquarters of a district then extending over more than five degrees of longitude from east to west. That the whole of the district does not count more than about five hundred households, including the semi-nomadic herdsmen and fishermen known as Loplik, sufficiently indicates the desert character of the whole territory. To the east it comprises the forbidding expanse of the dried-up salt sea bed to which I referred in the first chapter, and the Lop-nor marshes, which form the last remnant of that prehistoric sea. They receive the water of the dying Tarim river, and with it all that is left of the drainage of the huge basin called after it.

The territory is now known as Lop, just as it was when Marco Polo passed here, toward the close of the thirteenth

century, before crossing the "great desert of Lop," as he calls
it, on his way to Cathay, or westernmost China. Very poor
as its economic resources must always have been—for the
ground capable of cultivation is extremely limited—yet this
territory was very important to the Chinese in ancient times
as the land of passage through which led the line of their earliest advance into Central Asia. Hence the accounts in the Chinese Annals of the Former Han and succeeding dynasties often
mention the territory, first under the name of *Lou-lan* and
subsequently under that of *Shan-shan.*

Conclusive evidence shows that the small oasis of
Charkhlik was already the chief place of Lop when Hsüan-
tsang made his way through it on his return to China about
A.D. 645, and that it had been so for several centuries before.
Its archeological remains proved scanty, as might be expected
on ground which had remained cultivated for a long time or
been reoccupied after abandonment, as it is now again today.
All the same, Charkhlik was a place of importance to me; for
it was at this last inhabited locality that I had to make my
preparations for my long-planned exploration of the ruined
site of ancient Lou-lan, situated in the desert to the north of
Lop-nor and first discovered by Dr. Hedin in 1900.

In the next chapters I shall describe the trying but very
fruitful and interesting labors accomplished on my second
and third expeditions into that forbidding and now utterly
waterless desert. But before I do so I may give some account
of the discoveries which attended my excavations at the ruins
of Miran. I first reached them after setting out from Charkhlik on December 7, 1906, for the Lop desert. Having by some
rapid trial digging ascertained their importance, I returned to
them by the close of January for thorough excavation. The
site proved a very desolate spot, situated about fifty miles to
the northeast of Charkhlik at the foot of the absolutely barren
gravel glacis which stretches down from the K'un-lun mountains toward the westernmost portion of the Lop-nor marshes.

The latter had probably within historical times receded considerably to the north of the position occupied by the ruins.

A small stream known as Jahan-sai, which had once been used to irrigate the area, still passes within a few miles of the ruins. Near its banks the people of Abdal on the Tarim had established a small colony where they could cultivate wheat without abandoning their life as fishermen on the river. They had no habitations there at the time, but in the narrow jungle belt by the river our camels and ponies could find such grazing as dry reeds, dead leaves of wild poplars and thorny scrub could offer. Thus we were spared for a time the usual anxieties about transport of water. But none of our party is ever likely to forget the misery we endured during those three weeks of incessant hard work from the icy gales which blew almost incessantly. There were days when all my assistants were on the sick list with the exception of my ever alert and bright Chinese secretary, Chiang Ssŭ-yeh.

My first view of the site was obtained from the top of a completely ruined mound showing solid masonry of sun-dried bricks. As a tunnel dug into it by "treasure seekers" showed, it undoubtedly marked the remains of a Buddhist stupa, or relic tower. Its top commanded an excellent view of other ruins which, rising over the wide level flat of gravel eastward, looked like low islands on an inland sea. The old fort of which Tokhta Akhun, my hardy Loplik guide, had spoken as the principal ruin of the site, looked quite imposing from afar. But when I had approached it and was eagerly clambering over the badly breached walls of its west face I was struck at once by their inferior construction as suggesting a comparatively late date.

The trial excavation started along the interior face of the east wall soon confirmed this, but at the same time revealed that a rich mine was here awaiting antiquarian search. In inverse proportion to the small size and roughness of the half-underground hovels brought to light was the amount of the rubbish which seemed to fill them to the roof. From the very start of the digging, pieces of paper and wood inscribed in Tibetan cropped up in numbers. The layers of refuse of all kinds left behind by all the occupants continued to yield such records, complete or fragmentary, right down to the bottom. The first day's work brought the total up to two hundred. Similarly, the remains of discarded implements of all sorts, fragments of ragged clothing, arms, etc., were abundant. Everything pointed to the conclusion that these deep deposits of rubbish, rich in archeological plums—and remarkable, too, for their dirt—had accumulated during a protracted period of Tibetan occupation. Historical evidence from the Chinese Annals of the T'ang dynasty justified my assigning this occupation to the eighth or ninth century of our era.

On the following morning I proceeded on a reconnaissance to a ruin about a mile and a half away to the northeast, which Tokhta Akhun had spoken of as showing remains of sculptures. The ruin proved to be that of a Buddhist temple. Above the debris encumbering the sides of the base that alone survived, there still showed remains of fine stucco relievos arranged for architectural decoration. On clearing a small portion of the base on the east side, I lighted upon fragments of stucco sculptures of large size. Then I felt quite assured that the temple dated from a period far more ancient than that of the Tibetan fort. A number of observations made it appear *a priori* very probable that here a site of considerable antiquity had after abandonment been reoccupied, as I had noted before at the site of Endere, between Niya and Charchan.

It seemed hard to leave behind such a promising site, even for a time, without exhausting it. But a variety of practical considerations, mainly connected with climatic conditions, made the postponement imperative. And here I may point out, by the way, that only by such carefully planned adaptation to the widely different climatic conditions prevailing in the various regions did it become possible to extend our geograph-

ical and archeological explorations over the vast areas covered
by the surveys of my second and third expeditions. So it came
about that the clearing of that desolate Tibetan stronghold
could not be resumed by us until my return from the absolute
desert by January 23, 1907. Camp was then pitched close under the walls of the fort. But the hope that they would afford
some protection from the icy winds ever sweeping this desert
glacis of the mountains proved vain; so frequently they veered
around to catch us.

The ruined fort quite fulfilled the promise held out by
the first experimental digging. The rooms and half-underground hovels which had sheltered its Tibetan garrison during
the eighth to the ninth century A.D. were rough enough in design and construction but proved to contain in some respects
the most remarkable refuse accumulations it has ever fallen to
my lot to clear. In the midst of inconceivable dirt, sweepings
from the hearth, litter of straw, remnants of ragged clothing
and broken implements, there were to be picked up in plenty
Tibetan documents on wood and paper, fragments in many
cases but often quite complete. From a single small apartment
still retaining in parts its smoke-begrimed wall plaster we recovered over a hundred such pieces. The rubbish reached in
places to a height of close on nine feet.

Evidence of a varied and often rather unsavory kind
seemed to indicate that the rooms serving as casemates continued to be tenanted to the last, while the refuse accumulations on the floor kept steadily rising. Nothing but absolute
indifference to dirt could have induced the occupiers to let
room after room of their closely packed quarters be turned
into regular dustbins, choked in some instances up to the roof.

I have had occasion to acquire a rather extensive experience in clearing ancient rubbish heaps, and know how to diag-
nose them. But for intensity of sheer dirt and age-persisting
smelliness I shall always put the rich "castings" of Tibetan
warriors in the front rank. More than a year later, when clearing the remains of a small ruined fort on the Mazar-tagh hill

north of Khotan, more than five hundred miles away, I correctly disgnosed its Tibetan occupation by the smell of the refuse even before finding definite antiquarian evidence. Among plenty of curious finds at the Miran fort I may specially mention here only the very abundant relics of defensive armor in the shape of lacquered scales of leather. They evidently belonged to different suits of scale armor and varied in size and ornamentation.

It was hard to find time for the examination of such technical details during the days when icy gales were almost constantly blowing. On the top of the dominating east rampart, where I had to stay most of the time to watch the excavations proceeding in different places, the onslaught of the wind was felt to the full. Whenever I descended to the diggings I enjoyed my share of the blinding dust made up largely of disintegrated filth. The worst of exposure and discomfort was felt near the southeastern corner of the fort, where the protecting wall curtain had been breached by wind erosion and fallen. And just there two fairly large rooms presented a particularly rich mine of refuse and records.

The great mass of the Tibetan documents on wood and paper of which in the end we recovered here over a thousand, has proved on examination by such competent scholars as Professors F. W. Thomas and A. H. Francke to consist of miscellaneous office papers, more often than not of a petty kind. They are reports, applications, indents and the like, all couched in the language of everyday life. Tibetan literature, while abounding in canonical Buddhist texts, possesses exceedingly little of early secular writing. This gives distinct interest to this mass of miscellaneous documents, quite apart from the manifold glimpses they yield of local conditions at the time when the Tarim basin had passed for a century under Tibetan domination. A great number of the records treat of military affairs, mentioning frontier posts in need of supplies or help, troop movements, etc.

Among the numerous localities named I have been able

to identify the "Castle of Great Nob" with Charkhlik and the "Castle of Little Nob" with Miran itself. The name *Nob*, like Hsüan-tsang's *Na-fu-po*, obviously corresponds to the medieval and modern *Lop* applied to the whole territory. Other evidence furnished by those records has made it possible to prove that the far earlier ruins at Miran, to which we shall presently turn, mark the site of Yü-ni, which the Chinese Annals mention as the "old eastern town" of Shan-shan.

The absence of even the slightest scrap of Chinese writing among all these records is a significant indication of the total disappearance of Chinese influence and control in the Tarim basin from the last third of the eighth century onward. But, on the other hand, a crumpled-up little package of papers in "Runic" Turkish script supplies distinct proof that this distant corner, too, of the Tarim basin had seen something of those valiant Western Turk tribes who, whether as allies or as rivals of the Tibetans, had a main share in bringing down Chinese domination in Central Asia. The late Professor Thomsen, the famous decipherer of the Orkhon inscriptions in the earliest known Turkish tongue, has published these papers and shown that they date approximately from the same period and contain long lists of persons, apparently Turkish soldiers, to whom warrants or passports were issued.

There can be no doubt that the Tibetan stronghold was intended to guard the direct route from the southern oases of the Tarim basin to Tun-huang on the westernmost confines of China proper. This route passing south of Lop-nor had, like the one to the north of it, with which I shall deal later on, been used as a main line of communication into China from the times of the Han dynasty onward. Hsüan-tsang, and centuries after him Marco Polo, had followed this track through the desert. So there was enough to invest this trying desert track with historical interest for me. But before I myself set out by it from Miran, my work at this site was rewarded by the discovery of art remains far older and of far wider interest than those relics of Tibetan occupation.

These came to light from the debris mounds of some Buddhist shrines surviving wind erosion and scattered over the bare ground in the vicinity of the fort. These shrines, as conclusive archeological evidence showed, must have been in ruins long before the Tibetan occupation led to the erection of the fort. At the ruin to which my attention had already been directed on my first visit to the site, two stories could be clearly distinguished. Destruction, mainly by wind erosion, had completely removed the stucco decoration from the upper one. But when we came to clear the lower one from the encumbering masses of debris, there came to light half-engaged columns of strikingly Persepolitan look and scanty remains of life-size statues which once filled the niches between them. As the heavy debris was being removed along the passage which once enclosed the whole oblong fane, we soon came upon a colossal head in stucco representing a Buddha. It measured fully seventeen inches across the temple. As the material was merely a coarse clay mixed with straw, the lifting and subsequent safe packing of this heavy mass of sculpture was no easy task.

This and several other colossal heads subsequently unearthed all showed with equal clearness modeling in Greco-Buddhist style. The origin of this and several other colossal heads was revealed when the clearing of the passage showed its outer wall to be lined by the torsos of six huge figures seated with folded legs. Across the knees they measured a little over seven feet. The surviving drapery of these colossal seated Buddhas proved how closely the sculptor in faraway Lop had followed the elaborate arrangement of the folds which the Greco-Buddhist style of Gandhara derived from classical models.

That the abandonment of the temple had taken place centuries before the Tibetan occupation became highly probable when close to the base of one statue I discovered a fairly large fragment of a Sanskrit palm-leaf manuscript in Brahmi characters. The material showed that the manuscript had been written in India, and the type of the Brahmi script that its date could not be later than the fourth century.

But the influence exercised by classical art was revealed still more impressively when I started exploration at a cluster of mounds suggesting much-decayed stupas about a mile to the west of the fort. On clearing the smallest of these mounds, I came upon the remains of a solid structure, square outside but circular within. It had once carried a dome and enclosed a small stupa. Heavy masses of debris fallen from the vaulting and the upper portion of the rotunda walls completely blocked the circular passage around the stupa base. Fragments of painted stucco cropped up here rapidly. It became evident that the interior walls of the rotunda had once been adorned with frescoes. Yet when the digging there reached a level of about four feet above the floor and a delicately painted dado of winged angels (Fig. 6) began to show on the wall, I felt completely taken by surprise. How could I have expected by the desolate shores of Lop-nor, in the very heart of innermost Asia, to come upon such classical representations of cherubim?

As in eager excitement I cleared head after head with my bare hands, I rapidly convinced myself that the approach to classical design and color treatment was closer in these wall paintings than in any work of ancient pictorial art I had seen so far, whether north or south of the K'un-lun. Much in the vivacious look of the large fully opened eyes, in the expression of the small dimpled lips, etc., brought back to my mind the fine portrait heads of Greek girls and youths to be seen on painted panels from mummies of the Ptolemaic and Roman periods found in Egypt.

I was still wondering how to account for the distinctly classical style in the representation of these winged angels and their apparent loan from Christian iconography when the discovery in the passage of remnants of colored silk streamers supplied definite evidence for the dating. They were obviously votive offerings, and the writing of the Kharoshthi inscriptions found on them resembled exactly that on the wooden and leather documents from the Niya site. The gift of the inscribed streamers, with the writing still remarkably fresh and black, could not have preceded the abandonment of the shrine by any great length of time. Hence it followed that Miran, like the site of Niya, must have been abandoned about or soon after the close of the third century A.D.

I cannot describe here other minor finds supporting this conclusion, but must refer briefly to remarkable fragments of frescoed plaster which were found leaning in closely packed layers against a portion of the wall still standing in the southeast corner of the passage. They had once decorated the higher wall faces and, sliding down on the debris already accumulated below, had escaped destruction, soon to be covered up and protected by sand. It was a very ticklish task safely to lift and recover these terribly brittle panes of mud plaster with their friable surface of thin stucco painted in tempera.

I need not describe here how this task was accomplished in spite of the very trying conditions of work, and the safe packing done with such scanty materials as I could improvise. My satisfaction was great when, on unpacking the cases more than two years later, I found that the great care taken had allowed all these remains of painted mud plaster to reach the British Museum in safety. There it became possible for my devoted friend and assistant, Mr. F. H. Andrews, to assure their preservation by an ingenious method of mounting on plaster of Paris reinforced with expanded aluminum. By carefully joining up various fragments, we recovered thus considerable portions of fresco compositions forming part of the painted friezes which once decorated the rotunda wall higher up.

All the fresco remains thus preserved represent typical scenes of Buddhist iconography. Thus, in one picture, the figure is obviously the Buddha dressed in the mendicant's red-brown robe, standing with his right hand raised in the well-known "gesture of protection." By his side stand six disciples with heads shaved as monks. The scene is clearly laid in a garden or grove, but not enough is left to determine the particular legend illustrated from Buddha's life story.

However, it is the artistic treatment in composition, design and coloring, rather than the iconographic purport, which gives to all the fresco remains from the Miran shrines their special interest and great value. Buddhist as the subjects are, all details in the artistic presentation are derived from Hellenistic models. It may suffice here to point to the large straight eyes of the teacher and disciples, so different from the elongated slanting eyes which all figures painted later in Central Asia and the Far East display. Equally significant is the drapery, the peculiar pose of the curving fingers emerging, as it were, from a toga, etc. As regards methods of technique, a most striking testimony is supplied by the regular employment of "light and shade" wherever flesh is painted in these frescoes. The use of chiaroscuro, so well known to classical art, has never before been observed in the old pictorial work of India, Central Asia or the Far East.

Varied and instructive as the surviving fragments of those frescoed friezes are, it is the fine winged-angel figures of the dado which have from the first appealed to me most. The seven of them which had survived have all been brought safely away and are now divided between the British Museum and my collection at New Delhi. While in all externals the aim manifestly is at a homogeneous effect befitting a heavenly fraternity, a strong individual element is cleverly introduced in the faces. Such details as the varied expression in the eyes, the pose of the head, etc., can be adequately studied only in the originals or in the full reproductions fortunately available in my *Serindia*. But I may at least touch upon one indication of the skill with which the painter-decorators at Miran adapted designs, borrowed from the West and, no doubt, often used, to peculiar structural conditions. Care was taken so to fit the pose of the winged busts in the dado to the position they occupy low down on the wall of the circular passage that their raised gaze may just catch the eyes of the worshiper as he performs the ceremonial circumambulation of the stupa.

Taking into account certain youthful winged forms met with in Greco-Buddhist relievos, it appears highly probable that these figures of the Miran dado must be traced back to the young winged Eros of Greek mythology as their ultimate ancestor. But this descent lay, no doubt, through intermediate stages, influenced by Oriental conceptions. To put it quite plainly, the figures of the Miran dado curiously suggest an affinity to the angels of some Early Christian church. But it is well to remember that the idea of angels as winged celestial messengers was familiar to more than one religious system of Western Asia before the rise of Christianity.

Nowhere in the Hellenized Near East do we know at present of graphic representations of angels from a sufficiently early age to throw light on the question as to where and when the cupids of classical mythology underwent transformation into the type of winged figures seen on the Miran dado. But it is easy to explain how those angels came to figure in the decoration of a Buddhist shrine on the very confines of true China. The Greco-Buddhist sculpture of Gandhara shows that figures copied from the winged Eros were actually used there to represent that class of celestial attendants which Buddhist mythology has borrowed from early Hindu lore and knows by the name of Gandharvas. If a visitor to the Miran shrine ever cared to inquire from its guardians about the significance of these winged beings so curiously reminiscent of figures he might have seen before in distant regions like Syria, Mesopotamia or Western Persia, the local guardians could readily have labeled them Gandharvas.

But we may well feel in doubt as to whether this iconographic explanation is really needed, for on excavating a mound only some sixty yards off, I discovered there a Buddhist shrine of exactly the same rotunda type decorated on its passage wall with a dado showing figures altogether secular and frankly Western in character.

In this ruin, too, the rotunda held in its center a stupa enclosed by a circular passage, both somewhat larger than in the shrine first described. That both shrines dated from approximately the same period was proved at the outset by the discovery of a similar angel bust painted on what little survived of the wall of an outer square passage. The stupa within had suffered badly from the burrowing of treasure seekers, but gilt fragments of fine wood carvings which once adorned its top were recovered from the debris with which the fallen dome had choked the circular passage. The clearing of this passage by the side of its eastern entrance revealed that what remained of the passage wall was decorated with frescoes arranged in a frieze with a dado below it. On the former there soon emerged some short inscriptions in Kharoshthi script and Indian language by the side of two figures. There was thus definite proof that these shrines and wall paintings dated back to the early centuries of our era.

On the west side, facing the entrance, a segment of the enclosing wall had been completely leveled down by early treasure seekers. Hence the frescoes were now found extending over two detached hemicycles. Owing to greater decay, the one on the northern side retained but little of the upper frieze, but in the frescoed dado below it was easy, in spite of faded colors, to recognize a remarkably graceful composition quite classical in design (Fig. 7). Its connecting feature was a broad festoon of wreaths and flowers carried by youthful figures, true *putti*. Among these, wingless cupids alternated with figures wearing the Phrygian cap and unmistakably copied from the Persian god Mithra worshiped throughout the Roman Empire. In the hollows of the undulating festoon there rose alternatively heads and busts of men and girls. All of them, by the expression of the faces, the dress and the objects carried in their hands, seemed as if meant to convey frank enjoyment of life. No relation whatever to Buddhist worship or mythology was to be traced either in these figures or those far better preserved which were seen between the garland-carrying *putti* in the southern hemicycle of the dado. Among them were graceful girls, richly adorned with flowers, carrying a decanter and cup; playing on a guitar, etc. (Fig. 7). In their faces Greek features seemed to mingle with others strangely reminiscent of Levantine or Circassian types of beauty, while the elaborate hairdress pointed to the Near East or Iran.

Still more remarkable perhaps were the strikingly varied types presented by the male busts. There were youths with heads quite Roman in look; their right hand was raised with some fingers stretched out and others bent under, just as if engaged in the classical game of Mora. Other busts with heavy beards, abundant hair and rich dress were unmistakably meant to represent barbarians from the north or west. The expression of the eyes, the broad lips, the low forehead seemed to convey frank devotion to the good things of this world; and a transparent goblet raised against the breast marks it still more plainly. In marked contrast to these representatives of Western and Northern manhood was to be seen the bust of a young Indian prince, clean-shaven and richly adorned with jewelry. An unmistakable expression of softness conveyed by the features and dreamy-looking eyes, quite as much as by the peculiar peaked headdress, vividly recalled the well-known type which in the Greco-Buddhist sculpture is used for the representation of Prince Gautama before he became the Buddha.

The utter desolation around greatly heightened the effect of this bright cycle of figures. They looked to me as if meant to symbolize the varied pleasures of life. How strangely contrasted with the discomforts and cares of the protracted la-

bors we were carrying on in dreary wastes holding nothing
but traces of a dead past! With that cycle of youthful figures
before me, I might well have felt tempted to believe myself
rather among the ruins of some villa in Syria or some other
Eastern province of the Roman Empire than among those of
a Buddhist sanctuary on the very confines of China.

Yet a look at the painted frieze, about eighteen feet long,
which survived on the southeastern wall segment, sufficed to
dispel any doubt. There on a field of true Pompeian red was
to be seen a procession representing the Jataka legend of
Prince Vessantara, well known among the stories of the Buddha's previous births. Starting from the left of the entrance is
shown the pious prince riding out of the palace gate, banished
by his royal father for undue prodigality in charitable gifts.
Before him a classical quadriga carries his equally pious wife
and his two sons. Then the scene shifts to the forest where the
prince, now seen on foot, presents his miraculous wish-grant-
ing white elephant to four Brahman mendicants who meet
him asking for alms. The wall, being broken farther on, did
not allow me to follow the rest of the story. But fresco fragments surviving above the dado on the northern hemicycle
proved that there had been represented the hermit life led
by the princely couple after their retirement into the jungle,
and finally their happy return to their royal home with which
the pious story ends.

Both frieze and dado were clearly painted by the same
hand. But while in the frieze the painter was manifestly following the conventional representation which Greco-Buddhist art had long before adopted for that particular legend,
he was left free by the quasi-secular character of the dado to
take there his inspiration from the contemporary art of the
Roman Orient. This impression has received distinct support
from what a short inscription in Kharoshthi painted on the
thigh of the white elephant has fortunately revealed to us
about the painter of the frescoes. As interpreted by Abbé

Boyer, s.j., the distinguished French scholar and a valued collaborator on all my Kharoshthi materials, it records the name of the painter as *Tita* as well as the amount of the payment he received for his work. There is some doubt as to the words indicating the amount, but none about the name, and as "Tita" is a form which cannot be accounted for etymologically in any Indian or Iranian language, I feel no hesitation about recognizing in it the rendering which the Roman name Titus would necessarily receive in Sanskrit and Prakrit.

We need feel no surprise to find this name Titus, which was in popular use during the early centuries of our era throughout the Roman Orient, borne by a painter-decorator whom his calling had carried so far east on the way to China. For, from a record of Marinus of Tyre, preserved in Ptolemy's *Geography*, we know that men of much the same origin, Roman Eurasians, as it were, were accustomed to visit the "land of the Seres," *i.e.* China proper, in connection with the silk trade, and that long before the probable date of the Miran shrines.

It was easy to make sure by repeated tracings of exact copies of this and another short Kharoshthi inscription on the frieze which refers to Prince Vessantara shown below it. But climatic and other difficulties rendered it practically impossible for me at the time to secure such a photographic record of the frescoes as would do full justice to their artistic importance. I soon convinced myself that, owing to the peculiar brittleness of the plaster on which they were painted, any attempt to remove larger pieces of the frescoed surface would result in mere destruction, unless the wall behind were first systematically cut away to permit of safe detachment. Such a laborious task would have required at least a month, if not more. It was impossible then to spare this time without grave risk that the long journey on which I was bent through the Lop desert to Tun-huang would be rendered impracticable by the melting, as the season advanced, of the ice of the salt springs on which, at a number of stages, we should have to depend for water. So, reluctantly enough, I had to leave this difficult task for later.

My regret at this necessity proved only too well justified. When in March 1908 I was able to let Naik Ram Singh return for that task from the neighborhood of Khotan, my skillful and ever-plucky "handyman" reached the site only to fall there a victim to that fell disease of glaucoma before he could start on his task of removal. The heroic way in which the brave Sikh stuck to the attempt even after he had gone blind first in one eye and then in the other is a tragic story, too long and too sad to tell here in detail.

When I myself in January 1914 regained the ruined site, I found to my dismay that the care both myself and later again Naik Ram Singh had taken to have the interior of the shrine safely buried again under sand and debris had not sufficed to protect it. An ill-managed attempt to remove the frescoes was made, some years after my discovery had been reported, by a young Japanese traveler who lacked preparation, technical skill and experience equal to his archeological zeal. The attempt was thus bound to result in mere destruction, as was proved only too clearly by the shattered fragments of painted hard plaster which I found littering the passage floor below the southern hemicycle. This hapless effort after "archeological proceeds" had fortunately been abandoned before it extended to the northern hemicycle, and the frescoed dado of this we succeeded in removing without damage after prolonged and exacting labor. But of the greater portion of the paintings I had first brought to light here, my photographs, imperfect as they are, and my notebooks have alone preserved a record.

CHAPTER VIII

Explorations at Ancient Lou-lan

IT WAS AT THE SMALL OASIS of Charkhlik, as already related, that in the first days of December 1906 I had to make preparations for my long-planned expedition to the ruins in the utterly waterless desert north of Lop-nor which Dr. Hedin had first discovered on his memorable journey of 1900. After exploring whatever remains we might trace there, I proposed to take my caravan across Marco Polo's "Desert of Lop" to Tun-huang by the ancient route which he followed and which had since fallen into oblivion for centuries. Everything pointed to the need of careful arrangements for transport and supplies if serious risks were to be avoided. Equally important it was to husband my time as carefully as possible; for work in waterless desert would be practicable only during the few months of winter when the cold would allow me to transport water in the form of ice.

The extremely limited resources of Charkhlik, a mere

village as befits the headquarters of a district almost wholly desert, made these preparations an exacting task. Within three days I had to raise a contingent of fifty laborers for the proposed excavations, with food supplies to last all of us for five weeks, and to collect as many camels as I possibly could for the transport; for we would have to carry water, or rather ice, sufficient to serve the needs of us all on seven days' march across the desert, then during a prolonged stay at the ruins, and lastly on the return journey.

The problem looked formidable enough when I found that, after exhausting local resources, I could raise the number of camels only to twenty-one, including my own seven, fine hardened animals, it is true, and some animals brought on hire from Charchan. The problem would have been still more complicated had I not been able to reckon as a convenient depot upon the small fishermen's hamlet at Abdal, near where the waters of the Tarim emptied themselves into the Lop marshes. There I could leave behind all baggage and supplies not immediately needed, to be available when the time came for the move through the desert to Tun-huang.

Fortunately Liao Ta-lo-ye, the Chinese magistrate of this forlorn district, proved most helpful. Soon I was joined, too, by two hardy hunters from Abdal—Mulla, a wiry elderly man, and burly Tokhta Akhun. Both had seen service with Hedin and were not frightened, like the rest of the men, by the risks of such a desert expedition. It was true that neither of them had ever approached the ruined site from the side of Abdal, and therefore could not be expected to act as guides beyond the point where we should leave the marshes. But they knew the nature of the ground we should have to traverse, and, inured to hardships by their experience as hunters, they were ready to face the wintry desert like men. Their prompt appearance on the scene put some heart into the local cultivators selected as diggers, who were thoroughly frightened by the prospect of having to leave their homes in the depth of winter for a distant and wholly unknown journey in the waterless desert northeastward. Their relatives were bewailing them as already doomed.

After very strenuous efforts we were able to start on the morning of December 6. As I reviewed my crew of laborers duly assembled by the edge of the last fields I was greatly struck by the strong Mongolian look in the faces of the Lopliks. These are the descendants of the autochthonous semi-nomadic stock of fishermen, as distinguished from the Turki colonists brought from the distant western oases. There the relatives of the men bade us farewell with shouts of *"Yol bolsun,"* "May there be a way." Rarely had this Turki "good-by" sounded to me so pregnant in meaning.

I have already related how trial excavations detained us for a couple of days at the ruined site of Miran, reached after two long marches across an utterly bare glacis of gravel. By December 10 we arrived at Abdal, the last little fishing hamlet on the Tarim. There our ponies as well as all supplies and baggage, not needed until the start for Tun-huang, were left behind in charge of Tila Bai, the most reliable of my Turki servants. My devoted Chinese secretary, Chiang Ssŭ-yeh, much to his regret, had also to remain behind, eager as he was to keep by me. His feet would not have been equal to the long tramps on the trying ground before us, and it was impossible to spare camels for his person and his impedimenta, slender as both were.

Next morning I started my desert column from Abdal after crossing the deep and still unfrozen Tarim. For one day we followed the incipient Lop-nor marshes eastward, and luckily found good thick ice already available in one of the fresh-water lagoons formed by the dying river. Every available camel was loaded with big bags full of ice, each load weighing between four and five hundred pounds. Four galvanized iron tanks full of water, also soon frozen hard, were to serve as a safe reserve. In addition we had some thirty donkeys laden with smaller bags of ice. They were to march on for two days beyond the last point where drinkable water or else ice was available and leave their loads there as a sort of halfway depot. Of course, they themselves would need water; but with a two days' thirst on them, and relieved of loads, they could be trusted to return quickly to the Tarim.

As to the camels, they were given a thoroughly long drink, six to seven big bucketsful each, and that would have to last them, for all that we knew, for some weeks. In the bitter cold of the winter they would feel the need of water far less than of grazing. No grazing could be expected for them, once the last living vegetation was left behind us, until they reached the reed beds of some salt springs to the north of the ruined site. But Hassan Akhun, my excellent head camel man on all my journeys, had duly provided in our equipment a few skins full of rape-seed oil in order to administer from time to time half a pint of this evil-smelling luxury to each of our own camels. It was the "camels' tea," so my camel factotum declared, in the cold of the winter, and it did indeed prove of great nutritive value when they had to go so long without any grazing.

After another day's march across a dreary salt-encrusted steppe, two more of my men were left behind at a pool near the Chainut-köl marsh where the water was just drinkable for animals and covered with thin ice. This was to form a kind of advance base with spare rations for the laborers. The route we now struck from this point to the north-northeast led necessarily near the one followed by Hedin, in 1900, in the reverse direction. But there was nothing to guide us except the position of the ruins as indicated in his route map and the compass. A notable change, moreover, had taken place in the physical aspects of this dismal ground since Hedin had traversed it from the north. The great newly formed lagoons in which the waters of the Tarim had in that year of an exceptional spring flood spread northward had since completely dried up. The water of the rare pools left behind in the salt-encrusted beds of these lagoons was so salt that in spite of the great cold it had not yet frozen.

By the evening of December 14 we had left the last depression with dead poplars and tamarisks behind us and camped between high sand cones covered with hoary tamarisk growth. There all the bags of ice brought on the donkeys were carefully stacked on the north side of the highest sand cone to form a depot, and the donkeys sent back in charge of two extra men. They were then to return from Chainut-köl and bring up the reserve food supplies of the laborers.

Starting off again, we passed very soon into that zone of excessive wind erosion which constitutes so striking a feature of the northern portion of the Lop desert. It consists of an endless succession of steep clay banks or terraces, separated by sharply cut trenches. These are known to the Lopliks by the convenient designation of "Yardangs." They have all been carved out by the winds with the help of the sand which they drive before them and which thus serves as their instrument of corrosion. These terraces or "Yardangs" invariably run from east-northeast to west-southwest and thus clearly mark the prevailing direction of the strongest and most persistent winds, which sweep down for the greater part of the year from the Mongolian plateaux into this the lowest portion of the Tarim basin, in obedience to the powerful atmospheric factor known as "aspiration."

The march across those terribly hard banks and trenches of clay over which our route took us at an angle was tiring men and animals badly. It was most trying to the camels' feet, their soft pads becoming easily cracked and lacerated on such ground. Thus at every camp several of the poor beasts had to undergo that painful if always effective operation of "resoling." It consists of sewing small pieces of oxhide on to the live skin so as to protect the sore spots. It is an operation requiring a good deal of skill, as the camel naturally resists it.

Fortunately Hassan Akhun was a great expert at it and ever ready to train the other camel men—though his methods of instruction were far from gentle, involving sometimes blows and kicks.

In the midst of this forbidding eroded ground we crossed at intervals shallow depressions usually marked by rows of fallen trunks of dead wild poplars. They could be followed by the eye winding away in the distance, just like branches of rivers before they lose themselves in the level expanse of the sandy desert. And, in fact, observations repeated on the different routes by which I successively crossed this part of the Lop desert, together with evidence furnished by our careful mapping of all such features, have led me to believe that these depressions with the strips of dead forest along them mark the terminal beds in which the waters of the Kuruk-darya, the "Dry River," which once irrigated the land around the ruined site of Lou-lan, had at different periods made their way into the marshes fringing the great dried-up Lop Sea. The topographical and archeological reasons for this belief have been fully set forth in *Serindia* and *Innermost Asia*. Here it must suffice to mention that they find support in interesting references furnished by Chinese historical records to this ancient delta and the dried-up sea bed eastward.

We had scarcely entered this desolate area when, on its wind-swept bare ground, flint arrowheads, knife blades and other small implements of the Stone Age, together with fragments of very coarse pottery, were picked up in frequent succession. The same happened again, after intervals, farther on. Considering that our route had to be kept as straight as possible, and search to the right or left was practically excluded, the frequency of such finds was conclusive evidence that belts of this area must have been occupied by man in late prehistoric times.

The very trying nature of the ground did not allow us to cover more than fourteen miles of march a day at the utmost, though I kept men and beasts on the move from early morning till nightfall. Nor was the maintenance of a correct course toward the compass point by which we were steering easy on ground so much broken. For the same reason I had to take care to have our track marked at points easily sighted from each other by signposts built up of dead wood or lumps of clay. These were to assure guidance for those who were to bring up our reserve store of ice and supplies.

We were nearing the end of a second troublesome march across this waste of eroded hard clay when a number of small metal objects, including Chinese copper coins of the Han dynasty, with plentiful fragments of well-finished pottery, lying on the ground gave assurance that our route led here through a belt which during historical times has known human occupation, at least in places. Yet we were, as our survey showed, still twelve miles in a direct line to the south of the ruins traced by Hedin.

By that time we were already in the clutches of an icy northeast wind which in the middle of the following night nearly blew my tent down. This bitter wind continued with short intervals during the whole of our stay in this region. With minimum temperatures rapidly falling below zero Fahrenheit it made life exceedingly trying for us all. Had it not been for the plentiful fuel supplied by the rows of bleached dead tree trunks to be found near ancient river beds, the men would have suffered even more than they did. Even with the sun shining brightly I could not keep head and hands warm with my thickest wraps and gloves while that piercing wind was blowing.

Chinese copper coins of the Han type, bronze arrowheads and other small objects had been picked up with increasing frequency on December 17, when at last in the afternoon, after crossing a broad and well-marked dead river bed, the first ruined mound indicating proximity of the site was duly sighted in the distance, exactly where Hedin's sketch map had

led me to expect it. The excitement among our band of laborers was great after the growing anxiety they had felt as
to the end of this long quest. Some eight miles across steep
clay banks and sharply cut trenches between them had still
to be covered before by nightfall I was able to pitch camp at
the foot of the ruined stupa which stands out in this weirdly
desolate landscape as the landmark of the main group of
ruins.

By next morning the excavations were started which,
carried on unremittingly for eleven days with a relatively
large number of men, enabled me to clear all remains traceable at the several groups of ruins. No time was lost in send-
ing off the camels. The majority were dispatched to the north,
where they might be expected to find grazing at least on reed
beds near a salt spring which was known to Tokhta Akhun
at the foot of the barren Kuruk-tagh hills. The rest were dispatched south to our halfway depot to fetch the supplies of
ice, etc., left there.

Looking around that morning from the high base of the
stupa, I had before me vistas which seemed strangely familiar
and at the same time strikingly novel. To the south and southwest there arose in small clusters ruins of timber and plaster-
built houses. These curiously recalled well-remembered ruins
at the Niya site, though here the winds had left far less cover
of protecting sand. Outside the area occupied by these ruins
there was nothing for the eye to rest on but an endless succession of sharply cut "Yardangs" of hard clay and deep-scoured
trenches, all running in the same direction as that relentless
northeast wind had sculptured them. It was, too, strangely
like a picture of the sea, but of one frozen hard and buckled
into innumerable pressure ridges.

Excavation was started at a ruined dwelling situated close
to the south of the stupa on the top of a terrace rising fully
eighteen feet above the wind-eroded ground. It was but a
scanty remnant of a well-built house, and the heavy timber

debris covering the slopes showed where rooms had completely disappeared through erosion of the underlying soil. Yet the search of the surviving portions sufficed to bring to light some Chinese documents on narrow slips of wood as well as on paper. Other documents were in Kharoshthi, written on wooden tablets in shape exactly corresponding to those at the Niya site, and some also on scraps of paper.

There was thus evidence from the start that the same early Indian language as found in the records of the Niya site was in common use also in this distant Lop region for indigenous administration and business. Considering how far removed the Lop region is from Khotan, this uniform extension of an Indian script and language to the extreme east of the Tarim basin was a discovery of distinct historical interest. Of a variety of other curious relics by which the search of that first ruin was rewarded I can only mention fragments of a woolen pile carpet, the earliest so far known, and a small bale of yellowish silk, fairly well preserved. Subsequent finds of wooden measures and of an inscribed silk selvedge have enabled me to prove that this bale shows us the regular width, nineteen inches, and the actual form in which that ancient and most famous product of Chinese industry used to be carried to the classical West.

From the start the wind-eroded bare ground near the ruined dwellings yielded an abundant crop of small objects in metal, glass and stone. There were fragments of bronze mirrors in abundance, often with good relievo decoration at the back, metal clasps, stone seals and the like. Beads of glass, paste or stone were picked up in plenty. The profusion of copper coins, all belonging to square-holed types of Han issue, was significant, suggesting a plentiful circulation of petty cash and that lively traffic which it usually indicates.

In a large structure to the southwest, partly built with sun-dried bricks, it was possible, notwithstanding far-advanced decay, to recognize the remains of a "Ya-mên" or Chinese administrative headquarters. In a small closetlike room which may originally have served as a prison cell, Dr. Hedin had found a considerable number of Chinese records on wood and paper, some dated between the years 264 and 270. Careful search of the whole structure yielded plenty more of such documents, including thin, curled pieces of wood, obviously shavings from slips of the regular size which had been scraped down for fresh use.

Smaller houses close by, built exactly in the same manner as the residences of the Niya site though more roughly, had probably served as quarters for officials of the local non-Chinese administration; for here Kharoshthi tablets of the familiar shape prevailed, and style and contents bore close resemblance to those of the Niya documents. But the richest haul was made in a big rubbish heap, over one hundred feet across, outside the western end of the "Ya-mên" building. Amidst layers of stable litter and other refuse this unsavory quarry, still retaining its pungent odors, yielded up abundant Chinese records both on wood and paper. Evidently they had been swept out from office rooms as "waste papers." Often they had been torn up, or else in the case of wooden slips they showed signs of having been used as "spills" to light fires with.

Kharoshthi documents, on wood, paper and silk, had also found their way, though in smaller numbers, into this general deposit of refuse. A very interesting find and unique at the time was a torn piece of paper inscribed in an "unknown" script, recalling Aramaic. This has proved since to be a relic of that Sogdian language and script, hitherto completely lost, which in the early centuries of our era was used in far-off Sogdiana, the region of the present Samarkand and Bukhara.

The interpretation of the Chinese records recovered was accomplished by my lamented great Sinologue friend, M. Chavannes, in a masterly publication issued at the Oxford University Press and including all Chinese documents from my second collection. Their contents, like those previously found by Dr. Hedin, conclusively prove that the site was that of a station designated as *Lou-lan* from the ancient name of the whole territory. This formed the western bridgehead, as it were, on the earliest route which the Chinese had opened toward the close of the second century B.C. into the Tarim basin.

The great majority of the dated documents belong to the years between A.D. 263 and 270, and thus coincide with the reign of the Emperor Wu-ti of the Chin dynasty, who, after the downfall of the Later Han, reasserted Chinese supremacy in the "Western Countries." The latest document is of the year A.D. 330. Its date is expressed in a regnal period that in China had come to a close fully fourteen years before. It is thus evident that the little station must have been completely cut off from intercourse with the central authorities of the Empire. The final abandonment of the site, and of the desert route for which it had served as a terminal station, was by that time obviously very near.

Small as the station was and limited the local resources of the whole tract, yet there is enough evidence in the Chinese documents to show the importance of the traffic it saw as long as the route remained open. There are fragments of reports emanating from or directly addressed to the "Commander-in-Chief of the Western Regions," and of records relating to military action on a stage manifestly not local. But the majority of the documents refer to petty details of administrative routine as carried on by those who looked after the cultivation, food stores and transport of a small Chinese military colony. The difficulties about making it self-supporting are curiously illustrated by repeated orders urging the reduction of food issues to officers and men.

The Kharoshthi documents, of which the text has now been published by Professor Rapson and his learned collaborators in France, show in character, language and other respects the closest agreement with those from the Niya site. From extract translations subsequently communicated to me I was able to establish that the indigenous designation of the locality was *Kroraina*. Of this the name *Lou-lan* was meant to be a rendering, the nearest which Chinese phonetics would permit of.

To the many miscellaneous relics which the clearing of that large rubbish heap, as well as the search of other ruined dwellings around, yielded I cannot refer here. But a curious fact illustrating the destructive force which has left its mark over the whole site calls for mention. Careful examination of some much-broken narrow terraces visible here and there to the south and north of the area occupied by the ruins showed that they had once formed part of ramparts built of stamped clay with intervening layers of tamarisk brushwood. This was the regular method of construction used by the ancient Chinese engineers for defensive works in this region and was specially adapted to withstand wind erosion.

Yet of this circumvallation, which formed originally a square of about 1020 feet inside, only fragments survived even on those sides which, built exactly to follow the direction of the prevailing east-northeast wind, were least exposed to its destructive force. The other two sides which directly faced this had been wholly ground down and literally carried away by erosion. It was only after the experience gained of similar breaching at sites far away to the east that I fully realized what the wind had accomplished here, and was thus able on my second visit to the Lou-lan site in 1914 to recognize such scanty traces of the walls facing east and west as had not been almost completely effaced.

By the evening of December 22 our work at the ancient fortified station was completed. There remained now to be explored another group of ruins about eight miles away to the west. These had been first discovered by Dr. Hedin. But as he had been able to visit them from the Lou-lan station only once and in the course of a single day, and had only five men with him to help in exploring them, there was obviously scope left for systematic excavation. The main point was whether we could retain adequate time for it. Our ice supply was diminishing rapidly. My anxiety was increased when Tokhta Akhun returned from the spring at the foot of the Kuruk-tagh with the report that its water was so salt that no ice had as yet formed on it. Yet the minimum temperatures during our stay at the ruins had fallen as low as 45° Fahrenheit below freezing point. For the same reason the camels had refused to drink from it. Fortunately the return of the camels from our half-way depot enabled us to shift our camp to those ruins on December 23.

The excavations strenuously carried on there during the following five days with our contingent of laborers, in spite of cases of illness still counting thirty men, proved very fruitful. Here it must suffice to mention only a few observations and finds of special interest. The careful clearing of a small Buddhist shrine yielded abundance of fine pieces of wood carving, including beams of over seven feet long, showing decorative motifs of a distinctly Hellenistic or Greco-Buddhist type.

Wind erosion had worked terrible havoc here, too, and at some large dwellings about a mile off to the southeast. Yet we recovered at the latter plenty of interesting relics. They included fine pieces from elegantly carved and lacquered furniture; fragments of carved wooden panels with motifs almost Roman in style; decorated textiles such as a well-preserved slipper adorned with tapestry designs unmistakably Western, etc. Near another small Buddhist shrine there survived dead fruit trees of an ancient fenced orchard, the only proofs of ancient cultivation to be traced at the site. There were other indications also that the settlement once existing there and around the fortified station had derived its importance far more from the traffic with China which passed through it than from its local resources.

My desire to trace the line followed by this traffic through the vast expanse of unexplored desert eastward was eager enough. But any attempt at this very difficult task was precluded at the time. Our ice store was getting very low. Increasing cases of illness among the men showed how exposure to the continual blasts was telling on them. So when, by December 29, 1906, the exploration of all structural remains at the western site also was completed, the main body of the men was sent back to Abdal along with the "archeological proceeds" in charge of Surveyor Rai Ram Singh. Rheumatism brought on by exposure to the icy winds had already put him more or less *hors de combat* before our arrival at the site.

I myself with a much reduced party set out through the unexplored desert to the southwest. A seven days' trying tramp brought us safely to the ice of the Tarim. Progress was far more difficult than on the journey from Lop-nor, owing to the steadily increasing height of the ridges of drift sand encountered. No more ruins, only occasional relics of the Stone Age, were met on the way. Even the rows of dead trees which marked old river courses, so frequent before, here soon disappeared. The resulting difficulty about fuel made itself seriously felt while minimum temperatures fell to 48° Fahrenheit below freezing point. Interesting geographical observations attended this journey, which ultimately carried us back to Charkhlik and Miran; but of them no account is needed in this place.

CHAPTER IX

Tracking the Ancient Route
Across the Dried-up Lop Sea

IN THE NEXT CHAPTER I shall give an account of the long desert journey which in February and March 1907 brought me by Marco Polo's route from Lop to Tun-huang and led to the discovery of the ancient Chinese border wall near this westernmost oasis of China proper. This journey had allowed me to locate with certainty the eastern starting point of that forbidding desert route to Lou-lan, which for centuries had served China's earliest intercourse with Central Asia and the West. But an attempt to trace it right through was possible only from the side of Lou-lan. From there also it was bound to prove a formidable task. So I had to wait until seven years later when my third expedition allowed me to undertake it.

On January 8, 1914, I arrived at Charkhlik. Once again the little oasis had to serve as the base for my explorations in the Lop desert. But my difficulties were greatly increased by an event which, as a small but significant result of the troubles

caused in Turkistan by the Chinese revolution, may receive
here brief mention. Before I started on New Year's Eve
from Charchan for Charkhlik, I learned that a band of Chinese
"revolutionaries," in other words, gamblers and adventurers,
had left a short time before for Charkhlik and was reported to
have attacked and captured the district magistrate of Charkhlik. The Chinese subdivisional officer of Charchan had been
helpless to prevent the outbreak. So he considerately provided
me with introductions, one to the unfortunate Amban, assuming that somehow he had regained freedom and authority,
and the other to the leading spirit of the "revolutionaries,"
whom he shrewdly guessed to have been installed by them in
office.

In the course of the ten marches to Charkhlik, mainly
along the Charchan river, we did not meet with a single way-
farer. This struck me as strange at the time. On my arrival, I
found that neither of the two introductions could be presented. When the little band of revolutionaries had captured
and then cruelly put to death the hapless magistrate, their
leader had set himself up as Amban *ad interim*, while the local
Mohammedans looked on with indifference. But within a
week a small detachment of Tungan troops had arrived from
faraway Kara-shahr. Stealthily introduced into the oasis by
the same adaptable local headmen, they had surprised the revolutionaries while asleep and killed or captured all of them.
This local upheaval had left no Chinese civil authority whatever, and in its absence no effective help could be hoped for
from the easygoing Lopliks and their indolent headmen.

I greatly chafed at the consequent delays encountered in
raising the supplies, labor and camels needed for my carefully
planned explorations. Yet in reality the revolutionary disturb-
ance was to prove a boon in disguise. After my start from
Charkhlik I was obliged to devote nearly two weeks' strenuous labors at the site of Miran to rescuing what was left of
those fine wall paintings, which I have described in Chapter VII

as discovered in the larger of two ruined rotundas. While thus engaged, I received information from Sir George Macartney, the British Consul-General at Kashgar, that an obstructive edict had issued from the Chinese provincial headquarters ordering the district authorities to prevent surveying work on our part. It was meant virtually to put a stop to all my intended explorations. The intercession of the British Minister at Peking had been immediately invoked by that ever-watchful friend. But meanwhile I should have to contend, if not with an attempt at forcible interference, yet with Chinese passive obstruction, so easy to apply in my circumstances.

Fortunately the expected prohibition from Charkhlik never came. As I found out later, I owed this lucky escape to the opportune "revolutionary" outbreak. It had disposed of the legitimate district magistrate before he could take any action. His rebel successor, who had taken charge of the Ya-mên and found the orders there, had more urgent and profitable business to attend to before he was killed himself. Subsequently the military commandants, in strict observance of Chinese official rule, had carefully abstained from attending to civil affairs and kept the Ya-mên papers sealed up until the new magistrate had arrived from the distant headquarters at Urumchi and taken charge of the seal of office. But what a relief it was when I had safely collected all I needed and could set out for the waterless desert where there was no possible risk from human interference!

My tasks included the excavation of any ruins which the intended fresh explorations in the dried-up delta of the Kuruk-darya and the search for the ancient Chinese route once leading eastward of Lou-lan might reveal. In order to assure adequate time for the latter rather hazardous undertaking, it was essential to effect excavations rapidly and therefore to take along as many laborers as I could possibly manage to keep supplied with water, or rather ice. What with big loads of ice sufficient to assure the minimum allowances of water

for thirty-five people for a month, with food supplies of one
month for all and of an additional month for my own men,
and with indispensable outfit to afford protection in the wintry desert exposed to icy gales, the thirty camels I succeeded
in raising, including our own fifteen, were by no means too
many. It goes without saying that everybody had to walk.

By February 1, 1914, I had safely started this large column from Miran. Next day we took up our supply of ice
packed in bags from a terminal lagoon of the Tarim. Thence
four marches brought us to my immediate goal, a large ruined fort which had first been sighted some years before by
Tokhta Akhun, my faithful old Loplik follower. Wind erosion had deeply scoured the ground outside and in places had
completely breached the very solid enclosing rampart. It was
built of alternate layers of brushwood fascines and stamped
clay, after the fashion observed before in the ancient Chinese
border wall west of Tun-huang. Plentiful relics in the shape
of architectural wood carvings, implements, coins, etc., were
recovered by clearing what remained of dwellings within.
They proved occupation to have ceased about the same period as at the Lou-lan site. A well-marked dry river course
passing the fort was easily traced by the rows of fallen dead
trees lining its banks. As proved by its direction, it was a southern branch of the Kuruk-darya, the "Dry River," which had
once carried water to the Lou-lan site.

By following up this river branch, we came upon a second and smaller fort, and to the north of it upon scattered remains of an extensive settlement. Its timber-and-wattle dwellings had suffered greatly through wind erosion. Yet where
consolidated refuse heaps had helped to protect the original
floors we found ancient records on wood and paper in two
early Indian scripts, Kharoshthi and Brahmi, as well as in Chinese and Early Sogdian. There were other interesting remains
also, such as a fine lacquered casket, fragments of figured fabrics in silk and wool, of wooden agricultural implements, etc.

This settlement, too, must have been abandoned like the Lou-lan site not later than the beginning of the fourth century A.D.

The exact antiquarian evidence here obtained had its special value in helping to date a variety of physical features observed in the immediate vicinity of the ruined settlement. These throw light on the hydrography and early occupation of this part of the Lop region during historical times and those immediately preceding them. To the latter period belonged the abundant finds of stone implements, such as neolithic arrowheads and jade celts, picked up on eroded ground near by.

On the two long marches which brought us to the Lou-lan site we passed once more a succession of old river beds. All were lined by rows of fallen dead "Toghrak" (wild poplar) trees and clearly marked by their direction as belonging to the delta once formed by the Kuruk-darya, the "Dry River." Finds of Chinese Han coins and of small metal and pottery fragments mingled freely in places with relics of the Stone Age on the bare ground scoured by the wind erosion. The route we followed was different from that of my first visit in 1906; but finds and observations alike fully confirmed the conclusions then arrived at.

It was long after nightfall on February 10 that, struggling across that unending succession of steep Yardang terraces so difficult to cross for the camels, we reached the ruined Chinese station of Lou-lan. From our base camp at the familiar stupa ruin I pushed out reconnaissances into the unknown desert to the east and northeast, while our diggers were kept at work with good results on small outlying ruins and deeper deposits of refuse which had escaped attention during the stress of my previous visit. Among the finds made in the course of this renewed clearing were more documents on wood and paper in Chinese, Kharoshthi and the Iranian language known since my discoveries of 1906-07 as Early Sogdian.

Quite as interesting were the series of close observations

I was able to make on ground immediately adjoining the ruined site as to the levels at which a temporary return of water, subsequent to the abandonment of the Chinese station, had from time to time arrested the process of denudation and wind erosion by allowing desert vegetation to grow again and thus afford protection to the clayey soil. These observations clearly showed that the process, striking as its effects everywhere are, had not been constant during the 1600 years which have passed since the site was abandoned to the desert. The water, which accounted for the appearance here and there in depressions of scanty tamarisk scrub and reeds since dead again, could only have come from the Dry River. In fact, on returning in 1915 to the Kuruk-darya in the desert, farther west where its bed could be clearly followed along the foot of the utterly barren Kuruk-tagh, the "Dry Hills," I found that within it brackish water could be reached by digging shallow wells in some hollows. Hence I could not feel altogether surprised when I learned on my fourth journey in the Tarim basin (1930-31) that a recent great hydrographic change affecting the course of the Tarim had caused the greater portion of its summer floods to meet the Konche-darya much farther north than before and thus to deflect the united waters of both once more into the Dry River and toward the area of ancient Lou-lan. The hoped-for chance of studying this latest change affecting the Lop basin has, I regret, been denied to me through Chinese obstruction.

The time for more exciting work came when by the middle of February I could turn to the main task which had drawn me back to this desolate ground of Lou-lan. It had been duly prepared for by reconnaissances made mainly with the help of Afrazgul Khan, the young but zealous and intelligent Pathan draughtsman who had joined me as a Sepoy from the Khyber Rifles and who has since, by his merits, risen high in the service of the Survey of India. Those reconnaissances, on ground untouched by human feet for many centuries, led to the discovery of a succession of remains to the northeast which clearly indicated that the ancient Chinese trade and military route, which I was anxious to trace toward Tun-huang through the desert, had followed that direction, at least in its initial portion.

The nearest among those remains was an ancient burial ground situated some four miles from the Lou-lan station on the top of an isolated clay terrace, or *mesa*, rising some thirty-five feet above the eroded ground. On the sides of the mesa, graves had been partially exposed and destroyed by wind erosion undercutting the banks and causing them to fall. But the top of the mesa had been safe from this destructive agent, and there a series of large grave pits, revealed by rapid clearing, yielded a rich antiquarian haul in quite bewildering confusion.

Mixed up with human bones and fragments of coffins, there emerged funeral deposits of all sorts, objects of personal use such as decorated bronze mirrors, wooden models of arms and household implements, Chinese documents on paper and wood, and, above all, a wonderful variety of fabrics which delighted my eyes. Among them were pieces of beautifully colored figured silks, fragments of rich tapestry work and embroidery as well as of pile carpets, by the side of coarse fabrics in wool and felt. It soon became evident that remnants of garments of all sorts had been used here for wrapping up bodies. I could not have wished for a more representative exhibition of that ancient silk trade which had been a chief factor in opening up this earliest route for China's direct intercourse with Central Asia and the distant West.

It was easy to realize from various indications that the contents of these pits must have been collected from older graves which wind erosion or some similar cause had exposed or was threatening with complete destruction. Consequently the relics here saved, in obedience to a pious custom still practiced among Chinese, can safely be assigned to that period of the

Han dynasty's rule which followed the first expansion of Chinese trade and power into Central Asia about the close of the second century B.C.

The mass of beautifully figured silks, both polychrome and damasks, here recovered have since proved quite a revelation as regards the artistic style and technical perfection of the products of Chinese silk weaving which traveled westward through Lou-lan while trade still followed this route. These relics of Chinese textile art, from the time of Christ and before, claim special interest because they have been preserved for us on the very route of the earliest silk trade. But equally important is it for the student of those early relations between the Far East and the West to note that among the decorated fabrics there are found fragments of exquisitely worked tapestries in wool which display a style unmistakably Hellenistic. Whether they are of local make or imports from Central-Asian territories farther west, we have in them striking illustration of a cultural influence which that ancient desert route also served for centuries, but in the reverse direction.

The many interesting details revealed by the examination of the technique, material and designs of these specimens, the earliest so far known of China's decorative textile art, have been dealt with in *Innermost Asia*. But among the tapestries showing classical influence there is a fine fragment of a Hermes head quite classical in design. Another tapestry piece curiously reflects the mingling of Chinese and Western art influences, and obviously was produced in Central Asia. Here decorative motifs in the border, unmistakably classical, are combined with the figure of a winged horse which is well known from Chinese sculptures of Han times.

Continuing to the northeast for another twelve miles, we soon left behind the last dry river bed, once fed by the Kuruk-darya and still marked by trunks of wild poplars and tamarisks dead for centuries. Then we came upon the ruins of a small walled *castrum* which, as close examination showed,

had served as an advanced *point d'appui* for Chinese missions
and troops where they first reached habitable Lou-lan territory from the side of Tun-huang. Its walls, built with alternate layers of carefully secured reed fascines and stamped clay,
and remarkably well preserved after two thousand years' exposure, showed such close agreement in all constructive details with the westernmost extension of the ancient Han border wall in the desert of Tun-huang that there could be no
doubt about its dating, just as this does, from the first military
advance of the Chinese into the Tarim basin. It represented
the western bridgehead, as it were, of the route by which
that advance was made possible.

The walls of the *castrum*, constructed with the same
technical skill as on the ancient Tun-huang *Limes*, had with-
stood well the attacks of that most formidable enemy in this
region, wind erosion. Its destructive force, at work for 2000
years, had not succeeded in seriously breaching these massive
walls. But inside the circumvallation the force of the wind
had wrought terrible havoc, scooping out hollows down to
twenty feet and more below the ground level. However, in a
refuse heap sheltered by the north wall, dated Chinese records
survived, belonging like most of those found at the Lou-lan
station to the period preceding the final abandonment of the
route, soon after the end of the third century A.D.

Beyond this large fortified station other remains were
traced. Of special interest was a small ruined fort discovered
some three miles to the northeast on the top of a precipitous
mesa fully one hundred feet high and commanding a distant
view over the desolate waste around. The elevated position,
together with the absolute aridity of the climate since ancient
times, had assured here a truly remarkable state of conservation to the bodies of men and women found in graves outside
what was evidently a look-out post occupied by indigenous
Lou-lan people. Several of the bodies were wonderfully well
conserved, together with their burial deposits. The peaked felt

caps decorated with big feathers and other trophies of the chase, the arrow shafts by their side, the coarse but strong woolen garments, the neatly woven small baskets holding the food for the dead, etc., all indicated a race of semi-nomadic herdsmen and hunters, just as the Han Annals describe the Lou-lan people when the Chinese found them on the first opening of the route through the desert.

It was a strange sensation to look down on figures which but for the parched skin seemed like those of men asleep, and thus to feel brought face to face with people who inhabited and, no doubt, were content with this dreary Lop region 2000 years ago. The characteristics of the men's heads showed close affinity to that *Homo Alpinus* type which, as the anthropometrical materials collected by me have proved, still remains the prevailing element in the racial constitution of the present population of the Tarim basin. The distant view gained from this elevated point made it certain that we were here near the eastern extremity of the ground once reached by life-giving water from the river. Beyond to the east there lay the boundless expanse of shimmering salt, marking the dried-up Lop sea bed.

Apart from their direct interest, the discoveries briefly indicated had a special importance as furnishing me with a safe starting point and some guidance for the difficult task still before me, that of tracing the ancient Chinese route through the forbidding desert eastward. But it was impossible to set out at once. Incessant toil in the waterless desert with constant exposure to its icy winds had exhausted our Loplik laborers, hardy plants as they were. When the last digging at the outlying ruins to the northeast had been done, I had to take them back to our Lou-lan base camp whence they could return in safety to the world of the living.

There at the ruined station I was to my great relief rejoined by my valiant old travel companion, Rai Bahadur Lal Singh, whom I had sent from Miran to make a survey along the dying Tarim to the Konche-darya and then down the bed of the Dry River to Lou-lan. With him arrived also that plucky hunter, Abdurrahim, from the Kuruk-tagh, who, with his lifelong desert experience and his magnificent camels, brought fresh strength to our party. It may serve to illustrate the stamina of his animals that the baby camel to which one of them gave birth at the Lou-lan site subsequently traversed with us all those waterless wastes of salt and gravel unharmed and after the first few days on its own legs.

The topographical indications I had deduced from the position of the remains discovered in succession seemed to point to the ancient route having lain to the northeast. Yet this bearing would lead us at right angles away from the line on which, as our preceding mapping showed, we should have to look for the direct route to the eastern starting point of the route beyond the termination of the ancient Chinese border wall. It was an observation distinctly discouraging for the search we should have to make for the ancient route; for the ground ahead was sure to prove devoid of all resources for human life, including water.

Careful preparation was essential for ensuring safety on such a journey through an absolute wilderness. Its estimated length of at least ten days' march was bound to put to a severe test the endurance of our brave camels, already hard tried by the work of the preceding weeks. So it became necessary at this stage first to take my party northward to the distant salt springs of Altmish-bulak at the foot of the Kuruk-tagh. The three days' march led to the discovery of interesting remains at small Chinese burial grounds on the gravel glacis overlooking the ancient riverine belt. Then a few days' halt at Altmish-bulak had to be allowed for our camels to gather fresh strength by grazing at reed beds and by the chance of a drink after three weeks. To us humans, too, this little patch of vegetation seemed delightful.

After replenishing our ice supply and taking a carefully

arranged store of fuel, we started on February 24 for our re-spective tasks. The one allotted to Lal Singh was to survey the unknown northeast shores of the great salt-encrusted basin representing the dried-up ancient Lop sea bed. I myself, ac-companied by Afrazgul, proposed to search for the ancient Chinese route where it left the edge of the once inhabited Lou-lan area and to trace it over whatever ground it might have crossed in the direction of Tun-huang. It was a fascinat-ing task, combining geographical and historical interest, but one attended also by serious difficulties and risks.

From what I knew of the general character of the ground before us, it was certain that we could not hope for water, nor over most of it for fuel to melt our ice with, be-fore striking the caravan track leading from Charkhlik to Tun-huang. It meant some ten days' hard marching, and there was a limit to the endurance of our brave camels, al-ready hard tried by the preceding weeks' work in absolute desert. It was impossible to foresee what physical obstacles might be met and delay us in this wilderness so devoid of all resources. There remained the problem how to hit the line of the ancient route and to track it onward through ground which all through historical times had been more barren, per-haps, than any similarly large area of this globe. For a careful search of any relics left behind by the ancient traffic there would be no time. Much if not most of the object in view had to be left to good fortune, together with what hints I could deduce from previous observations. Fortune served me better than I had ventured to hope.

Physical difficulties soon presented themselves as we made our way south by two trying marches, across a perfect maze of steep clay terraces and hillocks encrusted with hard salt, and by February 25 reached the vicinity of that outlying little fort. There I was fortunate enough to discover more re-mains which confirmed my conjectural conclusion that the initial bearing of the route lay to the northeast. At the very edge of the area with signs of dead vegetation I came upon a towering mesa bearing on its top the remains, almost completely eroded, of an ancient watch tower of the type familiar to me from the Chinese border wall beyond Tun-huang. We had evidently reached here the extreme eastern limit of the area to which the waters of the Dry River had once carried life. Beyond this there were no ruins to guide us; for we were now passing into ground which all through historical times must have been as devoid of plant or animal life as it is now. As we left behind the withered and bleached fragments of the last dead tamarisk lying on the salt soil, I felt that we had passed from the land of the dead into ground that never knew life—except on the route which we were to track.

But as we started northeastward by the compass across absolutely barren wastes of clayey detritus or salt crust, chance came again and again to our help in a way which at times seemed almost uncanny. Finds of early Chinese copper coins, small metal objects, beads and the like seemed as if meant to assure us that we were still near the ancient track by which Chinese missions, troops and traders had toiled for four centuries through this lifeless wilderness. These finds showed that I was right in my reliance on those ancient Chinese with their topographical sense having for good reasons selected this bearing, puzzling as it seemed at the time.

It must suffice here to mention what perhaps was the most striking and welcome of these finds. The last traces of dead vegetation marking the termination of the ancient delta had long been left behind when we suddenly found the old route line plainly marked by two-hundred-odd Chinese copper coins strewing the dismal ground of salt-encrusted clay for a distance of about thirty yards. They lay in a well-defined line running from northeast to southwest. The coins, square-holed, were all of the Han type and seemed as if fresh from a mint. Clearly they had got loose from the string which tied them, and gradually dropped out through an opening of the bag or case in which they were being carried by some convoy. Some fifty yards away in the same direction there lay scattered bronze arrowheads, all manifestly unused. Their shape and weight exactly agreed with the ammunition of Han times so familiar to me from finds along the *Limes* of Tun-huang. There could be little doubt that coins and arrowheads had dropped from some convoy of stores proceeding to Lou-lan in Han times. Their having remained on the ground is easily accounted for if we assume the convoy to have moved at nighttime and a little off the main track, but still in the right direction.

That day's long march was taking us past a far-stretching array of big mesas which, with their fantastically eroded shapes, curiously suggested ruined towers, mansions or temples. It was easy to recognize in them those wind-eroded mounds which an early Chinese text mentions near the northwestern edge of P'u-ch'ang, or the "Salt Marsh," *i.e.* the ancient Lop sea bed, and in which Chinese eyes saw the ruins of a mythical "Town of the Dragon." Finally, after continuing our northeasterly course for another day across bare clay and gypsum detritus, we arrived at a forbidding belt of salt-coated erosion terraces. They clearly corresponded to those which Chinese notices of the ancient route to Lou-lan repeatedly mention as the dreaded "White Dragon Mounds," and graphically describe. Progress between them was very trying for our poor camels' feet. They were sore already, and the painful process of "resoling," as described above, had to be resorted to night after night. But still worse was it to face the crossing of the bed of the dead Lop sea with its terrible surface of hard salt, which I knew to lie beyond.

I was just preparing to climb a prominent mesa which had served as our guiding point and to use it as a look-out, when a fortunate find on its slopes, of Chinese coins and a collection of metal objects, including a well-preserved iron dagger and bridle, showed that it had evidently served as a halting place on the ancient route. Inspection of the ground ahead confirmed the suggestion that it had been used for this purpose, because at its foot was the first piece of ground, tolerably level and clear of salt, which travelers would strike after passing the hard, salt-encrusted sea bottom beyond.

So I at once decided to head straight eastward for that bed, and the crossing effected next day proved that I had been rightly guided. The march across this petrified sea bed, with its hard salt crust crumpled up into big cakes aslant and with small pressure ridges between them, was most trying for men and beasts alike. But when this weary tramp of twenty miles had safely brought us to the first patch of soft salt in front of the opposite line of salt-coated terraces, and we could halt for a night's rest, I had reason to feel glad of my choice and grateful for the finds which had prompted it. As subsequent surveys showed, we had crossed the forbidding salt sea bed at its very narrowest point, and had thus escaped a night's halt on ground where neither beast nor man could have found a spot to rest in comfort.

It was, no doubt, this consideration which had determined the early Chinese pioneers in the choice of this line for their route. Archeological evidence of ancient traffic on it soon cropped up again in the shape of coins and other small relics when, through the opposite belt of "White Dragon Mounds," we had gained the eastern shores of the ancient salt marsh. Three marches along these shores, over ground easy but still devoid of any trace of vegetation, dead or alive, finally brought us to the last offshoot of a low desert range, which overlooks from the north the great bay at the extreme eastern extension of the ancient dried-up sea bed. Then, as we skirted its shore line, under steep cliffs looking exactly like those of a sea still in being, I had the satisfaction to find the ancient Chinese road still in one place plainly marked. For there a straight wide track worn by the passage for centuries of transport animals, and probably also of carts, cuts across a small bay of the salt-encrusted sea bed.

It was a great relief when on the ninth day from Altmish-bulak we came upon the first scanty scrub and reeds growing on sandy soil by the shore of the dried-up sea bed. Then finally a long march to the southeast brought us safely across the wide salt-encrusted bay, here showing patches of actual salt bog, to the lonely caravan track toward Tun-huang at the well of Kum-kuduk.

How traffic of such magnitude as the Chinese Annals indicate was organized and maintained on a route passing across some 120 miles of utterly barren ground, already in ancient times without water, fuel or grazing, is a problem I need not discuss here. It was an achievement fraught with momentous results for the interchange of civilizations. There is deep significance in the fact that it was due far more to prestige, economic resources and capacity for organization on the side of China than to any military prowess among its people or its rulers. It may well, in fact, be looked upon as a triumph of the mind over matter.

CHAPTER X

Discovery of an
Ancient Border Line

IT WAS ON FEBRUARY 21, 1907, after I had completed my excavations at the Miran ruins and the safe packing of their archeological yield, that I started on the long desert journey which was to take us from the dreary Lop-nor marshes right through to Tun-huang on the westernmost border of Kansu and China proper. It was the same route by which Marco Polo had traveled "through the desert of Lop." Six centuries before him it had seen a traveler scarcely less great, Hsüan-tsang, the pilgrim of pious memory, returning to China laden with Buddhist relics and sacred books after many years' wanderings in the "Western Regions."

Though less important and less direct than the ancient Lou-lan route, this desert track, close on 380 miles long leading south of Lop-nor, must have seen much caravan traffic during successive periods, only to be practically forgotten again when Chinese power westward weakened or a policy of rigid seclusion strangled trade. Thus after the last Chinese re-conquest of the Tarim basin it had to be rediscovered. Since then this route had been frequented again on occasion by traders from Khotan and Yarkand, but only during the winter months when the use of ice makes it possible to overcome the difficulties otherwise arising from the saltiness of the wells at a succession of stages.

The ground crossed on the seventeen long marches in which we accomplished this desert journey, still ordinarily reckoned as in the days of Marco Polo at twenty-eight stages, did not compare in difficulties with that encountered by us in our explorations around and past Lou-lan. Yet its lifeless solitudes—we did not meet a single human being on this journey —made it easy for me to appreciate the feelings of superstitious dread which have haunted old travelers following this lonely desert track.

These feelings are duly reflected in the accounts of Chinese Buddhist pilgrims and in notices of the Chinese annalists. But nowhere do we find them more graphically expressed than in Ser Marco's description of the "desert of Lop." I therefore feel tempted to quote it here from his immortal book as Sir Henry Yule translates it.

"The length of this desert is so great that 'tis said it would take a year and more to ride from one end of it to the other. And here, where its breadth is least, it takes a month to cross it. 'Tis all composed of hills and valleys of sand, and not a thing to eat is to be found on it. But after riding for a day and a night you find fresh water, enough mayhap for some fifty or hundred persons with their beasts, but not for more. . . .

"Beasts there are none; for there is nought for them to eat. But there is a marvelous thing related of this Desert, which is that when travelers are on the move by night, and one of them chances to lag behind or to fall asleep or the like, when he tries to gain his company again he will hear spirits talking, and will suppose them to be his comrades. Sometimes the spirits will call him by name; and thus shall a traveler ofttimes be led astray so that he never finds his party. And in this way many have perished. Sometimes the stray traveler will hear as it were the tramp and hum of a great cavalcade of people away from the real line of road, and taking this to be their own company they will follow the sound; and when day breaks they find that a cheat has been put on them and that they are in an ill plight. Even in the daytime one hears those spirits talking. And sometimes you shall hear the sound of a variety of musical instruments, and still more commonly the sound of drums. Hence in making this journey 'tis customary for travelers to keep close together. All the animals too have bells at their necks, so that they cannot easily get astray. And at sleeping time a signal is put to show the direction of the next march. So thus it is that the desert is crossed."

It was not such reflexes of old folklore beliefs which occupied my thoughts most as we passed by long marches along the dreary salt-encrusted shores of the great dried-up sea bed and then up the wide desert valley which divides the foot of the eastern Kuruk-tagh from the high sand ridges covering the glacis of the Kum-tagh in the south. There were plenty of interesting geographical observations to keep my mind occupied, especially after we had passed from what looked like the head of that desert valley into ground very puzzling at first sight.

There, in a wide basin enclosed to the north by the somber and absolutely sterile slopes of the Kuruk-tagh and in the south by high ranges of dunes rising to more than three hundred feet, we found a series of unmistakable dry lake beds, and between and around them a perfect maze of clay terraces remarkably high and steep. These lake beds proved to represent an ancient terminal basin of Su-lo-ho which now finds its end in large salt marshes more than fifteen miles farther south. The Khara-nor lake of the maps where the Su-lo-ho was previously believed to lose itself was proved to lie still more than a degree of longitude farther to the east.

The discovery of that more ancient terminal basin, now

dried up, is of considerable geographical interest. It presents a very instructive analogy to the riverine changes which have taken place in historical times in the terminal branches of the Tarim and Kuruk-darya. It suggests that at an earlier period the Su-lo-ho, which drains a great portion of the high snowy Nan-shan ranges, emptied itself into the great Lop Sea. Thus the drainage area of the latter then extended from the Pamirs right across innermost Asia to the watershed of the Pacific Ocean.

There was constantly with me the thought of the ancient traffic which the earliest Chinese route to the "Western Countries" through Lou-lan had seen since the days of that brave pioneer of China's Central-Asian expansion, Chang Ch'ien, and no less the thought of all the human toil and suffering it had witnessed. From brief notices in the Imperial Annals of the Han dynasty I knew that the Lou-lan route, as we may briefly call it, started in the east from a fortified border station, famous in early Chinese historical records by the name of "Yü-mên-kuan," the "Barrier of the Jade Gate." It took its significant name from that precious jade (*yü*) of Khotan which from early down to modern times formed an important article of trade export from the Tarim basin to China. But neither Chinese nor Western scholarship was aware of the exact position of this famous "Jade Gate."

Nor could I get any information about any ruins likely to mark the route leading to it in the course of the inquiries I had made at Charkhlik and Abdal. I knew, however, from a brief account which Monsieur C.-E. Bonin, of the French Diplomatic Service, had published of his unsuccessful attempt in 1899 to follow the desert route from Tun-huang to Charkhlik, that he had passed some ruined watch towers and even remains of a wall running along them before he had to turn back from some marshes met west of the Khara-nor lake. M. Bonin's passing notice suggested the probable antiquity of those ruins, but in the absence of any map or route sketch it could not help to locate them.

Fortunately, observant old Mulla of Abdal, the true modern pioneer of the route, had told me that I might come across the first "Pao-t'ais," as he called them—the term usually applied to small towers serving as signposts on Chinese roads—on the first march after emerging from that maze of high clay terraces or mesas. My hope was not disappointed. We were moving that evening of March 7 across a bare gravel plateau when a small mound, about a mile off the caravan track we were following, attracted my attention. On reaching it, I found to my joy that it was a relatively well-preserved watch tower, solidly built with bricks of hard sun-dried clay and some twenty-three feet high.

When I saw the familiar layers of tamarisk branches inserted at regular intervals between the courses, there could be no doubt about the great antiquity of this watch tower. It rose in an easily defended position on the very brink of a deep-cut, dry river bed. Adjoining it were the foundations of a small structure, badly decayed, probably the watchmen's quarters. Fragments of iron implements, carved wood and a piece of stout woolen fabric which I picked up quickly confirmed this. Later systematic survey has proved that this was a watch tower advanced beyond the westernmost section of the ancient protected border line.

The fodder supply carried for our ponies was now beginning to run short, and this made it imperative to gain the Tun-huang oasis, still five marches off, without undue delay. Next morning we had passed only three miles beyond where we had halted by the side of what proved the terminal bed of the Su-lo-ho, when I noticed another ruined watch tower on a gravel ridge at some distance away to the southeast. Letting the caravan move on by the well-marked track, I hastened up to the tower. It showed the same construction as the first. On the flat gravel surface around, there was no indication of other structural remains. But my attention was soon attracted by a line of reed bundles cropping out from the gravel soil close by. Following this a short distance along the plateau edge, I saw to my delight that the line stretched away perfectly straight toward another tower visible some three miles to the east and assumed the form of an unmistakable wall where it crossed a depression.

A little prospecting revealed that I actually stood on the remains of this wall. On clearing away the slight layer of drift sand, we soon came upon a regular wall constructed of horizontal reed bundles placed at regular intervals across layers of stamped clay, the whole consolidated by permeating salts. On the outside, and placed at right angles to the packed bundles within, there were fixed other reed bundles carefully bound after the fashion of fascines and forming a revetment. The reed bundles, or fascines, showed a uniform length of eight feet and a thickness of about eight inches. The care and solidity of this strange wall could not by itself furnish a definite clue to its age, but a lucky chance encouraged the hope of my finding the needful chronological evidence.

Within the reed bundles exposed by a little scraping on the top of the wall there turned up, together with small rags of colored silk, fragments of wooden boards and the like as well as a little label-like tablet of wood showing Chinese characters of remarkable clearness and of distinctly ancient look. There was no date, only the entry: "the clothes bag of one called Lu Ting-shih." My excellent Chinese secretary in his scholarly modesty would commit himself only to the statement that the characters looked older than those used since the tenth century A.D. Yet in my Sinologue ignorance I made bold to conjecture that they might be of Han times.

How these relics of manifest antiquity had got mixed up with the materials used for the wall was not a question to occupy me much at the time. What mattered was the clear sight I gained of more towers stretching away in a line both to the southwest and to the east. The need of following my caravan on the track toward Tun-huang made me turn eastward, and I had no reason to regret it. Proceeding from tower to tower, we found that strange wall cropping out in long stretches.

In places it was preserved up to five or six feet in height, in others ground down by erosion to what looked like a mere swelling on the flat gravel surface. But here, too, a little scraping revealed the same fascines of reeds or brushwood. Before I reached our camp in the evening, I had secured unmistakable proof that the watch towers were meant to guard a continuous border line. It recalled at once those *Limes* lines with which the Roman Empire protected its frontiers wherever barbarian inroads threatened them, from Hadrian's Wall in Northumberland down to the Syrian and Arabian marches.

It was a fascinating discovery which invited prolonged exploration. The line could be followed two more marches for a total distance of over fifty miles by the towers actually passed on the caravan track or else clearly sighted at varying distances to the north. More imposing ruins, too, were met as we moved on until the track toward the Tun-huang oasis obliged us to turn off across the bare gravel plateau to the southeast.

Before systematic exploration of all these remains in the desert west of Tun-huang could be undertaken, it was essential to secure needful supplies and also labor for excavations. So I now had to turn south to Tun-huang or Sha-chou, the "Town of the Sands," as its alternative name of later origin appropriately calls it. The surroundings of the small walled town of Tun-huang still showed plentiful evidence of the terrible devastations the oasis had suffered during the last great Mohammedan rising. It proved difficult to obtain even a minimum of diggers from its scanty and indolent population. But the two local mandarins, both the scholarly magistrate and the military commander, a dear old warrior, showed friendly interest in my aims and did all they could to help me. So by March 24 I was able to set out again for the desert with a dozen opium-smoking coolies, all the labor that could be raised.

In order to make sure whether the ancient border line continued to the east and there too, as I guessed, might lie

more or less along the southern bank of the Su-lo-ho and its
lagoons, I took my course first due north. But my search for
two days failed to reveal the hoped-for remains of the ancient
Chinese *Limes*. As subsequent investigations proved, the effect
of extensive inundations from the Su-lo-ho and its large tributary, the river of Tun-huang, such as we actually encountered, has there effaced its traces. But when we extended our
search farther to the east, I succeeded in hitting the line of
wall and watch towers again. My joy at this fortunate discovery was fully justified. Over a distance of some sixteen miles
the line could here be followed practically without a break.

Where the bare gravel surface of the low plateau over
which it had been carried, well above the flood level, gave
way in places to low dunes, we came upon a remarkably well-
preserved stretch of wall. Eight feet thick and practically intact on its sides, it stood here still to a height of over seven feet,
and the peculiar method of its construction could be studied
with ease. The alternating layers of fascines and stamped clay
had, owing to the salts contained everywhere in the soil and
the water of the ground, acquired quasi-petrified consistency.

In such a region the wall could hold its own against man
and Nature. Owing to the combined elasticity and cohesive
strength of the fascines, it could withstand better than any
other material the force of slow-grinding but incessant wind
erosion. As I looked at the wall rising before me with almost
vertical faces I could not help being impressed by the skill of
the old Chinese engineers. It must have been a formidable task
to construct so solid a wall across an extensive desert area,
bare of all resources and for the most part even of water. And
yet it was accomplished within a comparatively short period,
and as it proved in the end over a total distance of some four
hundred miles right away to the Etsin-gol.

But my satisfaction grew still greater when, from the
refuse layers traceable near most of the watch towers and
among the remains of small adjoining quarters, we recovered

an abundance of Chinese records on wood. Quite a number of the inscribed narrow slips proved to be dated, and our excitement was great when my Chinese secretary's decipherment showed that all these dates belonged to the first century A.D. It thus became certain that this ruined border line was occupied already in the Former Han dynasty's times, and that I had in my hands the oldest written Chinese documents so far recovered.

I had reason also to be pleased with what Chiang Ssŭ-yeh's rapid examination sufficed to make out of their contents. It showed that they greatly varied in character. There were brief reports or orders on matters of military administration; acknowledgments of receipt for articles of equipment or supplies; private communications. Fragments also of a school glossary and writing exercises seemed to be represented. But equally clear was it that the full interpretation of these materials would need protracted study. There were, in fact, plenty of puzzles in paleography and diction awaiting solution by the philological acumen of that great Sinologue, M. Chavannes.

It was easier to become familiar on the spot with the stationery aspect of these miscellaneous "papers," to use an anachronism. The most usual form was that of thin wooden slips always measuring about nine and a half inches in length and from a quarter to half an inch wide. The fact that a single vertical line often contained over thirty Chinese ideograms, *i.e.* words, illustrates the remarkable neatness of the writing which prevails. Besides the carefully smoothed slips of wood or bamboo, use had been made also for less formal communications of that abundant, if rougher, local writing material, tamarisk wood. Cut into fancy shapes, it was obviously good enough for mere copy-writing. With such the soldiers stationed at these desolate posts had evidently been used to beguile their time.

Plenty of "shavings" showed that the supply of proper

wooden stationery had its value and was used over and over again. There was other evidence also among the miscellaneous relics recovered from the refuse of the straits which seem to have beset the guardians of these remote posts in the desert. It could scarcely have been otherwise, since the records deciphered make it probable that the rank and file was composed mainly of convicts deported from distant parts of the Empire for service on this forbidding border.

By April 1 we had completed the search of all watchposts which a succession of icy sand storms raising a thick dust haze allowed us for the time being to trace eastward. The exhaustion of our small band of Chinese diggers would have in any case necessitated a return to our base at Tunhuang. After a day's halt there I set out with a fresh set of laborers and all supplies needed for prolonged work on the desert border in the west. My new route took me first to the small outlying oasis of Nan-hu, a mere hamlet, where I was able to locate the ruins of that ancient "Yang Barrier" which the Han Annals mention in conjunction with the "Barrier of the Jade Gate." It was a military station, intended to guard the alternative "southern route" into the Tarim basin. This passes along the high and utterly barren slopes of the easternmost K'un-lun, and still serves nowadays for occasional traffic when the desert route from Tun-huang to Charkhlik is closed from the late spring till the winter on account of the saltiness of the wells by the shores of the ancient dried-up sea bed.

The archeological observations to be made around peaceful little Nan-hu did not detain me beyond April 10. Then we moved off into the scrub-covered desert to the north, and by the second day struck the line of the *Limes* close to where our first camp had stood. I felt elated on being back again by the old frontier wall, and all the more glad for the chance of fully exploring its remains, since our discoveries along the section to the northeast of Tun-huang had definitely established its high antiquity. The length of the line to be carefully surveyed and searched was great, and what with climatic conditions increasingly trying and the distance from any local resources, the task was bound to prove hard. But it was fascinating work, and its reward proved more abundant than I could foresee.

It would be quite impossible within the limits of this book to attempt a systematic review of all the essential facts revealed by that busy month's explorations as to the way in which that oldest of all *Limes* lines was guarded, and as to the conditions of life that prevailed along it for centuries. All that the finds and observations on the spot and the interpretation of the hundreds of documents have disclosed has been fully recorded in my *Serindia*. Glimpses at characteristic ruins and brief references to the finds which they yielded must here suffice.

On the edge of the bare gravel plateau along which the westernmost section of the wall extended, there rose at varying intervals some of the best-preserved watch towers. They were invariably built solid, whether with bricks or stamped clay, and on a base from twenty to about twenty-four feet square; they tapered toward the top. This had once borne a small look-out room or platform protected with a parapet. In most cases the top could be reached only by clambering up ropes, holes still visible in the brick work serving as footholds.

The position for the towers had invariably been chosen with a sharp eye for the natural advantages which the ground offered both for defense and for look-out. Hence, significantly enough, the distances between the towers varied considerably as the ground outside the line could easily be kept under observation or not. In the same way advantage was invariably taken of any elevated position which might offer facilities for the transmission of optical signals. A carefully organized system of transmitting information by fire signals at night and smoke signals by day was maintained along the whole line. This is proved both by references in the documents and by actual evidence of the materials which I found provided for such signals.

Considering that 2000 years had passed since those towers were built, I might well have wondered at their remarkable preservation had there not been striking evidence on the very ground near them how little wind erosion, that greatest foe of ancient remains in a practically rainless region, could assert its force on this flat surface of gravel. Again and again I noted that the footprints left as I had ridden past more than a month before looked absolutely fresh. All the same, it was a surprise when, returning here seven years later on my third expedition, I was still able to recognize my own footprints and in some cases even those of my ever-active fox terrier Dash II.

Adaptation to all important natural features and careful use of whatever advantages they offered had obviously played a decisive part in the planning of this ancient line of defense. This was fully demonstrated by our survey, where the westernmost section of its wall proved to have terminated. So far the line of wall extended along the route toward Lop, which it obviously was meant to protect and watch. Then, close to the point where the Su-lo-ho bed is crossed, it turned sharply to the southwest, and after a stretch of some twenty-four miles ended on marshy ground. The explanation is that the *Limes* had at its turning point reached the extreme northeastern corner of the great terminal basin of the Su-lo-ho. This extends over an area of some three hundred square miles filled with lakes and marshes, quite impassable during most of the year. Thus the *Limes* could here rest its flank securely for a great distance upon ground that offered effective protection from attack by mounted men.

●
———

CHAPTER XI

Finds Along the
Ancient Chinese Limes

BEFORE PROCEEDING to describe finds of special interest among
the ruins of the Chinese *Limes*, reference may conveniently
be made here to the historical facts, already briefly mentioned in the second chapter, which throw light on the construction of this border line and explain its main purpose.
When the great Emperor Wu-ti had ousted the Huns from
their grazing grounds at the northern foot of the Nan-shan in
the year 121 B.C., military colonies were at once established in
that passage land which was to serve his "forward policy" toward Central Asia. The Han Annals tell us that at the same
time the construction of a wall was started westward in extension of the earlier "Great Wall" of China. There can be no
doubt that its main purpose was to protect the great highway
thus opened for trade and political expansion into the Tarim
basin.

As the Huns were still hovering all over the desert tracts

to the north, it was obviously essential to make this long line of communication safe both for trade and troop movements. The wall of the Emperor Wu-ti, intended to serve as the instrument of China's expansion westward, thus offers a striking analogy to the earlier *Limes* systems of the Roman Empire; for we know now that the lines of the Roman *Limes* were originally integral portions of the great strategic road system of the Empire where it approached its frontiers. The word *limes* served as the technical term for Roman military roads pushed forward from a base of operation on a frontier, and this justifies our use of it for their older Chinese counterpart.

We know from the Han Annals that by 108 B.C. a continuous line of posts and small forts was established from the present town of Su-chou as far as the "Jade Gate." This was at that time still placed somewhere east of Tun-huang. But after success had crowned the second expedition sent into the Tarim basin by the Emperor Wu-ti in the years 102-101 B.C., we learn that "military posts were established from place to place from Tun-huang westward to the Salt Marsh." These were meant to safeguard the passage of political missions and trade caravans and to assure their supplies en route. There can be no possible doubt that this Chinese historical notice, based on the contemporary record of the famous "father of Chinese history" Ssŭ-ma-chien, relates to the line of wall and watch stations explored by me.

We know that the Emperor Wu-ti's policy of commercial and military advance into Central Asia was pursued with relentless energy in spite of formidable physical difficulties. It seems therefore safe to assume the westward extension of the wall to have reached the terminal point mentioned at the close of the preceding chapter within a very few years of 101 B.C. All the same, it was no small satisfaction to me when the clearing of the modest quarters at one of the several towers, which guarded that western head of the *Limes*, brought to light a large inscribed tablet bearing a date corresponding to

94 B.C. It mentions the local name, *Ta-chien-tu,* by which this westernmost wall section is designated also in documents found elsewhere. As among these one is dated in 96 B.C., we have here definite evidence that the extension of the *Limes* must by that time have been carried right through to the extreme end of the wall.

This conclusion was fully confirmed when we came to explore those watch stations which, from the terminal point of the wall, stretched away to the southwest along the edge of the great marshy basin. The distances at which they were placed from each other clearly showed that they were meant to serve mainly as signaling posts along a portion of the line for which a natural flanking defense was provided by impassable marshes. High detached ridges of clay stretched out here like fingers from the gravel plateau into the wide marsh-filled basin. These offered ideal positions for conspicuous signaling stations, and the Chinese engineers did not fail to make the most of them. They had placed their towers here for more than twenty-four miles in an almost straight line as if they had fixed their position by sighting with a diopter.

There were interesting relics to recover at almost all these watch towers. But at none were they so abundant as at the ruin of a small post which was placed about two miles behind the line and evidently served for a kind of sectional headquarters. The arrangement of the modest quarters could be made out very clearly, as the plan shows. The wooden door posts at the entrance were still in position; the fireplace or oven, enclosed by a thin clay wall burnt red, still retained its ashes. Yet among the wooden documents recovered in the room, which was probably meant to accommodate an officer, one bore a date corresponding to May 10 in 68 B.C.

But far more important was the big haul of Chinese records made soon after we started the first experimental scraping of the refuse heaps which cropped up from the gravel-strewn slopes below the ruin. Here within an area only a few

feet square more than three hundred inscribed pieces were recovered. The contents of a small official archive had evidently been thrown down here together, and the very numerous dated pieces showed that these "waste papers" of an
ancient military clerk's office belonged to the years 65-56 B.C.
I cannot here mention more than a few among those which
have a distinct historical and antiquarian value from the light
they throw on the organization of this military border and
the life led along its course.

Several documents found here reproduce or quote Imperial edicts concerning the establishment of an agricultural
military colony in the Tun-huang region and the construction
of a "rampart" or wall to guard the border. Others refer to
the organization of the troops along it, giving the names of
different companies, etc. There are also reports and orders
relating to other posts and sections of the *Limes*. The mention
made of "indigenous officers" in a number of documents
proves that the enlistment of non-Chinese, *i.e.* barbarian, soldiers was resorted to here, just as it was on more than one
Roman border line. And curiously enough I found at a
neighboring signal post half of a wooden tablet inscribed in
that Early Sogdian language which was spoken about Samarkand and Bukhara. The piece had evidently served as a tally.
Curious, too, are numerous pieces containing elaborate Chinese calendars for the years 63, 59, 57 B.C., and the fragment
of a well-known Chinese lexicographical work. A great mass
of wooden "shavings" showed that here as elsewhere some
officer or clerk, eager to improve his penmanship, an important matter for Chinese until late years, had used improvised
tablets for writing exercises, by paring them down with a
knife again and again to obtain a fresh surface.

We must now leave this westernmost section, already occupied, as we have seen, from the time of the first construction of the *Limes*, in order to turn to a rapid survey of its remains farther east. Plenty of interesting observations and finds

were to be made also along what I may call the marsh sections of the *Limes*. Before, however, touching upon these I may briefly mention the watch station T. vIII met on the way eastward. When first seen by us it presented itself as a mere low mound covered with gravel. But its position pointed to a watch tower having once stood here. On excavation it proved to contain the debris of a brick-built tower which had, perhaps through faulty construction, completely collapsed and in its fall buried the walls and roof of the guard rooms adjoining.

When these had been cleared, there were found among other curious relics a measure in the shape of a bootmaker's foot rule marked with the inches of the Han period; and wooden seal cases with grooves arranged to hold a fastening string just as on the covers of Kharoshthi tablets from the Niya and Lou-lan sites. There was a wooden label stating that the box or bag to which it was once attached contained a hundred bronze arrowheads of a specified type belonging to the Hsien-ming company of the Jade Gate. Of such ancient ammunition for crossbows there were plentiful specimens picked up all along the *Limes*. But of special interest was a perfectly preserved wooden cover, provided with the seal socket and string grooves so familiar to me from the oblong wooden envelopes of the Niya site. As a small rim sunk on the under surface of the cover proved, it had served as a lid to a small box which the Chinese inscription in fine big characters declared to have been "the medicine case belonging to the Hsien-ming company." I was glad to let this proof of early medical care figure at the exhibition arranged in 1912 at the Wellcome Medical Museum in London.

From the small lake where our first camp by the border wall had stood, there extends a well-defined and very interesting portion of the Han *Limes* as far as the Khara-nor lake. The defensive line has here been carried across a succession of marshes and small lakes filling the depressions which descend from the gravel glacis in the south toward the Su-lo-ho. Farther east it stretches along the wide lagoons and marshes into which the Su-lo-ho expands after leaving the Khara-nor as well as along this large lake itself. This alignment had with much care been chosen by the old Chinese engineers in order to supplement their line by natural defenses, and thus to save labor in construction as well as effort in its protection. The Imperial edict, which one of the previously mentioned documents from the sectional headquarters station on the southwestern flank of the *Limes* quotes, had enjoined the governor of Su-chou "to examine the configuration of the places. Utilizing natural obstacles, a wall is to be constructed in order to exercise control at a distance."

Our survey of the *Limes* section extending from that small lake for a distance of about eighteen miles eastward showed with great clearness how thoroughly and intelligently those instructions of the Imperial order had been carried out. The wall had there been carried unfailingly over every bit of firm ground capable of offering a passage for the enemy's inroads and right down to the edge of the marshy inlets. The lakes and bogs across their bottoms necessarily took the place of the wall; for they provided a natural defense and thus saved the labor of construction over many miles. It is easy to appreciate this gain if we think of the huge difficulties of supplies and transport which must have attended the maintenance of adequate labor for building the wall in absolute desert.

The gain resulting from this use of the natural obstacles offered by impassable marshes must have been even greater along the section which stretches farther east to the Khara-nor lake and then along its southern shores. There this "wet border" formed by the Su-lo-ho marshes and by the large lake is so wide that the construction of a wall appears to have been thought unnecessary, except on two short stretches where the Su-lo-ho happens to flow in a well-defined narrow bed.

The topographical features just briefly indicated necessarily rendered our search for the line of the *Limes* at this point far more difficult. Once my ever-watchful Chinese secretary and Ram Singh, my very intelligent "handy man" from the Bengal Sappers and Miners, had been initiated into the task of clearing such modest ruins they could safely be left behind to direct this work at the posts traced. Thus I was free myself to start with a couple of my Turki followers on reconnaissance rides. They were needed to show me in advance the task which awaited us at each ruin and to enable me to select suitable camping places nearest to water. Never did I feel more the strange fascination of this desolate border than while I thus traced the remains of wall and watch stations over miles and miles of bare desert and past the salt marshes. There were, indeed, the towers to serve as guides from a distance. But what with the marshes and salt-encrusted bogs encountered between the tongues of the desert plateau, and the strips of treacherous ground along the edges of the marshes, it seemed to me at times like an obstacle race.

The search for the remains of the old wall was, of course, still more exciting. Over considerable stretches, where the direction coinciding with the prevailing wind and a sheltered position on lower ground had reduced the force of erosion, the wall still rose to a conspicuous height, in a few places up to twelve feet or so. Elsewhere it often needed a careful scanning of the ground to discover the low, continuous swelling which marked its line, together with the ends of neatly laid reed bundles cropping out from below the gravel.

Once we had hit the line on a particular stretch of higher ground it was easy to follow it right through to the nearest watch station eastward. The position for the towers had invariably been chosen with a sharp eye for the advantages of the ground commanding the nearest depressions. Where the clay terrace or knoll selected ensured by itself a wide outlook, the towers had not been built so high and access was therefore still practicable to the top. As I sat there amidst the debris of the small watch room usually provided to shelter the men on guard, and let my eyes wander over this great expanse of equally desolate marsh and gravel, it was easy to recall the dreary lives once passed here. No life of the present was there to distract my thoughts of the past.

Undisturbed by man or beast for so many centuries, there lay at my feet the debris of the quarters which the men exiled to this forbidding border had occupied. Near them were the often more extensive refuse heaps which had accumulated during this occupation. The thinnest layer of gravel sufficed to preserve here in absolute freshness the most perishable objects. Often a mere scraping of the slope with my boot heel or the end of my hunting crop sufficed to disclose where the detachments holding the posts had been accustomed to throw their refuse, including their "waste paper," or rather wood. Thus I soon grew accustomed to picking up records of the time of Christ or before within a few inches from the surface.

Never did I realize more deeply how little two thousand years mean where human activity is suspended, and even that of Nature benumbed, than when on my long reconnoitering rides the evenings found me alone at some commanding watch station. Struck by the rays of the setting sun, tower after tower, up to ten miles' distance or more, could be seen glittering as if the plaster coating which their walls had once carried were still intact. This plaster was meant, of course, to make the towers more visible from a distance. It had been frequently renewed, however, as shown by the many successive layers of white plaster which wall portions protected by debris still retained. How easy it was then to imagine that towers and wall were still guarded and that watchful eyes were scanning the deceptive depressions northward for that fleet and artful enemy, the Huns!

The arrowheads of bronze which we picked up in numbers near the wall and towers, as well as references occurring in the records found which Chiang Ssŭ-yeh would read out and interpret, were proof that attacks and alarms were familiar incidents on this border. Unconsciously my eye sought the scrubby ground flanking the salt marshes where Hun raiders might collect before making their rush in the dusk. Once across the chain of posts, the road lay open for them to any part of the Tun-huang oasis or the Chinese settlements farther east. Not only the notion of time but also the sense of distance seemed in danger of being effaced when I thought how these same Huns were destined some centuries later to shake the empires both of Rome and Constantinople.

But the slanting rays of the setting sun would reveal also things of the past far more real. The line of the wall then showed up quite distinctly for miles and miles even where it was decayed to little more than a low straight mound. It was then that the eye most readily caught a curiously straight furrow-like line running parallel to the wall and at a distance of about ten yards from it. Close examination showed that it was a narrow but well-defined track worn into the coarse gravel soil by the patrols who had tramped along it for centuries. Again and again the men recognized as clearly as I did this strange, uncanny track reappearing along wall sections miles away from the caravan route, wherever the remains of the wall were high enough to offer protection against wind-driven sand and pebbles.

On my first reconnaissances I had already made another curious observation equally puzzling at first sight. At quite a number of watch stations I noticed a series of queer little mounds, usually arranged in regular cross rows *quincunx* fashion or else in a line, but always at some little distance from each other. Closer examination showed that they all measured about seven to eight feet at their base and were built up entirely of fascines of reeds, laid crosswise in alternate layers. Their height varied from about one to seven feet and that at the same station. Sticks of wild poplar wood had been driven through the fascines in order to secure them when first stacked. No such strengthening was needed any longer. Through the action of the permeating salts the fascines had attained a quasi-petrified condition, and yet the fibers of each reed when detached were still flexible.

The dimensions of these fascines always corresponded to those used in the construction of the wall. This at first suggested that they were stacked ready for any urgent repairs. But then such stacks were to be found also at certain watch towers well detached from the line of the wall. The true explanation offered itself when I repeatedly found some of the fascines reduced by fire to mere calcined fragments. This made it clear that the fascines thus stacked were meant to be used for signals by fire or smoke. The Chinese records found have supplied plentiful evidence of a system of such signals having been systematically organized and used on this *Limes*.

As I have already said, it is impossible here to refer to all the individual finds of interest. But I may just mention that from a refuse-filled room at one of the watch posts on this section we recovered not less than eight neatly folded letters written on paper in that Early Sogdian language and script of which before my second expedition nothing was known. A few were found wrapped up in silk covers while others were merely fastened with string. The decipherment of these letters, a difficult task owing to the very cursive script and for other reasons, has now shown that they contained private communications apparently of traders visiting China from Central Asia. They must obviously have preferred the newly invented writing material, paper, to the wooden slips and tablets to which Chinese conservatism clung.

The microscopical examination made by the late Professor Von Wiesner, a leading authority on the history of paper-making, has proved that the material of these letters represents the earliest paper hitherto known. It was prepared from hemp textiles reduced to pulp exactly in the fashion which Chinese texts record as having been used for paper when it was first invented in A.D. 105. The discovery of these letters and of some paper fragments elsewhere on the *Limes* is in full accord with the fact that the latter can be proved by dated documents to have been guarded down to the middle of the second century A.D., except along its westernmost section. This appears to have been abandoned in the first quarter of the first century of our era during the troubled times of the usurper Wang Mang.

A retrenchment of the *Limes* made early in the first century A.D. is clearly marked by a later and less solid transverse wall running south from about the middle of the "marsh section." Just at this point there rises by the caravan route a ruined square fort of quite imposing appearance. Its walls of stamped clay, fully fifteen feet thick at the base, still stand to a height of over thirty feet. Its antiquity was suggested by the fact that, in spite of the great solidity of the clay, considerable portions of the outer faces had fallen. We found no datable remains within, but a small hillock less than a hundred yards off proved on excavation to be covered with the debris and refuse of an important ancient station. Abundant finds of Chinese documents soon proved that we had here struck the site of that famous "Jade Gate" at which we know that in Han times all traffic passing along the desert route was controlled. Curiously enough, many of the best-preserved tablets came to light on clearing a deep shaft which had probably long served as a dungeon and later on been turned into a dustbin. This is not the place to deal with the many curious details which the abundant documents found at this site reveal regarding the military organization, service, etc., of the *Limes*.

About three miles to the north, just where the transverse wall joins the old line, we hit upon the remains of a station which, judging from the plentiful records found in its refuse heaps and ranging over two centuries, must also have been an important headquarters. There we found *inter alia* interesting relics of the ancient silk trade in the shape of strips of silk inscribed in Chinese and Indian Brahmi. They give exact details as to the place of production, size and weight of the bales from which they had been cut off. Equally curious it was to find here also a neatly tied up little package containing a bronze arrowhead with the broken pieces of its feathered shaft. It was obviously, to use the proper official language as applied to the identical practice of modern military routine, a case of "one arrow (broken) returned into store in support of indent for a new one." There are numerous records among the documents from the *Limes* containing indents for the issue of fresh arrows as well as for crossbows to replace others returned in a damaged state.

About five miles to the east of the site of the ancient "Jade Gate" there rises close by the caravan road and well behind the line of the wall a very imposing ruin. With its three big halls adjoining one another in a continuous block and extending over a total length of some 560 feet, this structure was at first very puzzling. Its very thick walls of solid stamped clay, though still rising to fully twenty-five feet in places, showed but few openings and those evidently meant for ventilation. There was an outer enclosure and an inner one flanked by towers at the corners. The structural peculiarities led us before long to guess that this strange pile had served as a supply magazine for the troops stationed or moving along the wall and for officials and political missions traveling by the desert route. This has been fully confirmed by the Chinese records recovered from refuse in a corner of an inner enclosure; for these tell us of deliveries of grain, brought from the Tun-huang oasis; of suits of clothing stored, etc. So here we had found that advance base of supplies, which was so much needed both for the troops guarding the desert border and for those using the difficult route to or from Lou-lan.

Here we may take our leave of this western portion of

the ancient Chinese *Limes*. I had carried its exploration as far as the eastern end of the Khara-nor when, by the middle of May 1907, the increasing heat, scarcely relieved by recurring sand storms, together with other trials of the desert and the exhaustion of the men, obliged me to regain the oasis. In the following autumn I was able on my way back from explorations in the Nan-shan mountains to ascertain that the wall had its continuation eastward along the Su-lo-ho as far as the great bend of the river from the south near the oasis of Yü-mên-hsien. This has taken its name from a later position of the "Jade Gate."

But it was not until the spring of 1914 that my third expedition allowed me to carry my renewed systematic exploration of the *Limes* from Tun-huang right through to the Etsin-gol river, over a distance of some 320 miles. Where the *Limes* east of the oasis of An-hsi had been carried to the right bank of the Su-lo-ho and ran close to the deep-cut river bed, its remains were less well preserved; because the prevailing northeast winds, blowing down with the great violence from the gravel plateaux of the Pei-shan and dreaded by wayfarers, could there assert to the full their destructive force of erosion on the loess soil of the bare riverine belt.

Still farther to the east the *Limes* line was found to have lain nearer to the foothills of the barren Pei-shan. Striking evidence was afforded here, too, of the persevering energy and power of organization with which those military engineers of the Emperor Wu-ti had faced formidable natural difficulties. Thus some thirty miles to the northeast of the little oasis of Ying-p'an ("the garrison") we found the line of the *Limes* boldly carried into and through what since ancient times must have been a big area of drift sand. Where not completely buried by dunes, the wall, built here wholly of tamarisk fascines and of the usual thickness, still rose to a height of close on fifteen feet. It was easy to realize what efforts it must have cost to assure water and supplies for the men who were engaged in constructing and guarding this section of the *Limes*.

I need not here describe how we tracked the protective line farther through wastes of sand and rocky detritus to the border of Southern Mongolia. What has been told already of the *Limes* will suffice to show what great powers of systematic organization were needed for the rapid creation and continued protection of this passage for China's first advance into Central Asia. But the glimpses afforded of the forbidding ground over which this advance was successfully accomplished must also impress us with the magnitude of the human sufferings and sacrifices which the extension of the "Great Wall" and the subsequent bold enterprises of Han policy must have involved for the Chinese people.

Ancient Buddhist painting on silk, recovered from the "Caves of the Thousand Buddhas," Tun-huang. It shows the Bodhisattva Avalokitesvara, as seen in a dream, guiding a pious soul to his heaven.

Sir Aurel Stein's caravan marching over high dunes in Takla-makan Desert, south of Tarim Basin.

Caravan of camels crossing salt-encrusted bed of dried-up Lop Sea.

Painted panel representing Persian Bodhisattva (Rustam).

Ruined house, Niya site, first find-place of inscribed tablets, after excavation.

Frescoes of winged figures from dado of passage in ruined Buddhist shrine, excavated at Miran site.

Portion of frescoed dado, with lower part of frieze, on the south wall of rotunda in Buddhist shrine, Miran site.

The dado shows on the left a girl carrying jug and patera; on the right the bust of a young man; between them a wingless amorino carrying a garland. In frieze, the lower portions of four draped male figures and quadriga.

Painted clay figure of lady rider, from the tomb of Astana ceme-tery, Turfan.

CHAPTER XII

The Cave Shrines
of the Thousand Buddhas

WHEN IN THE YEARS immediately following my first Central-Asian expedition I was planning the second, it was my eager wish to extend it into Kansu, that northwestern frontier province of China. This wish was prompted largely by what my friend the late Professor de Lóczy, the distinguished head of the Hungarian Geological Survey, had told me of the sacred Buddhist grottoes situated to the southeast of Tun-huang and known as Ch'ien-fo-tung, the "Caves of the Thousand Buddhas." As a member of Count Széchenyi's expedition and thus a pioneer of modern geographical exploration in Kansu, he had visited them as early as 1879. Without being himself an antiquarian student, he had rightly recognized the artistic and archeological interest of the fine fresco paintings and stucco sculptures which he had seen there, and the glowing description he gave of them had greatly impressed me.

I found my expectations fully realized when within a few

days after my arrival at the Tun-huang oasis in March 1907 I
paid my first visit to the sacred caves. They are carved into
the precipitous conglomerate cliffs overlooking from the west
the mouth of a barren valley some twelve miles to the southeast of the oasis. A small stream descending from the westernmost portion of the Nan-shan range has cut its way here
through the foothills overlain by huge ridges of drift sand, but
now loses itself a short distance below the caves. On the cliffs
above the broad waste of rubble and sand on which the
streamlet debouches, there were first seen a multitude of dark
cavities, mostly small, like troglodyte dwellings of anchorites
retired to a distant Thebais. From the small size of most of
these recesses and the absence of wall paintings in almost all
of them, it seemed safe to conclude that they had served
largely as quarters for Buddhist monks.

Farther up there were to be seen hundreds of grottoes,
large and small, honeycombing in irregular tiers the somber
rock faces, from the foot of the cliff to the top of the preci-
pice, and extending in close array for over half a mile. This
bewildering multitude of grottoes all showed paintings on
their walls or on as much as was visible of them from outside. Among them two shrines containing colossal Buddha
statues could at once be recognized; for in order to secure
adequate space for the giant stucco images of the Buddhas,
close on ninety feet high, a number of halls had been excavated one above the other, each providing light and access for
a portion of the colossus.

In front of most of the shrines there had been originally
antechapels or porches of oblong shape carved out of the
rock. Owing to the fall of the outer wall the tempera paintings
with which the inside wall surfaces had always been decorated
were now often fully exposed to view. In many cases the
rock-carved antechapels, whether originally or on restoration, had been replaced by wooden verandas, generally much
decayed. The galleries and stairs serving for access to the up-

per grottoes or for communication between them had almost all crumbled away. Hence many of these shrines high up on the rocks had become inaccessible. But the disappearance of porches and verandas made it easy to see that the interior arrangements and decoration of these upper shrines did not differ in any essential way from those prevailing in the cave temples carved into the foot of the cliff.

Access to these offered no difficulty, even though the fine drift sand which neglect through centuries had allowed to accumulate had covered the ground in front and also the original floor of the entrance, often to a considerable height. So I could quickly familiarize myself with the ground plan and general structural arrangement of these shrines. They showed much uniformity throughout. From the oblong ante-chapel the cave-temple proper was entered through a high and rather wide passage, which alone admitted light and air to the interior. This consisted everywhere of a single rectangular cella, usually almost square, hewn out of the solid rock and provided with a high conical roof.

Within the cella I found generally a big rectangular platform decorated with painted stucco. Its center was usually occupied by the colossal stucco image of a seated Buddha, with groups of Bodhisattvas, saintly disciples and divine attendants on either side. These varied in numbers, but were always symmetrically arranged. It was only too easy to see how much of all this statuary in stucco had suffered in the course of centuries through the natural decay of its material, and even more from the hands of iconoclasts and pious restorers. But in spite of all this destruction, these cave temples still retained plentiful remains to attest the prolonged continuance here of the sculptural traditions which Greco-Buddhist art had developed and Central-Asian Buddhism transmitted to the Far East.

Where the heads, arms and often the upper portions of the statues in general had been destroyed by vandal hands and then been replaced in modern times, the contrast of these crude restorations brought out still more clearly the fine modeling of what survived elsewhere as well as the graceful arrangement of the drapery and the harmonious coloring of the whole. In the profusion of gilding, of which plentiful traces survived, as well as in the remarkable effort bestowed on those colossal figures of Buddha, I recognized features of Buddhist art well known to us from the Indian Northwest Frontier and the huge rock-carved "Buts" of Bamian to Khotan and beyond.

Still more impressive, perhaps, was the wealth and abundant artistic interest of the old paintings, throughout Buddhist in character, which cover the plastered walls of all the large shrines and of many of the smaller ones. For the most part they were found in remarkably good preservation. This was obviously due to the extreme aridity of the atmosphere and the absolute dryness of the rock-cut walls as well as to the strength and tenacity with which the plaster bearing the frescoes clings to the conglomerate surface. I use the term "fresco" for the sake of its convenient brevity; for with the exception of one small shrine all the wall paintings are executed in tempera.

In the antechapels and passages the mural decoration ordinarily consisted of rows of large Bodhisattvas or Buddhist saints moving in dignified procession. In many of the smaller cellas the wall paintings showed diapers of small Buddhas or Bodhisattvas just as I had seen them on the walls of shrines at Dandan-oilik and elsewhere. Combined with elaborate floral designs and tracery, they served also to adorn the ceilings of the large cellas. In these the walls generally bore large panels of frescoes bordered by floral scrolls of striking beauty. Painted dados, often representing worshipers, in some cases Buddhist monks or nuns, extended below these panels.

The panels were filled by elaborate compositions, containing large numbers of figures. Those which showed Buddhas surrounded by a multiplicity of Bodhisattvas, saints and other divine attendants were obviously representations of Buddhist heavens. Other panels displayed scenes, bewildering in their variety, which looked as if taken from mundane life. Short Chinese inscriptions inserted on cartouches suggested that these scenes were taken from sacred Buddhist legends. But only after similar scenes among the silk paintings which I recovered from the "Thousand Buddhas" had been submitted to expert examination in London could I feel sure that these mural paintings illustrated Jataka stories, legends from previous births of the Buddha.

Throughout these legendary scenes with their freely drawn landscape backgrounds, their Chinese architecture, the bold movement and realism of their figures, a distinctly Chinese style prevailed. It was the same with the graceful and often fantastic freedom of the cloud scrolls, floral tracery and other decorative motifs. But all the principal divine figures, just as those around them, multiplied in the schematic fashion dear to Buddhist piety, bore the unmistakable impress of Indian models transmitted through Central-Asian Buddhism. Hieratic tradition had preserved for these Buddhas, Bodhisattvas and saintly attendants the type of face, pose and drapery originally developed by Greco-Buddhist art, whatever modifications Chinese taste had introduced in technique of treatment and coloring.

In spite of this strong conservative tendency, there were different phases of development to be distinguished among these wall paintings. There were plentiful archeological indications to suggest that those in most of the larger shrines belonged to the times of the T'ang dynasty, from the seventh to the tenth century, when the sacred site, like the Tun-huang oasis itself, had enjoyed prolonged spells of prosperity. Since a fine stone inscription of T'ang times which M. Chavannes had published before from an *estampage* mentions the first consecration of the site in A.D. 366, remains of shrines even earlier than the T'ang might also be looked for. The search for such would not have been possible for me without Sinologue training and expert knowledge of Chinese secular art. On the other hand, it was easy to recognize fresco work later in style but still skillful and vigorous on the walls of antechapels and passages. These were necessarily much exposed to decay and damage, and restorations such as later inscriptions mention under the Mongol dynasty had here manifestly been frequent.

During the centuries that followed the downfall of the T'ang dynasty until the establishment of paramount Mongol power, these marches of China proper, then no longer within the "Great Wall," had been exposed to barbarian inroads both from Turkish tribes in the north and Tibetan races in the south. These vicissitudes must have sadly affected the splendor of the "Thousand Buddhas" shrines and the numbers of monks and nuns who ministered to their worship. Yet in spite of all changes and devastations, Tun-huang had evidently managed to retain its traditions of Buddhist piety even then; for as I examined one grotto after the other I could feel no doubt that it was the sight of these multitudinous shrines, and the first vivid impressions there received of the cult paid to the images, which had made Marco Polo put into his chapter on *Sachiu, i.e.* Sha-chou or Tun-huang, a long account of the strange idolatrous customs of its people.

The good folk of Tun-huang have indeed remained to this day attached with particular zeal to such forms of worship as represent Buddhism in the queer medley of Chinese popular religion. My first rapid visit to the "Thousand Buddhas" had shown me that the cave temples, notwithstanding all apparent decay, were still real cult places "in being." This was impressed upon me still more by the great annual religious fair which, just at the time of my return from the exploration of the remains of the ancient *Limes* in the desert by the middle of May, drew the villagers and townspeople of the oasis by the thousands to the site. I therefore recognized that considerations of prudence would make it advisable to limit my archeological activity at the site, anyhow at first, to the ample opportunities its fully accessible remains offered for the study of Buddhist art, *i.e.* to such work as could not reasonably arouse popular resentment with its eventual risks.

Yet when by May 21, 1907, I regained the sacred site, which by then had once more resumed its air of utter desolation and silence, and established my camp there for a prolonged stay, I confess what kept my heart buoyant were hopes of another kind. Very soon after my first arrival at Tun-huang a vague rumor had reached me about a great mass of ancient manuscripts which had been discovered by chance several years before hidden away in one of the cave temples. There they were reported to be guarded by a Taoist priest who had come upon them in a walled-up side chapel while restoring that temple. He was supposed to have locked them up under an official order, and there were reasons for caution in endeavors to secure access to the trove.

On my first visit to the caves the Taoist priest or Taoshih, Wang by name, was away on a begging tour in the oasis. So I had to rest content at the time with ascertaining from a young Tangutan monk, then the solitary dweller at the site, that the place of discovery of the manuscript hoard was a large shrine near the northern end of the main group of caves. The entrance had been formerly blocked by fallen rock debris and drift sand. While the priest was slowly carrying on the restorations upon which he was engaged for years with pious zeal and devotion, a crack in the frescoed wall of the passage revealed an opening that led to a small chamber excavated from the rock behind.

It was said to have been completely filled with manuscript rolls, written in Chinese characters but in what was supposed to be a non-Chinese language. The hoard, estimated at several cartloads, was now guarded behind a carefully locked door with which the recess had been furnished. All I could see of it then was a long and excellently preserved roll of paper which the young monk had borrowed to give luster to his improvised little private chapel. A cursory inspection of the beautifully penned Chinese text showed to Chiang Ssŭ-yeh that it contained a *ching*, or book of the Chinese Buddhist canon. There was no definite indication of age, but both paper and writing looked decidedly old. All further speculation had to be put off until access to the whole hidden library could be secured. It was sufficient encouragement at the time to find its existence confirmed.

On my return in May I found the Tao-shih awaiting me at the site. He looked a very curious figure, extremely shy and nervous. As ignorant of what he was guarding as he was full of fears concerning gods and men, he proved at first a difficult person to handle. The fact of my finding now the narrow opening of the recess completely walled up with brick work sufficed to warn me that rapid access to the great hoard was not to be hoped for. What my zealous Chinese secretary had ascertained of the priest's peculiar disposition fully supported this apprehension of serious obstacles. The temptation of gain for himself or his shrine through what money I might offer was not by itself likely to overcome his scruples, whether prompted by religious feeling or fear of popular resentment—or perhaps the effects of both. The new statuary and the other additions to the shrine for which he was responsible were coarse and gaudy enough. Yet I could not help being impressed by what the humble monk had accomplished by his single-hearted devotion to his task of religious merit, the restoration of the temple. It was certain from all we saw and heard that out of the charitable gifts he had laboriously been collecting for years for this cherished pious object he had spent next to nothing on himself and his two humble acolytes.

I need not tell here the whole story of our lengthy struggle with his objections, conscientious and otherwise. Wang Tao-shih's ignorance of all that constitutes traditional Chinese learning would have made it useless to talk to him about my scholarly interests. But there was fortunately other help to fall back upon—the memory of the great Chinese pilgrim Hsüan-tsang. And to this our success in the end was largely due, apart from Chiang Ssǔ-yeh's tactful diplomacy. Already the fact of my well-known attachment to the memory of the saintly travler had been helpful; for, curiously enough, the Tao-shih, though poorly versed in and indifferent to things Buddhist, was quite as ardent an admirer in his own way of "T'ang-sên," "the great monk of the T'ang period," as Hsüan-tsang is popularly known, as I am in another.

There was visible proof of the priest's devotion to the great pilgrim's memory in the pictures with which he had caused the new loggia facing the cave temple to be decorated. They illustrated quaintly enough those fantastic legends which have transformed my Chinese patron saint in popular Chinese belief into a kind of Münchhausen. It is true they are not to be found in the genuine *Memoirs* and biography of Hsüan-tsang. But why should this little difference matter? The priest was obviously impressed by what in my poor Chinese I could tell him of my own devotion to the great pilgrim, and how I had followed his footsteps from India across inhospitable mountains and deserts.

●
___

CHAPTER XIII

Discoveries in a Hidden Chapel

IN THE END Wang Tao-shih was induced at nighttime and in
secret to hand out to my zealous assistant some specimens of
Chinese manuscript rolls from the hidden store for our examination. And here a fortunate chance came to our aid in a
fashion which to the priest was bound to appear like a miraculous intervention on the part of my Chinese patron saint. Even
Chiang Ssŭ-yeh felt impressed by the portent when on close
examination those rolls proved to contain Chinese versions of
certain canonical Buddhist texts which the colophons declared
to have been brought from India and translated by Hsüan-
tsang. Was it not the spirit of the saintly pilgrim himself who
had at the opportune moment revealed the hiding place of the
great manuscript hoard in order to prepare for me a fitting
antiquarian reward?

Under the influence of this quasi-divine hint, the priest
summoned up courage that morning to open before me the

rough door closing the entrance to the rock-carved recess where the great trove had lain hidden. The sight disclosed in the dim light of the priest's little oil lamp made my eyes open wide. Heaped up in layers, but without any order, there appeared a solid mass of manuscript bundles rising to ten feet from the floor and filling, as subsequent measurement showed, close on five hundred cubic feet. Within the small room measuring about nine feet square there was left barely space for two people to stand on.

It was impossible to examine anything in this "black hole." But when the priest had brought out some bundles and allowed us to look rapidly through the contents in a room of the newly built porch, well screened from inquisitive eyes, the importance of the great mine here opened for research in many directions soon revealed itself. The thick rolls of well-made strong paper, about one foot high and sometimes up to twenty yards or more in length, which turned up first contained Chinese Buddhist texts. They were all in an excellent state, manifestly preserved more or less in the condition they were in when deposited.

Even before detailed examination of colophons had shown exact dates, reaching back in some cases to the beginning of the fifth century A.D., there were to be noted unmistakable signs of great age in the writing, paper, arrangement, etc. An extensive text in Indian Brahmi characters written on the reverse of a Chinese roll left no doubt about the bulk of the manuscripts dating from a period when Indian writing and a knowledge of Sanskrit still prevailed in Central-Asian Buddhism. I could not feel surprise at such relics of ancient cult and learning having escaped all effects of time while walled up in a rock-cut chamber in these terribly barren hills. They were hermetically shut off from what moisture, if any, the atmosphere of this desert valley ever contained.

Already the search of those first hours carried on in a state of joyful excitement showed how varied were the re-

mains awaiting here excavation of a novel kind. As bundle
after bundle was brought out by the priest to be opened by
us with an eagerness which it was hard to disguise, there
emerged also in plenty Tibetan manuscripts, long rolls as well
as whole packages of leaves, both belonging to the huge Buddhist canon of Tibet. These obviously dated from the period
of Tibetan domination which we know in this frontier region
of China to have extended from the middle of the eighth to
the middle of the ninth century. That the closing up of the
chapel had taken place some time after this period was clear
from a fine Chinese inscription on stone dated A.D. 851 which
the priest had first come upon within the recess and subsequently set up outside.

Mixed up with the Chinese and Tibetan texts and in utter
confusion there were plenty of oblong paper leaves with Indian script belonging to different manuscripts, some in Sanskrit, some in one or another of the indigenous languages
which the Buddhists of Turkistan had used for their translations of the sacred texts. None of my previous finds of such
manuscripts equaled these in extent or in excellence of preservation.

But even more grateful I felt for the protection afforded
by this strange place of deposit when, on opening a large
package, carelessly wrapped in a discolored sheet of stout canvas, I found in it paintings mostly on fine gauzelike silk or else
on linen. They were mixed up with miscellaneous papers as
well as a mass of small pieces from fine figured and printed
silk textiles suggesting ex-votos. Most of the paintings first
found were narrow pictures from two to three feet in length.
By their triangular tops and floating streamers they could at
once be recognized as having been intended for temple banners. When unfurled, these silk banners showed beautifully
painted figures of Buddhist divinities, retaining their harmonious colors in perfect freshness.

The silk used for these banners was invariably a transparent gauze of remarkable fineness. The risks attending the use of such a delicate fabric were demonstrated only too clearly when subsequently I came upon convolutes containing silk paintings much larger in size. Though provided originally with borders of stronger material, these large silk hangings had often suffered a good deal, obviously in the course of long use while displayed on the temple walls. They must have been closely and carelessly folded up at the time of their deposition, and were much creased and crumpled in consequence.

After centuries of compression, I could not have attempted to open them out completely at the time of discovery without obvious risks of further damage. But by lifting a fold here and there it was possible to see that the scenes represented were often elaborate and crowded with figures. It was scarcely surprising that the delicate and difficult process of unfolding and cleaning all the paintings, amounting in the end to hundreds, occupied expert hands at the British Museum for some seven years.

There was no time then to search for votive inscriptions nor for any closer study of the paintings. My main care was how many of them I might be able to rescue from their dismal imprisonment and from the risks of their present guardian's careless handling. To my surprise and relief, he attached little value to these fine art relics of T'ang times. So I could rapidly put aside "for further inspection" the best of the pictures I could lay my hands on at that first day's rapid search.

It was advisable not to display too much *empressement* at this stage, and such diplomatic restraint had its immediate reward. It seemed to confirm the priest in his indifference to relics of this kind. So, hoping apparently to divert by their sacrifice my attention from the precious rolls of Chinese canonical texts, he proceeded more assiduously to grope for and hand out bundles of what he evidently classed under the head of miscellaneous rubbish. The result was distinctly encouraging; for among the quantities of fragmentary Chinese texts there could be picked up in increasing numbers documents of clearly secular character, often dated; drawings and block prints on paper; small packages of leaves from texts in Indian writing as well as remains of pictures and fine silk textiles, manifestly all votive offerings. So Chiang Ssŭ-yeh and myself worked on without a break that first day until darkness.

The task all-important for the time being was to keep Wang Tao-shih from giving way to his fears and flutterings about hostile rumors, etc. I had taken care to assure him in advance of generous donations for his shrine. Yet he seemed constantly to vacillate between fears about his saintly reputation and a shrewd grasp of the advantages to be obtained for his cherished task. In the end we succeeded, thanks to Chiang Ssŭ-yeh's genial persuasion and such reassuring display as I could make of my devotion, genuine enough, to Buddhist lore and Hsüan-tsang's blessed memory.

But my satisfaction was great when devoted Chiang Ssŭ-yeh cautiously appeared toward midnight at my tent and brought himself the big bundle containing the "selections" of that first day. The Tao-shih had stipulated that nobody besides us three was to learn of the origin of these "finds" as long as I was on Chinese soil. Thus Chiang Ssŭ-yeh had to be the sole carrier for seven more nights, with loads which grew steadily heavier and then needed carriage by installments.

Those days of anxious work had resulted in the rapid search of all miscellaneous bundles piled up on the top and in the selection of non-Chinese manuscripts, documents, pictures and other relics of special interest. Then we attacked the solid rampart of hard-tied uniform packages containing Chinese manuscript rolls. This was a troublesome task in more than one sense. The mere labor of clearing out the whole closely packed room might by itself have dismayed a stouter heart than that of the Tao-shih. It needed discreet treatment and judiciously administered doses of silver to counteract his relapses into timorous contrariness.

The effort was rewarded by the discovery, quite at the bottom of those piles, of more miscellaneous bundles. From their contents, crushed as they were by the weight above, we recovered among other precious relics a beautiful embroidery picture and other remains of ancient textile art. Rapid as our examination of those hundreds of manuscript packages had to be, it led also to the recovery of more manuscripts in Indian and Central-Asian writings which had got somehow embedded among the great array of Chinese rolls. The search of all these could not be completed before the priest, seized by a sudden access of fear or compunction, departed for the oasis overnight, locking up the cave chapel with all its remaining treasures. But by that time most of the "selections for closer study," as our polite convention called them, had already been safely transferred to my improvised storeroom.

Fortunately the Tao-shih, on his visit to the oasis, gathered full assurance that our friendly relations had aroused no resentment among his local patrons and that his spiritual reputation had not suffered. On his return, he was almost ready to recognize that it was a pious act on my part to rescue for Western scholarship all those relics of ancient Buddhist literature and art which were otherwise bound to get lost sooner or later through local indifference. So negotiations could proceed about the compensation to be offered to the Tao-shih in the form of a liberal present to the cave temple which by his restoration he could claim to have made his own with all its contents known or unknown.

In the end he received a weighty proof of our fair dealing in the form of such a number of silver ingots or "horseshoes" as fully satisfied his honest conscience and the interests of his cherished shrine. I received gratifying proof of the peaceful state of his mind when, on my return four months later to the neighborhood of Tun-huang, he allowed Chiang Ssŭ-yeh on my behalf to acquire a considerable share also of the Chinese and Tibetan manuscript packages for a certain seat of learning in the distant West. But my time for true relief came when, some sixteen months later, all the twenty-four cases, heavy with manuscripts, and five more filled with carefully packed paintings, embroideries and similar art relics, had safely been deposited at the British Museum in London.

I need allude only briefly to the fate of what I had been obliged to leave behind of that great *trouvaille* in the good priest's insecure keeping. Nearly a year later the caves of the "Thousand Buddhas" were visited by that distinguished French savant Professor P. Pelliot. Aided by his exceptional command of Sinologue knowledge, he induced Wang Tao-shih to allow him to effect a rapid scrutiny of the remaining masses of Chinese rolls. In the course of this strenuous labor he was able to pick out such non-Chinese manuscript remains as had got mixed up with them as well as to select those Chinese texts which he recognized as of philological, antiquarian or other special interest. The priest, evidently reassured by his previous transaction with me, allowed Professor Pelliot to acquire a considerable portion of the 15,000-odd manuscript texts and fragments thus examined.

During the great French savant's stay at Peking in 1909, on his way back to Paris, the news of the important Chinese manuscripts brought away by him excited much interest among Chinese scholars of the capital. So before long an order was issued by the central government directing the prompt transmission of the whole library to the capital. The information I received when regaining Tun-huang in 1914 on my third expedition left unfortunately little doubt as to the sad but characteristic manner in which this order from headquarters had been carried out.

According to Wang Tao-shih, who then hastened to welcome me back as an old and cherished patron, the large sum of money assigned in compensation to his temple had completely vanished *en route*, being duly absorbed in transit through the various offices. The whole collection of manuscripts was taken away in carts, packed in a very perfunctory manner. A good deal of pilfering occurred while the carts were still waiting at the Tun-huang Ya-mên; for whole bundles of fine Buddhist rolls of T'ang times were in 1914 brought to me there for sale. Similar opportunities for rescuing relics from the great *cache* offered also at different places on my way to Kan-chou as well as in Chinese Turkistan. So one may well wonder how much of the materials thus carted away actually reached Peking in the end.

On the second visit of mine in 1914, Wang Tao-shih duly produced his public accounts, and these showed all sums he had received from me duly entered for the benefit of the shrine. Proudly he pointed to the pile of new chapels and pilgrims' quarters which those silver "horseshoes" had since helped him to erect in front of his cave temple. In view of the official treatment his cherished store of Chinese rolls had suffered, he expressed bitter regret at not having previously had the courage and wisdom to accept the big offer I had made through Chiang Ssǔ-yeh for the whole collection *en bloc*.

But, when faced with this official spoliation, he had been shrewd enough to put away in a safe place a nest egg, as it were, of such Chinese manuscripts as he conceived to be of special value. It must have been fairly large in extent, for there remained enough to allow me to carry away, as a fruit of my renewed pilgrimage to the site, five more cases filled with some six hundred Buddhist manuscript rolls—of course, against an adequately increased donation.

Thus has ended on my part the "Prieste's Tale" from the Caves of the Thousand Buddhas. But some account seems due of the results which the study of the abundant and important materials safely brought away thence has yielded. Some idea of their extent and varied interest may be deduced from the fact that though their examination was started very soon after my return to England early in 1909, with the eager help of quite a number of very competent expert collaborators, and though a large part of the results has since been published in my *Serindia* volumes and elsewhere, there are still certain tasks awaiting completion.

Obviously the plentiful remains of ancient Buddhist paintings and drawings which had once served for the decoration of the sacred caves or been deposited there as pious ex-votos have most claim to the interest of the general public. All of these art remains, numbering close on five hundred pieces, apart from small fragments, have been carefully treated by expert hands at the British Museum and rendered safe for future preservation. Descriptive lists of all of them have been embodied in my publication, *Serindia*, and characteristic specimens fully illustrated and discussed by Mr. Laurence Binyon and myself in the portfolio of *The Thousand Buddhas*. In a volume published by the British Museum, Mr. A. Waley has furnished a detailed catalogue of all these pictorial relics. A cursory account of them will be given in the next chapter.

It is impossible to find room here for a description of the manifold decorated silk fabrics comprising a great variety of figured silks besides tapestry work, embroideries and prints recovered from the walled-up chapel. So great is the abundance and interest of these fine products of China's ancient and justly famous textile art. But I may at least give some indication, however cursory, of the wealth of manuscript remains brought to light there. It will help to illustrate that remarkable interchange of influences from varied regions, races and creeds of which Tun-huang was the scene from Han times onward. Needless to say, most of the information this rapid synopsis can present is derived from the painstaking researches which a number of distinguished Orientalist collaborators have carried on for years.

The great mass of Chinese manuscripts proves that religious life at the Thousand Buddhas and also in the Tun-huang oasis, of which it has always been the most sacred site, was maintained mainly by Chinese Buddhists. The Chinese materials brought away by me in 1907 comprise about 3000 more or less complete rolls, many of great extent, and besides close on 6000 documents and detached text pieces. No wonder that their cataloguing, started about 1914 by Dr. L. Giles of the British Museum, after Professor Pelliot had been obliged to abandon this task, has only now been completed for the press. The great majority of the rolls contain texts of the Buddhist canon as constituted in China. The devoted labors of a Japanese scholar, Rev. K. Yabuki, have shown that there are among them works previously unknown or lost.

But in addition there are to be found many fragments of secular texts, otherwise unknown, bearing on history, geography and other branches of Chinese scholarship. There have been found hundreds of documents throwing light on local conditions of life, monastic administration and the like, all representing a category of records of which practically nothing has otherwise come down to us from that early period. The exact dates noted in the colophons of rolls and in the documents extend from the very beginning of the fifth down to the close of the tenth century A.D. From the examination of these dates and that of the materials gathered by Professor Pelliot, it results that the walling up of the great deposit must have taken place about the beginning of the eleventh century, probably at the time when the conquest of this border region by the Tanguts caused danger to the religious establishments of the site.

This great store of Chinese literary remains will yet claim painstaking researches for many years to come. I can refer here only to one or two of the interesting discoveries already made by European and Japanese scholars. In the large block-printed roll dated A.D. 868 is found the oldest specimen of a printed book so far known. The perfect technique displayed by the text and the frontispiece indicates a long preceding development of the printer's craft.

Even more important from another point of view is the discovery of Manichean texts in Chinese garb. Their study has furnished the safest basis so far available for the study of that strange syncretistic religion of Mani which embodies so many Christian elements. It was hitherto known almost solely from the writings of its Christian adversaries and from text fragments discovered at Turfan. Firmly established first in the Persian Empire of the Sasanides, Manicheism had for centuries been widely spread throughout Central Asia. Westward it penetrated even into Mediterranean countries, and in certain heretical sects of Eastern Europe its influence survived to the late Middle Ages.

The Tibetan manuscript rolls and documents approach the Chinese materials nearest in character and extent. They also, for the most part, contain Buddhist canonical texts. But the learned labors of Professor F. W. Thomas, of Oxford, have shown that among these Tibetan remains, too, interesting data can be gathered about local history and the like, while this region together with the Tarim basin westward was under Tibetan domination from the middle of the eighth to the middle of the ninth century. It was then that Buddhism in its Tibetan form first gained that footing in Central Asia which later on through the conversion of the conquering Mongols developed into the ecclesiastical predominance it still retains over a great part of Asia.

The plentiful manuscript remains in Indian Brahmi script have been completely catalogued through the labors of that nestor of Central-Asian philology, the late Professor Hoernle, and have proved to comprise texts in three distinct languages. Most of the texts are Buddhistic, but some medical. Among the Sanskrit ones I may mention a large palm-leaf "Pothi" which, as its material proves, undoubtedly came from India. It counts among the oldest Indian manuscripts discovered. One of the ancient languages of Central Asia, formerly "unknown" and now designated as Khotanese or "Saka," is represented by several dozen of "Pothis" and rolls, including a gigantic roll over seventy feet long. The manuscript remains of another ancient tongue, the Kuchean or "Tokhari," once spoken in the north of the Tarim basin and in Turfan, claim special interest, because this tongue has proved to be more nearly related to the Italic and Slavonic branches of the Indo-European language family than to those spoken in Asia.

In a geographical sense nothing, perhaps, illustrates better the variety of cross-currents of Buddhist propaganda once meeting at Tun-huang than the fact that there came to light from the Thousand Buddhas also texts in the Iranian language of ancient Sogdiana, the region of the present Samarkand and Bukhara. The Sogdian script is derived from Aramaic, and varieties of the same Semitic writing are used also in a series of manuscripts containing Turkish texts. Among these is a fine roll containing an early Turkish version of the confession prayer of the Manicheans.

Evidently Mani's church, which during T'ang times had carried its propaganda into China itself, had its worshipers also in Tun-huang. Its priests there, as elsewhere, could live peaceably by the side of Buddhist monks and would benefit by the attractions which the Thousand Buddhas presented as a popular pilgrimage place. But perhaps the most curious evidence of Manichean presence is afforded by a complete little book in that oldest form of Turkish script which, from its resemblance to the Runic alphabets of Northern Europe, is known as "Runic Turkish." It is a book of stories composed for divination, and the late Professor Thomsen, the famous decipherer of that script, has characterized it as the "most remarkable, comprehensive and also best preserved" of the rare relics that have come down of that earliest Turkish literature.

With this curious relic of a race and language that have spread from the Yellow Sea to the Adriatic, I may close this brief account of all the strange links between the ancient East, South and West which have come to light at that crossways of Asia that is Tun-huang.

●
___

CHAPTER XIV

Buddhist Paintings
from the Thousand Buddhas

THE PAINTINGS RECOVERED from the walled-up cave chapel of the "Thousand Buddhas" are so numerous and so varied in character that I cannot attempt here more than a rapid review of the chief classes as illustrated by characteristic specimens. In view of the importance attaching to these abundant materials for the study of Buddhist pictorial art as transplanted to China, a few remarks on the data bearing on their origin and chronology may precede that review.

In the first place, it is important to note that the evidence of dated votive inscriptions on paintings entirely agrees with that which, as already mentioned, dated Chinese texts and documents furnish as to the final closing up of the deposit having taken place about the beginning of the eleventh century A.D.

But the small, well-sheltered recess may have served for some time before as a place of deposit for all kinds of sacred objects no longer needed in the various shrines and monastic quarters. Anyhow it is certain that some of the objects were of considerable antiquity already at the time when the chapel was walled up. Thus among the thousands of the Chinese manuscripts and documents brought away, there are exactly dated ones reaching back as far as the early part of the fifth century A.D. Among the textile relics, too, there are some to which an origin centuries older can confidently be assigned.

We have seen that the great stock of Chinese texts and documents had received additions in languages used in regions far away to the south, west and north. Something of the same kind is seen also in the case of the pictorial relics. For among those I was able to rescue from the careless keeping of the priest there are a series of pictures, mostly banners or drawings, which are unmistakably of Tibetan or Nepalese, *i.e.* Indian workmanship. But their number is comparatively so small by the side of the abundant pictorial remains which we may safely attribute to Chinese hands that I need not include them in this rapid survey.

I feel that for the purpose of this survey illustrations are likely to be far more helpful than any explanations or general remarks I can offer. However deep my interest in those art relics is, I cannot claim the full competence of the expert as regards the religious art of the Far East. Nor would it have been possible for me to furnish that iconographic analysis of all the varied pictorial materials which I published in my *Serindia* and *The Thousand Buddhas*, had I not enjoyed the advantage of much help and guidance from expert friends such as Mr. Laurence Binyon, of the British Museum, and the late M. Petrucci, as well as from my assistants, Mr. Fred H. Andrews and Miss F. Lorimer.

What gives to the paintings from the Thousand Buddhas their great value for the study of Far Eastern art is the fact that they belong to the T'ang period, from the seventh to the tenth century A.D., when Chinese art was at its greatest height of power, and that scarcely any genuine specimens of Buddhist religious painting as then prevailing in China were previously known. It is true that but few of our Tun-huang paintings can be attributed to the hands of great masters. Most of them are only pictures produced in provincial workshops, to meet the demands of local devotees for votive offerings.

But our paintings, just because they were produced on the extreme western border of China proper and on one of the great crossroads of Asia, permit us to distinguish more clearly than might otherwise be possible between what the pictorial art of Mahayana Buddhism, first developed in the region of the Indian Northwest Frontier and then carried with Buddhist doctrine through Eastern Iran and Central Asia, contributed to the artistic tradition of the Far East, and what was derived from purely native genius and style in earlier Chinese painting.

We can clearly distinguish these two essential elements in a beautifully executed series of silk banners which represent legends of Sakyamuni in his last life on earth, that is before he became the Buddha. These and all the other banners are executed on a very fine gauzelike silk and are almost transparent. They were meant to hang free, probably in the antechapel or passage leading into the temple cella, and to obstruct the light as little as possible. Being painted on both sides, they could be properly viewed by pious visitors to the shrines whichever way they were swung by the wind.

Curiously enough, where the legends of the Buddha are represented in several panels of the same banner, no strict chronological order is observed. In the top panel of one banner there is on the right the future Gautama Bodhisattva in a previous birth paying homage to Dipankara Buddha and receiving from him the prophecy of his own future greatness. The figure, pose and dress of the Buddha closely reproduce hieratic tradition derived from India. Next below there is a condensed representation of the famous "Four Encounters"

of Prince Gautama which determine his start on the road toward Buddhahood and Nirvana. Then follows the scene of
the announcement of Gautama's birth in a dream of his mother
Maya, the future Buddha being shown as a baby carried by a
white elephant on a cloud. Finally below are Queen Maya
and a lady attendant, both in distinctly Chinese costume,
walking from the palace of Kapilavastu.

In another banner rich in color and of spirited drawing,
we have above a representation of the "Seven Jewels" which
Buddhist mythology associates with every "Universal Monarch" from his birth. Instead of explaining their significance,
which would take too long here, I find of special interest the
scene below, which shows the Bath of the Buddha after his
birth. The Nagas, or divinities of the Thunder Clouds, which
perform the laving according to Indian tradition, have been
duly transformed into Dragons by the Chinese painter.
Finally at the bottom there is the traditional scene of the
Seven Steps taken by the infant Bodhisattva immediately after
the Birth, to the astonishment of the court ladies around him
as they see a lotus springing up beneath each step.

The identical scene is depicted in the bottom panel of
another banner. The upper panels show traditional scenes of
the Buddha's nativity in correct succession. Above, his mother
Maya is asleep, in the same pose as when the Descent of
Gautama Bodhisattva is seen by her in a dream. Then she is
being carried in a palanquin to the Lumbini Garden; the rapid
movement of the bearers is excellently expressed with true
Chinese skill. The Miraculous Birth of the child from Maya's
side is depicted below in close conformity with Indian tradition. Yet the ingeniously delicate way in which the mother's
wide-hanging sleeve is used to screen the act, and the skillful
representation of the hills behind the garden, are significantly
Chinese.

Even more distinctively Chinese is the treatment of two
of the "Four Encounters" seen in a fragmentary banner. They

show Prince Gautama riding out of the palace of his royal father, above as he meets the old man, infirm and bowed down
by age, and below as he encounters the sick man lying on the
ground. Chinese inscriptions by the side are meant to interpret
the scenes.

Other scenes from the Life Story of the future Buddha
are those of episodes following the Prince's Flight from the
royal palace. In the upper panels of a banner is shown the
legend of Prince Gautama escaping from his palace at night
while the women and minstrels of his seraglio and the guards
outside the gates are overcome by sleep. On the cloud above,
meant to symbolize the scene as seen by them in a dream, the
future Buddha is represented galloping toward freedom from
worldly bonds on his favorite steed Kanthaka. Below, the
messengers vainly sent out by Gautama's royal father to call
back the fugitive are brought before King Suddhodana to receive punishment. Two purple-robed executioners stand behind.

In another banner everything in figures and landscape
is characteristically Chinese. Yet the touching pose of the
Prince's faithful steed Kanthaka as it takes leave of its master,
now about to retire from the world, exactly reproduces that
regularly adopted in the corresponding representations of
Greco-Buddhist relievos. Next we have the scene of the
Prince preparing to have his hair cut before retiring into the
forest. Below, an emaciated figure in the traditional pose of
Indian ascetics symbolizes the austerities practiced by Gautama
before finding the true way to illumination and delivery.

We find two scenes relating to the Prince's farewell to
his horse Kanthaka and his faithful groom Chandaka represented also in the top portion of another banner. Revealed in
its lowest portion, in an excellently composed scene, is the pur-
suit of the mounted messengers sent in search of the Prince.

The frankly Chinese fashion in which these traditional
subjects of the Life Story are treated contrasts strikingly with
the fact that the figures of Buddhas and Bodhisattvas or future

Buddhas alike conform more or less closely to the types as originally evolved in Greco-Buddhist sculpture and transmitted through Central-Asian art. The problem thus raised is of distinct interest. Whatever the right explanation be, we have here a curious parallel to the transformation which Christian legend has undergone at the hands of Italian or Flemish painters.

Among the pictures showing single Buddhist divinities, the representations of Gautama Buddha and those who preceded him in gaining Enlightenment and Nirvana are, significantly enough, very rare. Buddhist piety in China as elsewhere appears always to have been attracted far more by lesser and more nearly human divinities. These supreme figures are, however, treated with special conservative respect. Hence their drapery always reproduces with fidelity the type fixed after Hellenistic models by the Greco-Buddhist sculptures of the Buddha.

Pictures representing single Bodhisattvas, whether on silk, linen or paper, are on the other hand very numerous. There are marked differences in style and treatment, but the influence of Greco-Buddhist tradition is very noticeable throughout in drapery and ornaments. Significantly enough, Bodhisattva paintings of special artistic merit are to be found mostly among the numerous representations of Avalokitesvara, the Bodhisattva of Mercy. The position occupied by him in the Buddhist Pantheon of Tun-huang was in fact as predominant as that of Kuan-yin or "Kwannon," the so-called "Goddess of Mercy," is in modern Buddhist worship of China and Japan.

In a painting which shows Avalokitesvara standing in a characteristically Indian pose and holding a twining spray, the faded color only helps to bring out the excellence of the design and the delicate drawing of figure and face. Two forms of Avalokitesvara, almost life-size, show a dignity and grandeur of design which seem derived from an original executed by the hand of a master.

A fine paper painting of Avalokitesvara seated by the

water on a bank under willows and holding a willow branch in his right hand is of interest because, according to Japanese tradition, an emperor of the Sung dynasty (twelfth-thirteenth century) is supposed to have first seen in dream Avalokitesvara as here depicted. But our painting proves the subject to have been treated in China far earlier. The figure of the donor below has the wide-brimmed hat characteristic of tenth-century male costume.

Among other fine silk banners, showing Bodhisattvas who, in the absence of inscription or characteristic emblem, remain anonymous, are two remarkable for the grace of the delineation and the beauty of the rich coloring. One Bodhisattva stands on a bluish-green lotus, with hands folded in adoration. Figure, attire and ornaments conform to the conventions of the "Chinese" type of Bodhisattva. But the drapery of the garments, derived as always from Gandhara models, is treated with faultless ease, and the color scheme is very harmonious.

Still more interesting is the other Bodhisattva figure. The striking pose, combining dignity and sense of power with rapid movement, and the pronounced non-Chinese features of the Bodhisattva's face make it one of the most impressive figures in the whole array of this Buddhist Pantheon. The erect carriage of the body, the uplifted head and the weight thrown forward on the right foot admirably express force in movement. This is skillfully emphasized by freely swinging tassels and bells on the canopy. The features of the face with its curious scornful expression are equally removed from the Chinese type prevailing among these divinities and the Hellenistic type of Greco-Buddhist art propagated in its Indian adaptation. The strangely foreign look of the head is in strong contrast to the thoroughly Chinese workmanship displayed in the sinuous lines of body and garments. The whole conveys a delightfully puzzling impression.

Apart from Avalokitesvara, there are two other Bodhisattvas whose claim to special attention from worshipers is attested by numerous paintings. One of them is Manjusri. In a well-preserved banner he is presented in a manner distinctly Indian as regards physical type, pose and dress. His lotus seat is carried on the back of a lion, his regular heraldic mount, guided by a black groom intended here to represent an Indian. The pose of the body with its rather feminine contours and the dress with its short loin cloth and transparent skirt is characteristically Indian. The harmonious design and color scheme give life to the whole. The hieratic conventions distinctly suggest derivation from an Indian prototype which had reached China not from Gandhara and the Indian northwest but from the south through Nepal and Tibet.

Avalokitesvara's only possible rival in popularity among the Bodhisattvas in the Buddhist Pantheon of the Far East is Kshitigarbha, known as Ti-tsang in China and Jiso in Japan. In our banners he is easily distinguished by the shaven head of the monk and the barred mantle, representing the mendicant's garment. Through countless incarnations he has labored for the salvation of living beings. As the trusted protector of travelers, he is represented in a fine picture. Sitting cross-legged on an open lotus, he holds in his right hand the wandering mendicant's staff; head and shoulders are draped in the traveler's simple shawl, while the left hand carries a flaming ball of crystal to light up the darkness of Hell. With its simplicity of design and the harmonious quiet of coloring, the picture has a singular charm, expressive of serene beatitude.

Below, to the left, is seen the figure, broken away at the bottom, of a youthful donor. Neither the space facing it on the right nor the cartouche between has been filled. We find the same unfortunately only too often in these paintings intended for votive offerings. The purchaser, probably buying the picture while on the way to or at the sacred site, may not have been able to spare the time—or the additional money—to have a dedicatory inscription properly composed and painted in by a competent scholar with that regard for fine penmanship that Chinese custom has always exacted.

But Kshitigarbha is worshiped perhaps even more fervently as the Lord of the Six Worlds, including that of beings in Hell. As supreme Regent of the Underworld he may use his power to pardon and deliver souls from punishment in Hell. It is in this character that we see him seated on a rock with his mendicant's robe and headdress presiding over the ten infernal Judges. These in Chinese magisterial costume sit at their tables of office. Before Kshitigarbha a condemned soul, wearing the *cangue*, that Chinese instrument of punishment, is brought up by a mace-carrying demon. In a magic mirror he is made to see the crime for which he has been judged. Once again the space meant for a dedicatory inscription has not been filled, nor the cartouches meant for the names of the donors.

Before we proceed to more elaborate compositions, we may note a group of minor divinities which often figure in these large paintings. By the great number of separate banners they are proved to have made a strong appeal to the imagination of Buddhist worshipers in the Tun-huang region. They are the Four Lokapalas or Guardians of the Four Regions. They are invariably represented as warrior kings arrayed in gorgeous dress and armor with their feet resting on crouching demons. Their conception reaches far back in the Buddhist mythology of India and their iconographic representation can be traced from Greco-Buddhist art right through Central-Asian frescoes to the Far East.

On the painted pages of a paper album all four of them are depicted: Vaisravana or Kubera, ruling the North, with his emblems, the halberd and a small model of a shrine; Virupaksha, regent of the South, with the sword; Dhritarashtra, of the East, with bow and arrows; Virudhaka, of the West, with the mace.

Certain variations in the features and costume allow us to distinguish between a quasi Central-Asian and a Chinese type of representation adopted for these warrior kings. In one of the numerous banners of Virupaksha, Regent of the South, there is the fierce expression of the face, the straight eyes, the long-waisted slim body of the probably older type derived from Central Asia. The rich armor and dress is shared also by the Chinese type, which shows softer features with characteristically oblique eyes.

Another fine example of this type shows in the sweeping curve of the pose, the freedom imparted to the drawing by the treatment of the flowing drapery, the hand raised with fingers spread, qualities peculiar to Chinese artistic feeling. I can allude only in passing to the abundance of material for the study of ancient defensive armor which these pictures supply.

Vaisravana, the Protector of the Northern Region, takes foremost place among the Lokapalas of our paintings. This is fully accounted for by the early Indian notion which identifies him with Kubera, the Hindu god of wealth. He alone is found in pictures attended by his demon host. Thus in a fine painting executed by the hand of a master, we are shown Vaisravana advancing on a cloud across the heaving ocean and followed by an imposing suite of attendants, some human, some demonic.

I cannot pause to indicate all the numerous points of interest, artistic as well as iconographic, which this exquisite little picture offers. It impresses the eye by the sure delicacy of the drawing, the harmonious coloring and the perfect balance observed in the disposition of the figures. The Lokapala's crown recalls the royal headdress of a Sasanian "king of kings" and is unmistakably derived from Iran. In the majestically rolling waves of the sea and the mountain range on the horizon admirably conveying distance, special gifts of Chinese pictorial art find striking expression.

Among the large number of paintings which show us Buddhist divinities of higher rank depicted in specific functions or in hieratic assemblies is one which can serve as a significant illustration of the difficulties which at present beset the dating of such specimens of early Buddhist painting in China. It is a beautiful picture showing Avalokitesvara in the act of guiding a soul to his heaven (Fig. 1). It is a noble composition, drawn with grace and dignity. On account of the coiffure and dress of the lady whose graceful figure, bowed in devout reliance on the divine guide, symbolizes a devout soul, this fine picture had at first been assumed to date from post-T'ang times. The supposed indication has, however, been disproved by the remains of a very remarkable painted scroll discovered by me at Turfan in a Chinese tomb (see Ch. xvii) which can definitely be dated as belonging to the first quarter of the eighth century. This silk picture, unfortunately fragmentary, shows various secular scenes, and the coiffures and costumes of the ladies in them correspond very closely to those of the lady representing the soul in our painting. Instead of being later, the fashion depicted belongs to the earlier T'ang period.

Among the large pictures showing Avalokitesvara grouped with attendant divinities, one, a silk painting very rich in colors, deserves prominent notice. It is in a mixed style of painting in which Chinese workmanship is combined with elements contributed by Indian prototypes, Iranian and Central-Asian influences, and Tibetan taste. It shows Avalokitesvara with a thousand arms seated within a central disc, and outside it a number of attendant divinities symmetrically grouped. The halo around the Bodhisattva, who is shown with a single head but multiple arms, is formed by a multitude of hands. The palm of each of these is marked with an open eye to symbolize that Avalokitesvara is omnipresent with watchful eye and ready hand, able and willing to save all his worshipers at the same time.

In the upper half of the background are discs enclosing the haloed Bodhisattvas of Sun and Moon, while below them rather stiff blossoms and sprays descend through the light-blue sky. The lower half of the background contains beautifully drawn figures, conventionally designated as those of the "Sage" and the "Nymph of Virtue," both seated on lotuses and in adoring attitudes. Below them again there stride in violent movement two demonic figures, with fiery hair and grotesque features. Their close kinship to the Tantric monstrosities cherished by Tibetan Buddhism is unmistakable. In the tank between this pair there rise two armor-clad Nagas, divinities of the water, upholding Avalokitesvara's disc.

We find this scheme of the Thousand-armed Avalokitesvara and the divinities constituting his "Mandala" or assemblage treated still more elaborately and with a glorious richness of color in another large and fortunately fairly well-preserved painting. It measures fully seven by five and a half feet. I cannot go here into all the details of this very sumptuous composition. To the divinities depicted in the preceding picture there are added here more Bodhisattvas in symmetrically arranged groups, the gods Indra and Brahman of Hindu mythology, besides monstrous divinities of distinctly Sivaitic character. The bottom corners are occupied by larger groups of divinities, with a female deity in each. Below these again are shown pairs of gorgeously attired Regents of the Quarters. Here, too, the lower edge of the painting shows demonic figures straddling against a background of flames. The skill in the ordinance of the whole is great, and the wealth of color treatment equals it in effect.

Compared with these sumptuous Avalokitesvara pictures, a large painting that presents four forms of that Bodhisattva in a row above and the Bodhisattvas Samantabhadra on his white elephant and Manjusri on his lion below, looks rather stiff and plain. But it has an interest of its own; for it is the oldest exactly dated painting, the dedicatory inscription indicating the year A.D. 864. A quasi-antiquarian interest is imparted to the picture by the bottom panel showing the donors and their ladies, two of them nuns. The costume of the other two donatrices, with the moderate width of the sleeves and the absence of ornaments in the coiffure, distinctly differs from the fashion shown by the tenth-century pictures. It equally differs from the fashion displayed by the donatrix figures in pictures which we have good reason to believe are older.

The first of these pictures is not a painting at all but a beautiful hanging in silk embroidery. It measures fully eight feet in height and about five and a half feet across. It is only the reproduction by craftsmen, or probably rather craftswomen, of a work from a master's hand. But it stands out by the nobility of its design, the skill and care of its execution and its fine colors as one of the most impressive of our T'ang paintings. It represents Buddha Sakyamuni on the "Vulture Peak," famous in Buddhist legend and situated above the present Rajgir. The figure in every detail of pose and dress reproduces a type derived by hieratic tradition from an Indian sculptural representation. Yet in the composition of the whole picture is revealed the touch of a master.

By the side of the Buddha stand pairs of Bodhisattvas and disciples. In spite of the damage which the hanging has suffered, the fine heads of the latter have survived. Very fine is the drawing of the two graceful Apsaras or celestial maidens floating down on either side of the canopy, borne up by cloud scrolls and their billowing stoles.

What invests the figures of the donors and their ladies with special interest is their lifelike treatment, and still more their costume. The peaked and tailed caps of the men are of a type found on sculptures of the period immediately preceding the T'ang. Equally distinctive is the costume of the ladies, with the high-waisted skirts and long, close-fitting sleeves, and so also the plain coiffure. Here obviously is the fashion of the time when the embroidery picture was worked, and this time must certainly be older than that of our earliest dated picture of A.D. 864.

The quasi-chronological indications thus secured from

ladies' changing dress fashions may help to console us for the loss of exact datings in the case of the large and important class of paintings which show us Buddhist Heavens. But before discussing these I must briefly refer to the idea of rebirth which made these celestial abodes of very direct interest and attraction for the pious. The axiomatic Indian belief in successive reincarnations, as strong now as it always was, lies at the foundation of all Buddhist doctrine. The prime object of this is to show the way to escape from the endless chain of fresh births and subsequent sufferings and to attain salvation in Nirvana, *i.e.* the beatitude of final absorption.

Now, the Chinese popular mind does not appear to have ever taken kindly to this characteristically Indian pessimistic view of life with its aim at the extinction of individual existence. Chinese Buddhists, less philosophically inclined than Indians, have sought comfort in the belief that souls of pious people might as a reward for virtuous lives and spiritual merits be reborn in a Paradise and find blissful rest there, if not forever, at any rate for unmeasurably long periods. Pious imagination makes such rebirth in a Paradise take place quite poetically through the virtuous soul issuing as a baby from a lotus bud. And among the Tun-huang pictures we actually find some representations of such happy births of young souls.

Mahayana Buddhism while developing the worship of Bodhisattvas made them the spiritual sons of several Buddhas, and in due course assumed a separate Paradise for each of the latter. Avalokitesvara is thus the spiritual son of Amitabha Buddha, the "Light Unlimited," who has created a Paradise in the West, and rebirth in this Paradise of Amitabha should be particularly singled out as the hope and ambition of the pious. Thus we find his Paradise represented more frequently than others among our large silk paintings.

Among those devoted to this subject is one noteworthy partly because its simple composition allows us clearly to distinguish certain essential features of such Paradise pictures, and partly because there is good reason to assign an early date to it. The painting, remarkable for its strong but harmoniously blended colors, shows in the center Buddha Amitabha enthroned between the Bodhisattvas Avalokitesvara and Mahasthama. Below are seated two lesser Bodhisattvas. Behind the principal triad the six original disciples of the Buddha are ranged; their shaven heads mark them as monks. Above, on either side, a celestial maiden floats down scattering flowers. A very notable point of technique is the use of "highlights" to bring out the modeling of the flesh. It is a method undoubtedly derived from Hellenistic art and found only in one other painting.

A very definite proof of early dating is supplied by the figure of the donatrix on the left of the panel below, which, though intended for a dedicatory inscription, was unfortunately never filled in. The figure of this lady kneeling on a mat is one of singular charm, and obviously painted from life by a very skilled hand. The face and pose admirably express pious devotion. The lady's costume, with its pleated skirt and high empire waist, as well as her hair plainly done in a small knot on the neck, represent an early fashion closely resembling that seen in the embroidery hanging. It is, in fact, found on certain Chinese relievos of the seventh century.

Quite a number of characteristic peculiarities of this picture are shared by another large silk painting of Amitabha Buddha's Paradise. Here, too, we see the central Buddha seated on a lotus and flanked by his two principal Bodhisattvas and their attendants. From the lake on which the lotus floats there rise lotus buds enveloping pious souls about to be reborn. By the side of a panel intended for an inscription which has never been written in, there are shown small figures kneeling, two donors on the right and a lady on the left. The costume and hairdress of the lady shows the closest resemblance to that of the fine figure of the donatrix seen before.

The two pictures we have just examined with their comparatively simple schemes make it easier for us to make out the details and appreciate the artistic execution of the more elaborate paintings which show Buddhist Heavens, such as one that portrays for us the Paradise of Bhaishajyaguru, the Buddha of Medicine.

In the middle is the presiding Buddha seated on a lotus, in the pose of "Argumentation," and by his side the Bodhisattvas Samantabhadra and Manjusri surrounded by smaller attendant Bodhisattvas, all richly attired and with nimbuses. Immediately behind the Buddha are four saintly disciples with the close-cropped hair of monks. Above, in the background, raised in accordance with Chinese perspective, are the celestial mansions; pavilions above the lake are occupied by more divine figures.

Immediately in front of the Buddha is placed a richly decked altar with a gracefully posed nymph on either side making an offering. On a platform projecting from the main terrace a dancer performs between musicians. It is a scene typical of almost all the large Paradise paintings. Yet the enjoyments of music and dance it represents might well seem strange to those whom Buddhist doctrine as rooted in true Indian thought would lead to seek reward for good lives in beatitude far less worldly. The side scenes on the right treated in secular Chinese style represent different calamities from which the Buddha's aid may deliver his worshipers.

To the Buddha of Medicine may be assigned another very large and sumptuous painting. In spite of the damage it has suffered it has a claim to special interest on account of its noble design and delicate execution. The great assemblage of celestial beings is elaborately staged on symmetrically ordered terraces and courts, all richly decorated and rising above a lotus lake. Among the groups of unhaloed figures on each side, there are seen warrior kings in gorgeous armor, as well as demonlike figures.

On the large platform projecting from the main terrace

once more a dancer performs in rapid gyration to the strain of a celestial orchestra. A particularly playful character is imparted to this celestial ballet by the curious figures of two fat infants rapturously dancing to the music. They obviously represent newly born souls reveling in the joy of their celestial childhood. Two other reborn souls sit upright, but with an unconscious air, on lotuses rising from the lake in the foreground. Only passing reference can be made here to varied details of interest, such as the architecture of the double-storied pavilions rising on either side, or the small Bodhisattvas who are playfully seated on railings or otherwise taking their ease. The marginal scenes quite Chinese in style represent incidents of the last incarnation of Bhaishajyaguru.

But it is Amitabha's Paradise in the West which is the most popular of these Buddhist Heavens. The Bodhisattvas Avalokitesvara and Mahasthama seated by the side of the Buddha make up his regular triad. Between and below them there are seated lesser Bodhisattvas. On a projection of the terrace the dancer performs between six musicians. The stole waved in her hands and the fluttering bands of her headdress accentuate her rhythmic movement. A newly born soul seated on a lotus and about to join the celestial company floats up on either side to the terrace.

Briefest reference must suffice to two grand fragments of a silk painting which must have been intended when complete to cover the whole back of a vaulted chapel or of the aisle of an antechapel. Of the two pieces the better preserved one even in its broken state measures fully six and a half feet in height and about three and a half feet in width. Both pieces had formed the outer wings, triptych-like, of an exceptionally large arch-shaped picture which evidently represented a Buddhist triad.

One is of the Bodhisattva Manjusri mounted on his white lion, which a dark-skinned attendant, intended for an Indian but suggestive of a Negro type, leads. The sumptuous cortège surrounding the Bodhisattva comprises a host of divinities, among whom are recognizable Regents of the Quarters accompanied by their demon attendants.

The corresponding portion of a majestic procession is better preserved in what survives of the other great painting. Here two noble figures of musicians march with uplifted heads playing on flute and mouth organ. The curving lines of their bodies and the floating loose garments convey a sense of rhythmic motion in harmony with the whole subject. Delighted absorption in the music is admirably expressed in the face of the flute player, while intent concentration is rendered with equal mastery in the look of the musician on the right.

In pictures like these of Buddhist Heavens and of celestial processions with their exquisite detail, delicate drawing and glowing animation of color, we feel lifted into an atmosphere of divine peace, while at the same time we are enabled to enjoy the buoyant motion and floating strains of music which seem to pervade it. As with such sensations we take our leave of the specimens of Buddhist pictorial art as it was practiced and gathered at this far-off crossroads of innermost Asia, we realize what gratitude we owe to the fortunate chance which had preserved for us remains of that art in the hidden chapel of the Thousand Buddhas.

CHAPTER XV

Explorations in
the Nan-shan Ranges

BY THE TIME my work about the Tun-huang oasis was completed, the summer of 1907 had set in. So I was eager to exchange archeological work in the torrid desert plains for geographical exploration in the western and central Nan-shan, the great "Southern Mountains" of the Chinese. However, before I could seek their alpine coolness I had to visit An-hsi, three marches to the east of Tun-huang, where the great road coming from Kansu and the interior of China turns off toward Chinese Turkistan. Ever since the times of the Later Han, this route leading across the desert hills and plateaux of the Pei-shan had become the main line of communication to Central Asia. An-hsi has always been a position of importance on it; but there was nothing to be found there to reflect this importance, either in the desolate circumvallation of the place with its single straggling street or within the wind-eroded walls of a ruined town site outside it.

But I succeeded in tracing on the waste ground to the south remains of the ancient border wall through which Hsüan-tsang must have passed when, defying official prohibition, he made his clandestine start on the adventurous journey that was to take him to the Western Regions. I have told elsewhere the story how that bold enterprise at the outset nearly cost the pious pilgrim's life, when he lost his way in the desert to the north and narrowly escaped dying of thirst before reaching the distant oasis of Hami.

After depositing my collections of antiques in the safe-keeping of the forlorn Ya-mên of An-hsi, I moved toward the great snowy range south. On my way there I discovered a large ruined site near the little village of Chiao-tzŭ, between the lowest two of the barren outer ranges. Desiccation, whether due to some local change in climatic conditions or to a gradual reduction of the glaciers which the last glacial period has left behind on the high watershed range toward the northernmost Tibetan plateaux, has worked great changes in the physical conditions of this lower hill region. This was illustrated by the fact that the stream from which a canal still traceable had once brought water to the ruined town and the cultivated area around it has completely disappeared.

Archeological evidence showed that the walled town had been occupied down to the twelfth or thirteenth century A.D. All the more striking was the proof which its walls afforded of the effects of wind erosion since that period. In spite of very massive construction, all lines of walls facing east have been completely breached and in many places practically effaced by the driving and scouring sand, while the walls facing north and south, and thus lying parallel to the direction of the prevailing east winds, have escaped practically uninjured.

When I subsequently ascended the cañon-like valley in which the stream of Ta-hsi cuts through the second outer range, I came upon a very picturesque series of Buddhist cave temples, known as *Wan-fu-hsia*, the "Valley of the Ten

Thousand Buddhas," and still forming a pilgrimage place. In character and date they showed close affinity to the shrines of the "Thousand Buddhas" though far less numerous. Here, too, fine fresco compositions on the walls served to illustrate Buddhist pictorial art as practiced in "T'ang times" on these confines of China proper.

After surveying the great chain of glacier-crowned peaks which overlook the terribly barren detritus plateaux of the Nan-shan west of the Su-lo-ho, we made our way through a hitherto unexplored mountain tract where even at this favorable season want of water was a serious difficulty, to the famous Chia-yü-kuan gate of the still extant Great Wall. For centuries the passage through this wall, marked by an imposing fort, has been greeted by travelers coming from Central Asia as the threshold of true Cathay. All books and maps, in fact, whether European or Chinese, represent the line of wall which bends around the westernmost part of the large Su-chou oasis to the very foot of the Nan-shan, as the termination of the ancient Great Wall which protects the northern border of Kansu. Yet it was obviously impossible to reconcile a belief in the antiquity of this wall with the indications afforded by the remains of the ancient frontier wall I had discovered in the desert of Tun-huang and which I found to extend also to An-hsi and beyond it.

The problem was solved when on my third expedition I succeeded in tracing the continuation of that early Chinese *Limes* where it runs across desert ground to the Etsin-gol some fifty miles north of Su-chou. Its purpose had been to protect the whole belt of oases along the northern foot of the Nan-shan which, since Chinese expansion westward had commenced under the Former Han dynasty, was indispensably needed as a passage into the Tarim basin. The crumbling wall of stamped clay through which the traveler now passes by the Chia-yü-kuan gate has proved to be of late medieval date. It was built for the very opposite purpose, that of closing the great Central-Asian route at a time when China had resumed its traditional attitude of seclusion.

At Su-chou, the first town "within the wall," I had to overcome considerable difficulties before we could start by the close of July on our expedition into the Central Nan-shan. The local authorities were full of apprehensions about attacks of Tangut robbers, etc., and the collection of the necessary transport proved a difficult task. Generally, the Chinese settlers of the Kansu oases are swayed by a perfect dread of the mountains, which to them remain a *terra incognita* beyond the outermost range. We could obtain guides only as far as the broad plateau-like valley between the Richthofen and Tolai-shan ranges. There we found gold pits at an elevation of about 13,000 feet worked by small parties of more venturesome people from the side of Hsi-ning on the northeastern border of Tibet.

After leaving these exposed mining camps, we did not sight human beings until toward the close of August we came upon a small camp of interesting nomads of Turkish race grazing in the valleys south of Kan-chou. Fortunately the well-defined character of the four great ranges in which the Nan-shan rises toward the uplands around the Khara-nor and Koko-nor lakes made the want of all guidance less serious. The excellent grazing met with almost everywhere at elevations between 11,000 to 13,000 feet was a great boon for our hard-tried animals. This abundance of grazing must have made these very extensive open valleys very attractive ground to nomadic tribes of early times, such as the Yüeh-chih, the later Indo-Scythians and the Huns.

But we all suffered a great deal from almost daily downpours of icy rain and sleet, and from the extensive bogs we encountered at the head of the great valleys and even on the broad watershed plateaux toward the Pacific drainage. The natural difficulties were increased very considerably by the helplessness of our Chinese ponymen and what I may politely call their deep-rooted physical aversion from taking risks. Again and again they made organized attempts at desertion which threatened to leave us without transport, but luckily they could be suppressed without frustrating our plans.

By marches aggregating over four hundred miles, we managed during August to cross and survey in detail the three northernmost ranges of the Central Nan-shan, all rising to snowy peaks of 18,000 to 19,000 feet, between the longitudes of Su-chou and Kan-chou. In the course of these surveys all rivers descending to the oases as well as the Su-lo-ho were explored to their glacier-fed sources. The magnificent ice-crowned range which divides the headwaters of the Su-lo-ho from the Khara-nor and Koko-nor drainage was surveyed along its northern face, and proved to rise both in height of individual peaks (over 20,000 feet) and of crest line considerably above the northern ranges.

From the wide mountain-girt basin some 13,000 feet high containing the Su-lo-ho sources, we made our way over bog-covered uplands to the headwaters of the Ta-t'ung river, where we touched the Pacific drainage. Thence we regained the upper valley of the Kan-chou river and finally effected our passage through the Richthofen range over a succession of high transverse spurs to the city of Kan-chou. The total mountain area covered by our plane-table survey between An-hsi and Kan-chou amounted to close on 24,000 square miles.

Seven years later, in the summer of 1914, my third expedition brought me once again to this large city of Kan-chou and the great oasis at the foot of the Nan-shan of which it is the center, just as in the days when Marco Polo stayed there. It was to serve as our base for the new surveys which I had planned in the Central Nan-shan. Their object was to extend the mapping which we had effected in the high mountain near the sources of the Su-lo-ho and Su-chou rivers by surveys of the high ranges farther east containing the headwaters of the river of Kan-chou.

In conjunction with our labors in the Etsin-gol region to be described in the next chapter these surveys were intended to complete the mapping of a well-defined portion of north-western Kansu. This, inasmuch as it sends all its waters into an undrained basin, may well be claimed in respect of its general physical conditions as belonging to Central Asia rather than to China. Previous experience had prepared me for the reluctance of the local Chinese to venture far into those mountains and for consequent difficulties about securing transport. But a fortunate chance brought just then an old Chinese friend to the military command of Kan-chou in the person of worthy General Tsai, whose kindness I well remembered from my visit to Su-chou in 1907. His opportune help enabled us to set out for the mountains by the first week of July.

The route followed during the first marches acquainted me with a series of old Buddhist cave temples at Ma-ti-ssŭ and with other interesting Buddhist remains. They included fine bronze statues of large size which somehow had escaped Tungan vandalism in the temples of the pretty little town of Nan-kou-ch'êng at the foot of the mountains. We were now near a dividing line of distinct geographical interest. While to the west, cultivation, whether in the plains or along the foot of the mountains, is possible only with irrigation, we now came upon large terraces and alluvial fans which rainfall alone suffices to render fertile. The marked change in climatic conditions indicated approach to the watershed of the Pacific Ocean and the great river valleys of true China. In pleasant contrast to the manifold signs of destruction which the great Tungan rising had worked along the main route, it was pleasant to find examples of typical Chinese architecture surviving in these verdant foothills.

Following the route toward Hsi-ning and ascending through picturesque gorges to the pass of O-po, we reached the wide valley where the easternmost feeders of the Kan-chou river gather at an elevation of over 11,000 feet. Thence we were making our way westward over high alpine grazing grounds frequented in the summer by Tangut herdsmen and horse-breeders when I met with a serious riding accident which might well have put an end forever to all my traveling. My Badakhshi stallion suddenly reared and, overbalancing himself, fell backward upon me, with the result that the muscles of my left thigh were severely injured. Two weeks passed in great pain before I could raise myself from my camp bed and use improvised crutches. Fortunately the arrangements already made enabled my Indian surveying assistant, R. B. Lal Singh, to proceed with the topographical tasks I had planned. By exceptional efforts this indefatigable old travel companion succeeded in extending our Nan-shan surveys over an area quite as large as that mapped in 1907. Meanwhile, with my crushed leg still feeling the strain very badly, I managed at last to get myself carried down in a litter to Kanchou.

It was in the same sadly crippled state that I set out by the third week of August 1914 for the long-planned journey through the "Gobi" of the Pei-shan, the desert of "the Northern Hills," as the Chinese call it. The journey was to take me back to the northern portion of Chinese Turkistan for the work of the autumn and winter. The route chosen for it had never been followed before by any European traveler. It was to acquaint me with a desert area which in parts still remained unexplored. The approach to it lay past the small oasis of Mao-mei, where the rivers of Kan-chou and Su-chou unite to form the Etsin-gol of the Mongols. It is in the wide bed of the Etsin-gol, practically dry for a great portion of the year, that all the waters descending from the Central Nan-shan find their way northward before they finally lose themselves in a basin devoid of drainage, just as the Tarim does in the marshes of Lop-nor.

CHAPTER XVI

From the Etsin-gol to the T'ien-shan

I HAD PREVIOUSLY visited this region of the Etsin-gol in the spring of 1914 when coming from the exploration of the ancient *Limes* north of Su-chou to which I have briefly referred above. I was attracted to this portion of southernmost Mongolia by its geographical character, which suggested resemblance to that of the Lop basin, quite as much also by its historical past. For it had been once included in the wide dominion held by those early nomadic masters of Kansu, the "Great Yüeh-chih," the later Indo-Scythians, and by the Huns, whose successive migrations westward were destined to affect so deeply the history of Central Asia as well as of Europe and India. In the valley of the Etsin-gol, Nature, by affording water and grazing, has ever provided an easy route for raids and invasions from the Mongolian steppes into the line of oases which extends along the northern foot of the Nan-shan and provides the great natural highway connecting China with the Tarim basin and innermost Central Asia.

Starting from Su-chou early in May 1914, I followed the Pei-ta-ho, the river of Su-chou, down to the oasis of Chin-t'a, and thence tracked the line of the ancient Chinese *Limes* where it skirts the barren stony glacis of the southeastern extremity of the Pei-shan to the oasis of Mao-mei. This extends from the junction of the Su-chou and Kan-chou rivers for some distance down their united course known as Etsin-gol by its Mongol name. Beyond the northern end of this narrow cultivated belt the *Limes* wall with its watch towers comes down close to the left bank of the wide river bed. Obviously the line must have had its continuation in the sandy desert stretching east of the Etsin-gol. But when we came back in June from the Etsin-gol delta the summer heat had become too great to permit of tracking the line farther on this waterless ground.

It is here that the route of invasion from the Mongolian steppes cuts through the ancient border line drawn by the Chinese when they first occupied the passage land to the north of the Nan-shan. The ruined forts of imposing size and evident antiquity which we found here on both banks of the river were, no doubt, intended to guard the gateway for invasion here presented. One fort built with clay walls of exceptional strength looked an exact counterpart of the ancient frontier post of the "Jade Gate" as located by me seven years before on the *Limes* in the desert west of Tun-huang.

As we moved down by the Etsin-gol from that last outlying Chinese settlement we found the sandy bed of the river nearly a mile wide in places but absolutely dry at the time. Only at rare intervals could water be obtained from wells dug in deep hollows below the banks. Some ninety miles below Mao-mei the river passes through a low rocky spur thrown out by the Pei-shan and then spreads out in a delta extending for some 110 miles to the north before it terminates in a line of brakish lakes and marshes.

The conditions brought about here by a succession of

low-water seasons furnished a striking illustration of the appearance which the Lou-lan delta may have presented before the Kuruk-darya had finally dried up. Where river beds lined by narrow belts of jungle had been left dry for long years, we found many of the wild poplar trees already dead or dying. The wide stretches of ground separating the several beds showed but scanty scrub or else were absolutely bare. No wonder that we heard sad complaints in the scattered camps of the two-hundred-odd families of Torgut Mongols which are established in the Etsin-gol delta, about the increasing difficulties caused by inadequate grazing. Yet this extensive riverine tract, limited as are its resources, must always have been of importance for those, whether armed hosts or traders, who would make the long journey from the heart of Mongolia in the north to the oases of Kansu. The line of watch towers of later construction met at intervals afforded proof that this route into Mongolia had been frequented and guarded during late medieval times.

The analogy thus presented with the ancient Lou-lan delta impressed me even more when I proceeded to examine the ruins of Khara-khoto, the "Black Town," which Colonel Kozloff, the distinguished Russian explorer, had been the first to visit in 1908-09. There remained no doubt for me then that it was identical with Marco Polo's "City of Etzina." Of this we are told in the great Venetian traveler's narrative that it lay a twelve days' ride from the city of Kan-chou, "toward the north on the verge of the desert; it belongs to the Province of Tangut." All travelers bound for Kara-koram, the old capital of the Mongols, had here to lay in victuals in order to cross the great "desert which extends forty days' journey to the north and on which you meet with no habitation nor baiting-place."

The position thus indicated was found to correspond exactly to that of Khara-khoto, and the identification was completely borne out by the antiquarian evidence brought to light at the ruined site. This soon showed me that though the walled town may have suffered considerably, as local Mongol tradition asserts, when Chingiz Khan with his Mongols first invaded Kansu from this side about A.D. 1226, yet it continued to be inhabited down to Marco Polo's time and at least partially even later, down to the fifteenth century. This was certainly the case with the agricultural settlement for which it had served as a local center, and of which we discovered extensive remains in the desert to the east and northeast. But the town itself must have seen its most flourishing times under the Tangut or Hsi-hsia rule from the beginning of the eleventh century down to the Mongol conquest.

It was from this period, when Tibetan influence seems to have made itself strongly felt from the south, that most of the Buddhist shrines and memorial stupas dated, which filled a great portion of the ruined town and were conspicuous also outside it. In one of the latter Colonel Kozloff had made his important find of Buddhist texts and paintings. But a systematic search of this and other ruins soon showed that the archeological riches of the site were by no means exhausted.

By a careful clearing of the debris, which covered the bases of stupas and the interior of temple cellas, we brought to light abundant remains of Buddhist manuscripts and block prints both in Tibetan and the as yet undeciphered old Tangut language, as well as plenty of interesting relievos in stucco or terra-cotta and frescoes. The very extensive refuse heaps of the town yielded up a large number of miscellaneous records on paper in a variety of scripts, Chinese, Tangut, Uigur or Turkish. Among them I may specially mention a printed bank note of the Mongol Emperor Kublai, Marco Polo's patron, dating from the year 1260. Finds of fine glazed pottery, ornaments of stone and metal and other antiques were also abundant on wind-eroded ground.

There was much to support the belief that the final abandonment of Khara-khoto was brought about by difficulties of irrigation. The dry river bed which passes close to the ruined town lies some seven miles away to the east of the nearest branch still reached by the summer floods. The old canals we traced leading to the abandoned farms eastward are removed considerably farther. It was impossible definitely to determine whether this failure of irrigation had been brought about by a reduction in the volume of the Etsin-gol's water or been caused by a change in the river course at canal head with which the settlement had for some reason been unable to cope. Anyhow, there seemed good reason to believe that the water supply now reaching the delta during a few summer months would no longer suffice to assure adequate irrigation for the once cultivated area. Even at the Mao-mei oasis, over 150 miles farther up the river, and with conditions far more favorable for the maintenance of canals, serious trouble had been experienced for years past in securing an adequate supply of water early enough in the season. Hence, much of the once cultivated area had been abandoned.

While excavations kept me busy at the site of Kharakhoto, R. B. Lal Singh had carried our survey right down to the terminal basin of the Etsin-gol. There the delta ends in two lake beds at no great distance from each other but separated by a gravel plateau. This bifurcation had a special interest for me as it corresponds exactly to the one I had observed where the Su-lo-ho finds its end in the desert west of Tunhuang. The eastern of the two lakes, which for some time past had ceased to receive flood water, was very brackish, while the other, which is reached by the present main branch of the river, held fresh water, though it too is without drainage.

By the middle of June the rapidly increasing summer heat had obliged us to stop work on this trying ground and to turn toward Kan-chou. It was reached by a desert route leading due south of Mao-mei, while our hard-worked camels were sent off for their much-needed summer holiday to the Kongurche hills, northeastward on the border of independent Mongol territory. They subsequently rejoined us when, by the last days of August, I returned there from the Nan-shan still crippled by the effects of the riding accident related in the last chapter.

Then, on September 2, 1914, we started from Mao-mei on the journey which was to carry us right across the great desert area occupied by the ranges of the Pei-shan where its width is greatest, in the direction from southeast to northwest. The routes we followed for close on five hundred miles had never been surveyed. I knew that only at one point, the crossroads of Ming-shui, could we expect to touch ground the position of which was known relative to routes previously visited by Russian travelers. Wherever it could safely be done, we moved in two parties and by different routes in order to increase the extent of the area mapped. I was still unable to walk or to bear the strain of riding and was obliged to get myself carried on an improvised pony litter. This made the responsible task of directing our moves still more difficult.

At Mao-mei I had secured the only two guides available, both Chinese, who professed to have crossed the Pei-shan with caravans that had proceeded to Barkul, north of the T'ien-shan. But their local knowledge, even when combined, proved very inadequate, and after less than half the journey it gave out altogether. We were thus obliged to trust mainly to the guidance of the faint caravan tracks traceable, and often where these were confusing to take our direction from the compass. This greatly increased the difficulty of finding the rare springs and wells which alone render travel possible across this inhospitable region of bare rocky hills and detritus-covered valleys. The scarcity of water and grazing implied serious risks in this mode of progress. Only a single small Mongol camp was encountered in the course of twenty-eight marches, and there too no guide could be obtained.

At last, after passing the well of Ming-shui, the snowy massif of the Karlik-tagh, the easternmost great elevation of the T'ien-shan, came into view, far away to the northwest, and served as a rough direction. But serious difficulties still awaited us in the last barren hill range through which we had to make our way, owing to want of water and the very confused and in places rugged configuration of its valleys. When we had safely emerged from it through narrow, tortuous gorges which ever threatened to stop our camels and ponies far away from water or grazing, it was a real relief to look down on open Dzungarian slopes of bare gravel and to sight far away in the distance a tiny dark spot suggesting vegetation. It was the little village of Bai for which I had wished to make all the time, and after four weeks of continuous travel it was no small satisfaction to have safely reached it without the loss of a single animal. There was reward for our troubles in the extensive and accurate surveys carried by new routes across a vast area which, barren as it is, presents distinct interest in its geographical features.

A rapid journey then carried us during October along the northern foot of the eastern portion of the great T'ien-shan range, already bearing its first winter snow, to the tracts of Barkul and Guchen. The ground crossed here, topographically better known, had a special interest for me, as it helped to acquaint me with the peculiar physical conditions of a region through which many of the great historical migrations westward, like those of the Great Yüeh-chih or Indo-Scythians, Huns, Hephthalites, Turks and Mongols, must have successively passed. These valleys and plateaux of Dzungaria are favored by a climate far less dry than that of the Tarim basin. They offer in many parts good grazing grounds and have often played an important part in the history of Central Asia.

Again and again they have in ancient times afforded a temporary home to nomadic tribes. These could never have maintained their flocks and herds in the arid plains of the Tarim basin. But from across the T'ien-shan they were always able and ready to carry out raids into it and to exact

tribute from the settled population of its oases. It was interesting to me to observe a curious if faint reflex of those great
tribal movements in the numerous camps of Mohammedan
Kazaks, fine men of Turki speech and Kirghiz race, whom
the Mongols had driven south under Chinese protection after
they had secured the "independence" (under Russian aus-
pices) of Outer Mongolia. It was instructive, too, to note the
studious care taken by the Chinese authorities to restrict as far
as possible the movements of these nomadic guests and thus
to guard against the risk of great currents of migration being started.

Winter had already begun to set in when we reached the
town of Barkul, and the shelter of its oldest temple where we
found quarters close to an important epigraphic record of
Han times, was very welcome after the icy blasts we had
encountered since the Pei-shan. Then, after passing through
Guchen, a center of caravan trade toward China and Mongolia, I visited and surveyed near Jimasa the remains, extensive but badly decayed, which mark the site of the ancient
capital of this territory. Under the names of Chin-man and
Pei-ting it often figures in the history of Chinese domination
in Central Asia. The economic and political connection of
this part of Dzungaria with the important oases of the Turfan basin to the south had been a very close one from an early
historical period.

Turfan was to be the field for my winter's labors, and I
was glad to reach it by the most direct route, hitherto unsurveyed. It led me across a rugged portion of the T'ien-shan
range rising to numerous snowy peaks by a pass close on 12,-
000 feet. The journey confirmed once more the accuracy of
the early Chinese itineraries in which this route is described.
At the same time it brought home in a striking fashion the
difference in climatic conditions which prevail on the opposite sides of the range.

The Dzungarian slopes are clothed higher up with a belt of

magnificent conifer forest, and lower down afford abundant grazing. On the other side, the descent to the south lay through utterly barren valleys of bare rock and detritus. It was a fit preparation for the aridity of the deeply depressed Turfan basin, where irrigation alone permits of plant growth and civilized human existence.

CHAPTER XVII

●
___

Among the Ruins of Turfan

THE FIRST WEEK of November 1914 found the several parties into which my expedition had been divided since leaving the Etsin-gol safely reunited at Kara-khoja, an important oasis in the center of the Turfan depression. Archeological and geographical reasons combined had made me choose this small but economically and historically important district as the base and chief ground for the explorations of that winter. On the physical side the Turfan basin derives special interest from the fact that within close topographical limits and thus in a concentrated form, as it were, it exhibits all the characteristic features of its great neighbor and counterpart, the Tarim basin. To this may be added the fact that in its terminal salt lake it contains what is one of the deepest depressions below sea level on the land surface of our globe. Hence a detailed survey of this area on a comparatively large scale, extended as far as limits of time would permit, was bound to claim my attention. The briefest description must suffice here.

The undrained basin of Turfan lies between the snowy Bogdo-ula portion of the T'ien-shan in the north and the much decayed hill ranges of the Kuruk-tagh, those truly "Dry Mountains" in the south. Along the foot of the latter stretches the deepest portion, descending to close on a thousand feet below sea level, of a great fault trough which forms the most striking feature of the basin. With its salt lake and marshes dried up for the most part it recalls the Lop sea bed on a small scale. From the barren slopes of the high mountain range to the north there stretches downward a wide, waterless glacis of gravel corresponding to that of the K'un-lun east of Khotan. Above its foot rises an utterly barren chain of hills thrown up by the same mighty geological dislocation which created the fault trough below it. The forbidding look of this hill chain, glowing red with its bare deposits of sandstones and conglomerates, explains its Chinese name of "Hills of Fire."

It is solely from the foot of this fault ridge that the oases of the depression secure their supply of water. It is utilized to the utmost for irrigation and accounts for their rich produce. Curiously enough, most of the irrigation thus secured depends not upon the surface flow from springs in which the drainage from the T'ien-shan heights comes to light again but upon an elaborate system of "Karezes" or underground wells and canals which tap the subterraneous drainage from the mountains. The climate of the basin is extremely arid and, owing to the low level of the trough, very hot during the greater part of the year. This warmth of climate, together with the assured supply of water provided by springs and "Karezes," makes it possible in the oases of the basin to reap two annual harvests. The fertility of the soil when irrigated under such favorable conditions is great, and accounts for the abundance of produce in cereals as well as in fruits and cotton.

But these favorable agricultural conditions would, in view of the limited area capable of cultivation, not suffice to account for the flourishing trade of Turfan at the present time nor for its wealth in the past, as attested by history and the abundance of ruins, were it not for the facilities which Nature has provided for intercourse and exchange of produce with the region to the north of the T'ien-shan. There moister climatic conditions provide ample pastures, and with them those resources of livestock, wool, etc., which Turfan lacks. Passes open all through the year both to the west and east of the Bogdo-ula massif allow of easy economic exchange.

The interdependence thus created between the Turfan basin and the tracts extending between the present Urumchi and Guchen is reflected throughout the political history of these territories. Thus in Han and T'ang times we find Cis-montane and Trans-montane Chu-shih, as the Chinese called them, always closely linked in their political fate, whether dominated by the Huns and Turkish tribes from the north or else under Chinese control. It was the same after the T'ang power in Central Asia had made its final stand just in these regions by the close of the eighth century A.D. The struggle had ended when Pei-t'ing, the capital of "Posterior" or Trans-montane Chu-shih, succumbed A.D. 790 to the combined attacks of Tibetans and Turks.

When by the middle of the ninth century the great Turkish tribe of the Uigurs had broken Tibetan power on the northwestern marches of China and established their domination over the greater part of Eastern Turkistan, Turfan and the tract due north of it became for centuries the cherished seats of their rulers. Originally nomadic, the Uigurs proved more than any Turkish tribe in Central Asia capable and eager to adapt themselves to civilized life. Residing on the northern slopes of the mountains during the summer, their rulers could keep up for a long time what was pleasant in their traditional ways of life, while drawing upon the settled population of the fertile Turfan oases for the material and intellectual resources with which to strengthen their power and to enjoy the pleasure of its possession.

The period of Uigur rule over Turfan lasted until the Mongol conquest early in the thirteenth century and in cultural respects did not undergo essential change even later. The record of a Chinese imperial envoy, Wang Yen-tê, who visited the Uigur king in A.D. 982 has left an interesting account of the flourishing conditions prevailing in Turfan, the abundance of Buddhist convents, the presence of Manichean priests from Persia, as well as of the intelligent and capable character of the Uigurs. Yet he found old pastoral traditions still favored by the rulers, who annually proceeded to the northern slopes of the T'ien-shan for their residence. Though the Uigur chiefs under Mongol domination turned to Islam, yet Buddhism was still prevalent in Turfan as late as A.D. 1420, when Sultan Shah Rukh's embassy on its way to China passed through it.

This long-continued practice of Buddhist cult, together with the protection from violent cataclysms which Turfan enjoyed under undisturbed Uigur rule, had allowed many remains of pre-Mohammedan civilization, including objects of cult, literature and art, to survive there comparatively well cared for to within four or five centuries of our own time. At the same time, owing to the special geographical conditions affecting irrigation in the Turfan basin, there has been no appreciable change within historical times in the extent of the cultivated area. Hence there are no sites there which once abandoned to the desert like that beyond the Niya river, or those of Lou-lan, have remained uninhabitable and practically inaccessible ever since, to preserve for us undisturbed remains of everyday life datable within narrow chronological limits. These circumstances, coupled with the immunity from complete devastation and consequent abandonment which the important localities of the territory have enjoyed, explain why the plentiful ruins of the pre-Mohammedan period in the Turfan basin are practically all found within the area of actual cultivation or in the immediate vicinity of still occupied towns and villages.

Easily accessible and conspicuous as they are, the abundant ruins of Buddhist times had not failed to attract the attention of Russian travelers toward the close of the last century. Subsequently they became the scene of extensive archeological operations by successive expeditions, Russian, German and Japanese. Among them those conducted by two very distinguished German scholars, Professors Grünwedel and Von LeCoq, between 1902 and 1907 had been exceptionally fruitful. Yet my own short visit of 1907 had shown me that those ruined sites of Turfan were not yet completely exhausted.

So I was glad to make Turfan the base and chief ground for our combined archeological and geographical labors of the ensuing winter. R. B. Lal Singh, ever pining for fresh work, was sent off for surveys in the great and as yet partly still unexplored desert area of the Kuruk-tagh, while with the second surveyor the detailed survey of the Turfan basin was taken in hand. With my remaining two Indian assistants I had already started the archeological work that was to keep us busy for the next three and a half months.

The ruined town known as Idikut-shahri or as "Dakianus' Town," which adjoins the large village of Kara-khoja, was the first scene of our excavations. It has long ago been identified as the site of Kao-chang or Khocho, as it is called in early Turkish, which was the Turfan capital during T'ang rule and subsequently under the Uigurs. Massive walls of stamped clay enclose here an area nearly a mile square, but of irregular shape, containing the ruins of very numerous structures, all built of sun-dried bricks or stamped clay. Turfan with its very scanty tree growth, apart from fruit trees, could supply but a minimum of timber. Most of them were Buddhist temples and monastic buildings, and a number of them of quite imposing dimensions. For generations past these debris-filled ruins had been quarried by the cultivators of the adjoining villages for the sake of manuring earth, and many of the smaller structures thus dug into had subsequently been leveled to gain more ground for cultivation.

Since the fruitful excavations made here first by Professor Grünwedel and then by the late Professor Von LeCoq, both of the Ethnographic Museum of Berlin, the destructive operations of the villagers had been further stimulated by the desire to secure manuscript remains and antiques as valuable by-products for sale to European travelers and others at Urumchi and occasional Chinese collectors. Of such finds it was possible to acquire a fair number. But for me it was more satisfactory to find that in some of the ruins deeper strata of debris had escaped exploitation. Their systematic clearing was rewarded by a variety of small but interesting remains, such as fresco pieces, fragments of paintings on paper and cloth, stucco relievos illustrating Buddhist art at Turfan; and also pieces of decorated textiles. Small manuscript fragments in the Uigur, Tibetan, Chinese and the modified Syriac script used by the Manicheans also turned up.

Long-continued occupation of the site renders the exact dating of such detached finds difficult. All the more useful was the discovery of a large hoard of well-preserved metal objects, including decorated mirrors, various ornaments, household utensils, etc., as the numerous Chinese coins found with it permit the date of its deposit under the Sung dynasty to be fixed with approximate accuracy. The domed sepulchral structure in which the hoard was found must have been already in partial ruin when the *cache* was made at the beginning of the twelfth century.

After rapid surveys of smaller ruined sites in the eastern portion of the Turfan basin, including that of the imposing pile of the Buddhist fane known as the "Tower of Sirkip," I turned to the ruins in the picturesque gorge above the village of Toyuk. There numerous rock-cut grottoes, once occupied by Buddhist and perhaps other monks also, honeycomb precipitous cliffs of the wildly eroded hill chain rising above the small stream that waters a flourishing little oasis famous for its grapes and raisins. Where the slopes are less steep, narrow terraces have been built, bearing ruins of small Buddhist shrines and monastic quarters. At the uppermost of these the second German expedition had made important manuscript finds.

Stimulated by these to monkey-like emulation, native searchers for antiques and "treasure" had subsequently wrought terrible havoc among ruins which had previously remained more or less untouched. Lower down, however, we succeeded in tracing remains which had been protected by heavy covering masses of debris, and the employment of large numbers of diggers to clear them was easy. After the difficulties to which my previous explorations at desert sites far away from habitations and water had accustomed me, conditions of work at the ruins of Turfan seemed to me, as it were, quite "suburban." In the end, we recovered at Toyuk a considerable quantity of fine pieces of frescoes and stucco relievos. Fragments of Chinese and Uigur manuscript texts were numerous.

From Toyuk I proceeded by the middle of December to the important site of Bezeklik, below the village of Murtuk. It occupies a conglomerate terrace on the steep west bank of the stream watering the Kara-khoja oasis, where it breaks in a narrow wild gorge through the barren hill chain overlooking the main Turfan depression. There an extensive series of ruined temple cellas, partly cut into the rock, had their walls decorated with paintings in tempera dating from Uigur times and representing scenes of Buddhist legends and worship in considerable variety of style and subject. In richness and artistic merit they surpassed any similar remains in the Turfan region and recalled the pictorial wealth of the "Thousand Buddhas" of Tun-huang. In 1906 Professor Grünwedel, with his intimate knowledge of Buddhist iconography and art, had carefully studied these fine mural paintings, and a considerable selection of fine fresco panels was then removed to Berlin, as one particularly well-preserved set had been previously by the late Professor Von LeCoq.

For centuries the frescoes had been liable to casual injury at the hands of iconoclast Mohammedan visitors. During recent years they had been exposed to further damage from local people, who in vandal fashion cut out small pieces for sale to Europeans. The risk of further destruction in the near future was only too obvious. Careful systematic removal therefore presented the only means under existing conditions of saving as many characteristic specimens as possible of these fine remains of Buddhist pictorial art as developed in Central Asia. For this long and difficult task I could fortunately utilize the trained skill and manual experience of my "handyman," Naik Shamsuddin. Valiantly helped by Afrazgul Khan, he successfully accomplished it in close on two months of continuous hard work. Carefully drawn plans had been prepared for their guidance.

The safe packing of the fresco panels, which filled in the end over a hundred large cases, was carried out in strict accordance with the technical methods I had first applied in the case of the wall paintings from the Miran temples. I cannot describe here how these large panels of friable mud plaster were secured against damage on their long journey to India with the result that, in spite of the risks implied by transport on camels, yaks and ponies over a total distance of close on 3000 miles and across passes up to a maximum of more than 18,000 feet, they reached their destination safely. The setting up of the Bezeklik frescoes in the building erected for their accommodation at New Delhi has taken up most of such time as my artist friend and assistant, Mr. F. H. Andrews, had, during the years 1921-28, been free to devote to the arrangement of the antiquities brought back from my third expedition.

Meanwhile, about Christmas I was able to pay a rapid

visit to Urumchi, the provincial headquarters on the other side of the T'ien-shan, chiefly for the purpose of seeing again my old Mandarin friend, scholarly P'an Ta-jên, then holding high office as Financial Commissioner of the "New Dominion" (Hsin-chiang). On all my three expeditions he had done his best whether near or far to help me in my labors. I owed it to him that a threatened resumption of obstructive tactics on the part of the provincial administration was averted. I feel all the more satisfaction at having had that chance of expressing my gratitude to this kind patron in person, because before my return in 1930 he had passed away, highly respected throughout the Province as a just administrator—and as one who died poor in spite of all his great charges.

In January 1915 work near Murtuk had progressed sufficiently to allow me to apply myself to a task which proved as fruitful as it was novel to me and in some ways unpleasant. Below the point where the gorge descending from Murtuk debouches on a gravel-covered waste, and above the large village of Astana, adjoining Kara-khoja from the west, there extends a vast ancient burial ground. It is marked by small conical mounds covered with stones, and by low lines of embanked gravel which form enclosures around scattered groups of such mounds. These mounds indicate the position of tomb chambers which are cut at a considerable depth into an underlying hard stratum of fine conglomerate or sandstone. A narrow rock-cut passage, originally filled in again, led down to a short tunnel-like passage giving access to each tomb and itself closed with a brick wall.

Most of these tombs appeared to have been plundered, according to local information, during the great Mohammedan rebellion of the last century and Yakub Beg's subsequent regime, but probably also earlier, mainly in search of valuables deposited with the dead. But as our investigations proved, the solid wood of the ancient coffins must also have been prized as a very useful by-product; for fuel, whether from trees or cattle dung, is very scarce in these Turfan oases. Drift sand had completely closed up again the passage of approach to the tombs thus opened, and this, with the utter aridity of the climate, accounts for the wonderful preservation in which their contents were found by us. Only during recent years, since the revolution in China had relaxed Chinese feeling about the desecration of the dead, had the tombs attracted attention from local antique hunters. Their operations had not proceeded far, but they gave useful assurance as to the absence of local prejudices. This allowed me, in fact, to secure a very useful guide in a certain Astana villager who, through protracted practice in this macabre line of business, had acquired uncanny familiarity with such abodes of the dead.

Willing labor could be obtained in plenty, and allowed very numerous tombs to be opened in rapid succession. The systematic search of each has conclusively demonstrated that the cemetery contains burials from the very beginning of the seventh to the second quarter of the eighth century A.D. This period comprises the last reigns of the local dynasty ruling Turfan territory before the Chinese reconquest in A.D. 640, as well as the century following which saw T'ang rule firmly established over Eastern Turkistan. Kao-chang, marked by the ruins near Kara-khoja and Astana, was then an important administrative center and garrison.

The chronological evidence is supplied by Chinese funeral inscriptions on bricks which were found intact near the approaches of numerous tombs. As interpreted by Dr. Giles and Professor Maspero, they record the names of the dead, with exact dates of the burials and details about their life, etc. With that evidence agree also the dates found on a mass of Chinese documents which turned up in certain of the tombs. Judging from their contents, which deal with petty matters of official routine, such as records on establishments of horses kept on postal routes; registers of correspondence; reports on malpractices of subordinates, etc., they could have found their way into the tombs only as waste papers. In fact, in one of the few coffins which had remained unopened such a package of miscellaneous papers was clearly seen to have been used as a "filling."

The dryness of the climate accounts for the remarkable state of preservation in which most of the bodies and the objects deposited with them were found. The variety of such objects was great, and almost all of them help to acquaint us with many aspects of the daily life led in Turfan at that period. They included neatly worked models of household furniture and utensils as well as many painted stucco figurines intended to represent the attendance to be provided for the dead in another world. Among them were found carefully modeled figures of ladies showing interesting details of dress (Fig. 8); armed horsemen in numbers to serve as a cortège; native servants in characteristic costume.

There were also spirited and well-executed representations of horses, recalling the elegant type of the present Badakhshi breed still highly prized on both sides of the Pamirs. Richly caparisoned, they show us the "horse millinery" then in use, much of the designs in its elaborate decoration still surviving in the modern saddlery of the country. Equally well modeled from life were the numerous figures of camels. Other and larger stucco figures found in alcoves near the entrance of the tombs show composite monsters meant, like the *tu-kuei* figures of Chinese sculpture, to keep off evil spirits from the abode of the dead.

Among the articles of food deposited for the use of the dead, the most interesting perhaps were collections of fancy pastry exhibiting a great variety of shapes. Their state of conservation was remarkable, especially as their receptacles had evidently been disturbed by plundering hands. Considering the brittleness of this elaborate pastry, it was no easy task to pack and transport it safely. Among the articles for personal use found with the dead there were ladies' toilet outfits which must have been actually in use.

The custom of wrapping around the bodies raglike pieces of fabrics, mostly silk, has provided us here, just as at those oldest burial relics of the Lou-lan grave pits, with a wealth of most interesting materials for the study of ancient textile art. Their value is greatly enhanced by the fact that in the Astana tombs all such finds can be dated with approximate accuracy. Among these textiles there abound figured silks, both polychrome and damasks. The variety of designs shown by them is great and helps in a very striking fashion to illustrate the position which Turfan and probably other oases of Chinese Turkistan occupied at that period as places of trade exchange between China and Western Asia. For by the side of figured silks with purely Chinese designs there were found here plenty of others showing features of decorative style peculiar to the silks produced in Iran and elsewhere in the Near East during the period (third-seventh century) conveniently designated as Sasanian.

Such "Sasanian" figured silks were particularly used as face covers of the dead. Among them I may specially mention one showing a finely designed boar's head, highly stylized, within the typical Sasanian pearl border. It is a very powerful piece of work and looks curiously modern. That Western designs at that time distinctly influenced Chinese taste is clearly demonstrated by other figured silks in which characteristic "Sasanian" motifs are used in pieces of unmistakably Chinese manufacture. They may possibly have been produced for export.

A strange illustration of this contact between the East and the West was furnished also by gold coins imitated from Byzantine issues which we found placed after the fashion of the classical obolus in the mouth of the dead, while Persian silver coins minted by Sasanian kings of the sixth century covered their eyes. But a find of true artistic value which may be mentioned here in conclusion was Chinese. It consisted of remains of a beautiful silk painting divided into several panels and when intact forming a scroll. It had evidently been deposited as a cherished possession of the dead, to be broken later into pieces by a plunderer's hand. It showed exquisitely painted scenes of ladies variously engaged in a garden. As an authentic specimen of secular painting of the T'ang period, when Chinese art was at its highest, this picture even in its fragmentary state claims great value.

Our plentiful "archeological proceeds" from Turfan had to be packed with great labor before I could start my big convoy of antiques, making up fifty camel loads, under the care of Ibrahim Beg, the most reliable of my Turki followers, for its two months' journey to Kashgar. When by the middle of February the detailed survey of the Turfan depression was also nearing completion, I was free to bring our work in the Turfan basin to an end by a close examination of the curious site of Yar-khoto, situated island-like between two deep-cut ravines to the west of the modern town of Turfan.

There an isolated and naturally strong plateau bears the remains of a maze of ruined dwellings and shrines carved out for the most part from the loess soil. They mark the position occupied by the earlier capital of Turfan territory during Han times and offer quite an imposing appearance. But owing to the ease with which the fertile loess soil within the ruins could be extracted by the villagers around for manuring earth, there were few layers of debris left here to invite systematic excavation. So when Chinese obstruction was beginning anew to assert itself directly against my archeological activity, I was glad to set out south into the Kuruk-tagh for fresh exploratory tasks in the desert.

CHAPTER XVIII

From the Kuruk-tagh to Kashgar

INTERESTING AND FRUITFUL as our archeological work in the Turfan depression had been, I felt all the time a strong longing for a return to the open air of the desert. But my leg had not yet recovered from the summer's accident in the Nanshan, and could not have faced long tramps such as fresh explorations in the Lop desert would have called for. So I had to be content for a time with what satisfaction Rai Bahadur Lal Singh's safe return toward the close of January from his expedition into the "Dry Mountains" brought me. In the face of great difficulties and risks, my indefatigable surveying assistant had accomplished important work since he had left me early in November.

After reaching Singer, the only permanent homestead in that vast area of barren plateaux and hills of the Kuruk-tagh, he had, in accordance with my instructions, carried triangulation southeast to the vicinity of the Lou-lan ruins in the wind-eroded Lop desert. There he had waited patiently, amidst icy gales and with temperatures falling well below zero Fahrenheit, until the dust-laden atmosphere cleared at last and allowed him to sight high peaks of the snowy K'un-lun range to the south. The object I had asked him to aim at was a connection of his triangulation in the Kuruk-tagh with peaks he had been able to "fix" a year before in the course of the survey operations carried along the northern slopes of the K'un-lun. He had spared no efforts and pains for this purpose. But considering the great distance, over 150 miles, which now separated him from that range right across the Lop basin, as well as the time that had elapsed since his previous work there, it was perhaps scarcely surprising that when it came at the Dehra Dun Survey Office to the computation of his theodolite observations, his identification of a particular peak sighted only once, and then too in a slight haze, proved erroneous.

Undismayed by the difficulties encountered, Lal Singh had then pushed into the unexplored and absolutely sterile region to the northeast of Altmish-bulak. Fortunately he had secured from Singer the company and assistance of Abdurrahim, that experienced hunter whose help had proved so valuable to us a year before, when I tracked the ancient Chinese route from Lou-lan to Tun-huang. They carried ice to keep their small party supplied with a minimum of water in this utterly arid region. But the fuel brought from Altmish-bulak had given out for several days, and they had to brave the bitter cold of the nights without a fire before Lal Singh decided to turn again westward from beyond the 91st degree of longitude. He then picked up an old desert track which had once been used by hunters of wild camels from Hami, and followed it down to the salt marsh that fills the deepest portion of the Turfan basin. The careful observations with the mercurial barometer taken along it have made it possible to determine its depression below sea level (close on 1000 feet) with greater accuracy than before. In spite of all he had gone through, Lal Singh would allow himself but the briefest rest at our base and by the first week of February set out afresh for the Kuruk-tagh, this time to survey its western parts.

I myself by February 16, 1914, left Turfan for the Kuruk-tagh and, having at Singer picked up Abdurrahim's youngest brother as a guide, examined the few places in the valleys westward, where traces of earlier occupation could be found. The succession of remarkably rugged ranges and deeply eroded valleys between them strangely contrasted with the appearance of worn-down uplands presented by most of the Kuruk-tagh. But here, too, the difficulty in finding water was great. Then over absolutely barren gravel wastes I made my way southeastward to the foot of the Kuruk-tagh. There wild camels were repeatedly encountered. This desolate tract, like the desert west of Tun-huang, seems to form a last refuge for these exceedingly shy animals.

Taking my supply of ice from the salt spring of Dolan-achchik, I proceeded south into the wind-eroded desert and mapped there the course of the "Dry River" which had once carried water to Lou-lan over the last portion left unsurveyed in the preceding year. The season of sand storms had now set in, and their icy blasts made our work very trying. It was under these conditions, fitly recalling the previous winter's experience at the grave pits of Lou-lan, that I explored two ancient burial grounds of small size discovered on clay terraces overlooking the ancient riverine plain. The finds closely agreed with those which the graves at the farthermost post to the northeast of the Lou-lan station had yielded the year before. There could be no doubt that the people buried here had also belonged to that autochthonous population of hunters and herdsmen whom the Chinese annals describe as living in this dreary Lou-lan region before the route leading through it was abandoned in the fourth century A.D.

The objects found in these graves strikingly illustrated how wide apart in civilization and modes of life these semi-nomadic people of Lou-lan were from the Chinese frequenting that ancient highroad. As a point of special interest I may mention that the twigs found invariably tied in small packages into the coarse woolen shrouds have prove to belong to the Ephedra plant, an alkaline product of which in recent years has passed into Western medical use as a powerful drug. How the Ephedra plant, of which the taste is exceedingly bitter, has become in the Zoroastrian cult of the Parsis a substitute for the sacred Haoma plant and the Indian Soma, the juice of which is praised in the earliest Aryan texts as a sweet intoxicating drink dear to gods and men, is rather a problem.

I had been eagerly looking out along the foot of the Kuruk-tagh for traces of Afrazgul, whom at the beginning of February I had dispatched from Turfan for a difficult supplementary task of exploration in the Lop desert. Considering the truly forbidding nature of the ground and the length of strain put on the four brave camels sent with him, I had reason to feel anxious about the safety of the little party, since he was overdue at our appointed rendezvous. So it was a great relief when, the day after my return to Dolan-achchik, he rejoined me with his three plucky Turki companions, including doughty Hassan Akhun, my old camel factotum.

After gaining Altmish-bulak by the most direct route from the north and taking his supply of ice there, he had examined certain ancient remains in the extreme northeast of Lou-lan for which I had not been able to spare time on the previous year's march. Then, striking southwest from the point where the ancient Chinese route entered the salt-encrusted bed of the dried-up Lop Sea, he had by very trying marches traced its shore line to the northernmost of the lagoons then reached by the spring floods of the Tarim. Finally, after crossing the area of formidable high dunes traversed by me in January 1907, but in another direction, he gained the foot of the Kuruk-tagh. From this exceptionally difficult exploration, which had kept the party from contact with any human being and even the sight of a living animal for a month and a half, he brought back an accurate plane-table survey and detailed diary records, besides interesting archeological finds.

We subsequently moved westward to the point known as Ying-p'an, situated near to the point where the ancient bed of the "Dry River" was found to turn off from the Konche-darya, the river from Kara-shahr, as it then flowed. Interesting remains of a ruined fort and a small temple site, first noticed by Colonel Kozloff and Dr. Hedin, were proved by the evidence of finds to belong to a fortified station. A Chinese record mentions it under the name of *Chu-pin,* on the river carrying water to Lou-lan in the early centuries of our era. The station was obviously meant to guard an important point of the ancient Chinese route where its line is crossed by the track still leading from Charkhlik to Turfan. That it held a Chinese garrison was shown by the remains found in some well-preserved tombs.

On my subsequent journey to Korla leading through the desert northwestward I was able to explore the remains of an ancient line of watch stations extending for over a hundred miles along the foot of the Kuruk-tagh. In these watch towers, some of them remarkably massive, it was easy to recognize the same characteristic features of construction with which I had become so familiar in the course of my explorations along the ancient Chinese *Limes* of Kansu. The towers obviously dated back to the time, about 100 B.C., when the Emperor Wu-ti caused the route leading from Tun-huang toward Lou-lan to be protected by his wall and line of watch stations.

From the great height of these towers and the distances between them, as well as from other indications, it could safely be inferred that they were primarily intended for the transmission of fire signals. The importance of this ancient highroad must have been greatly reduced after the extension

of Chinese control to the north of the T'ien-shan had opened
the route via Hami and after the route via Lou-lan had been
abandoned. But the finds of coins, torn Chinese documents
on paper and the like, made among refuse heaps near the
towers, showed that the line marked by these towers was
still frequented in T'ang times.

The need of signaling arrangements must have specially
made itself felt here in Han times; for it was mainly from
this northeastern corner of the Tarim basin which holds the
oasis of Korla that those Hun raids must have proceeded
which we know from the annals of both the Former and
Later Han dynasties to have more than once threatened the
Chinese hold upon Lou-lan and the security of the route leading through it. Korla marks the eastern end of the line of
oases which stretches along the foot of the T'ien-shan, and
which from ancient times to the present day has served for
the great northern highroad of the Tarim basin. But Korla is
also the point nearest to the great valley of Kara-shahr which
debouches within half a day's march from it. This valley descends wide open from the great plateaux of Yulduz at its
head, favorite grazing grounds of nomadic races from Huns
down to the Mongols of the present day, and has at all times
formed the easiest approach for nomadic raids and invasion.

The Kara-shahr valley at its southern end and near the
town from which it takes its name widens out into a subsidiary basin occupied for the most part by the large lake
known as Baghrash-köl. It is from this lake, which acts as a
big natural reservoir for the waters of the Kaidu-gol or Kara-
shahr river, that Korla derives its abundant supply of irrigation, and the Konche-darya that considerable and constant
volume of water which enabled it in ancient times to act as a
main feeder of the Dry River for the greater part of the year.

For reasons probably connected with its present, mainly
Mongol, population the naturally fertile area fringing the
Baghrash lake holds nowadays but comparatively little culti-

vation. But as the Chinese records show, it was different in ancient times when this territory of Yen-ch'i was of economic and political importance. There is evidence of this to be seen in the great extent of the ruined circumvallation known as Baghdad-shahri which marks the position of the old capital close to the northern shore of the lake. There the effect of subsoil moisture impregnated with salts, together with atmospheric conditions less dry than in the Tarim basin proper, has completely destroyed all structural remains. But a better field for archeological work was offered to me on my second expedition when, in December 1907, I was able to clear an extensive collection of ruined Buddhist shrines known to the local Mohammedans by the name of Ming-oi, the "Thousand Houses." They dot some low rock terraces jutting out from the foothills of the T'ien-shan to the north of the outflow of the lake.

The disposition of the ruins in long rows of detached cellas, varying in size but all similar in plan and construction, facilitated systematic clearing with a large number of laborers. Apart from the destructive effect of rain and snow, the temples had suffered much damage from a great conflagration. This, in view of the finds of coins reaching down to the ninth century A.D., may well have been connected with the earliest Mohammedan invasions which followed it. But in spite of iconoclastic zeal and climatic conditions, the excavations were rewarded by plentiful archeological spoil. The deep layers of debris filling the interior of the larger cellas and their circumambulatory passages yielded a great quantity of excellent small sculptures in stucco, which had once adorned relievo friezes on the walls. The heat of the conflagration had helped to preserve them by imparting terracotta-like hardness to the plaster stucco which otherwise would probably have suffered badly from the prevailing conditions of the local atmosphere. From some of the vaulted passages we recovered interesting fresco panels which a timely burial had saved both from fire and moisture. Of the lavish adornment with votive gifts which these shrines once enjoyed, there survived evidence in finds of painted panels and delicate wood carvings once richly gilt.

The style of these art relics, with rare exceptions like the wooden statuette of a Lokapala or "Guardian of the Quarter," which is a fine specimen of T'ang carving, displays clearly the predominent influence of Greco-Buddhist art as developed in the extreme northwest of India. But what imparts a very special interest to most of the stucco sculptures, for the student of the history of this art as transplanted to Central Asia, is the curious tendency which the modeling of the heads and the representation of certain attitudes shows toward a treatment reminiscent of Gothic sculpture. It seems the result of a parallel development, all the more curious and noteworthy because wholly unconnected in its course, though perhaps related in its ultimate causes.

It was also on my second expedition that an occasion offered in January 1907 to test the popular belief current in Korla as in other oases along the northern rim of the Tarim basin about "sand-buried towns," supposed to have been sighted in the desert stretching to the south. It is true that the desert between the line of these oases and the riverine belt of jungle which accompanies the Tarim and its northern affluents from the side of Kucha and Bugur is comparatively narrow and nowhere overrun by high sands. But the belief is all the same widely held.

Persistent affirmations of Korla hunters about walled towns, etc., they had seen induced me to make a short expedition into the unsurveyed desert area between the Inchike and Charchak river beds to the southwest of Korla. Geographically it was interesting, as showing the changes brought about by shifting river courses. But in the end it revealed that those elaborate reports had no more substantial foundation than the existence of some Mohammedan tombs and of rude shepherd huts by the side of dry river beds. My *soi-disant* guides were quite *bona fide* in their own way and genuinely sorry that my supposed magic arts, on which they had based their hope of discovering those ruins and their buried treasures, did not prove strong enough to overcome the evil spirits hiding the walled towns which their imagination, fostered by old folklore, had before let them see—invariably during a sand storm!

On my third expedition Korla served in the first days of April 1915 as a convenient place of meeting for the several parties in which we had worked since Turfan. From there we set out again some days later for the long journey to Kashgar. Lal Singh's task was to keep close to the T'ien-shan and to survey as much of the main range as the early season and the available time would permit. Mohammed Yakub, the second surveyor, was sent south across the Konche and Inchike rivers to the Tarim with instructions to survey its main channel as it lay at the time to the vicinity of Yarkand. With him I let go most of our camels in order that they might benefit by the abundant grazing in the riverine jungles after all the privations they had gone through since the autumn of 1913. I myself, for the sake of antiquarian tasks, had to keep in the main to the long line of oases which fringes the southern foot of the T'ien-shan.

Through this line there still passes the main trade route of the Tarim basin, just as it has always done since ancient times. Well known as is this highroad, extending over some six hundred miles from Korla to Kashgar, it yet allowed me to gather plenty of useful observations both on the present physical and economic conditions of the oases and on their historical past. But opportunities for actual exploration were restricted for a variety of reasons; so my account of this journey may be brief.

Continued occupation coupled with intensive irrigation has allowed but few structural remains to survive within the smaller oases, while on the desert ground around or between them there was not enough drift sand to aid in the preservation of antiques. Thus at the oasis of Bugur, five marches to the west of Korla, where I believe the ancient Lun-t'ai, mentioned in the Former Han Annals as the seat of the Chinese Protector General of the whole Tarim basin, to have been situated, no ancient ruins whatever could be traced. But in the clayey desert beyond it, toward Kucha, I found a series of massive watch towers along the caravan route clearly proving that the ancient Chinese highroad must have followed this identical line.

At Kucha the highroad reaches an oasis which after Kashgar is the largest at the south foot of the T'ien-shan. Apart from the size of the cultivated area and its economic resources which the irrigation facilities derived from two considerable rivers assure, Kucha enjoys also the advantage of a geographical position particularly favorable for trade; for the highroad is joined here by routes leading north across the mountains to rich tracts of Dzungaria, while to the south Khotan can be directly reached by the route that crosses the Taklamakan desert along the bed of the Khotan river. All this accounts for the importance, political as well as cultural, that has attached to the territory throughout historical times. This importance is reflected by numerous and impressive remains of temples and cave shrines which illustrate the flourishing conditions of Buddhist religious establishments in Kucha and the ample resources of the population that maintained them.

Situated for the most part at points where the rivers debouch from the foothills and not far from the main routes, these ruins could not fail to attract early attention. They had in consequence been thoroughly explored by German, French and Russian expeditions even before my second journey had allowed me in 1908 to pay a short visit to Kucha. Thus most of the very interesting wall paintings which once adorned the cave shrines of Kizil and Kumtura had found their way to the Berlin Museum of Ethnography to form the subject of important publications by Professors Grünwedel and Von LeCoq. The finds of manuscripts which rewarded those explorations had also been of considerable value; for though limited in extent they have acquainted us with the tongue of ancient Kucha, which, like that once spoken in the Turfan area, has proved to belong to the Indo-European language family and to be more closely related to the Italo-Slavonic branch than to the Aryan.

Notwithstanding the limitations resulting from these earlier labors, there was enough of useful archeological and geographical work to keep me occupied during three busy weeks spent within and around the Kucha oasis. With Afrazgul Khan's help a careful survey was made both of its actually cultivated area and of that which, by the evidence of numerous old sites found scattered in the scrubby desert to the south, east and west, must have once formed part of it. At several of these sites archeological finds of interest were secured affording definite evidence as to the period of occupation reaching back to Buddhist times. The survey thus effected furnished strong grounds for the belief that the area over which the Kucha oasis extended in T'ang times must have demanded for its cultivation means of irrigation greatly in excess of those now available.

The conclusion seemed clearly indicated that the discharge of the two rivers feeding the canals of Kucha has considerably diminished since the Buddhist period. But here as in the case of the Khotan oasis, which in many respects shows aspects curiously corresponding to those of Kucha, antiquarian evidence does not allow us definitely to answer the questions to what extent this diminution was the direct cause for the abandonment during historical times of once irrigated ground and by what stages it proceeded. But the fact itself of the reduced volume of water in these rivers deserves to be kept in view when considering the much-discussed problem of "desiccation" in Central Asia.

On my first brief visit to Kucha in January 1908 I had

started from here for the difficult and in some ways distinctly risky journey which carried me south from the Tarim across the forbidding wastes of the Taklamakan to where the Keriya river dies away amidst the dunes. In *Desert Cathay* I have fully recorded the anxious experiences we went through on that rather adventurous journey, and even if I could spare room here to relate them afresh, it would mean too great a digression from the ground that concerns us here.

By the beginning of May I started from Kucha westward, not without regret at having to leave the verdure of its fine orchards and its attractive people, genial and polite, just as the Chinese records describe them in ancient times. Afrazgul Khan was sent to map the old and shortest route to Aksu which leads through the scrubby desert to the south of a barren outer hill chain, and being now waterless for several marches is now practically abandoned. In order to visit a couple of minor Buddhist sites I myself had to follow the highroad through the subsidiary basin of Bai. This lies to the north of that hill chain, and is watered by the river which flows to Kucha from near the glacier pass of the Muz-art on the T'ien-shan.

The torrid heat of the Turkistan summer had begun to set in by the time we reached the long-stretched oasis of Aksu. So I was not altogether sorry that this narrow belt of cultivation along both banks of the Taushkan river descending from the northwest offered no ancient remains to explore. The tract does not appear to have been of importance in ancient times, and has received its present population of rather uncouth Dolans from a late immigration of an originally semi-nomadic Turkish tribe.

Our six long marches beyond, toward Maral-bashi, led mostly through desert ground within sight of bare mountains belonging to an outlier of the T'ien-shan which encircles the small oasis of Kelpin. On my second expedition I had carried in May 1908 a survey across those barren ranges, and after emerging from them traced a line of ruined watch stations marking the line of the ancient highroad where it ran through what is now absolutely waterless, sandy desert well to the north of the present route. The change of a terminal bed of the Kashgar river beyond Maral-bashi accounts for this diversion of the old caravan route.

In the neighborhood of Maral-bashi, another settlement of Dolans, where the courses of the Tarim and Kashgar rivers closely approach each other, detached rocky ridges, last off-shoots of the T'ien-shan, rise island-like from a wide riverine plain still marshy in places. A couple of them, situated just where the present road passes the village of Tumshuk, bear some ruins of Buddhist shrines dating back to T'ang times. They were duly visited, but as they had already been cleared by M. Pelliot and Professor Von LeCoq, they could not detain me. In the autumn of 1913 I had already explored the remains of a small Buddhist site in a similar position much farther to the north. Together with other archeological indications it suggested that the main course of the Kashgar river, which the modern caravan route from Maral-bashi to Kashgar hugs first on its left and then on its right bank, had probably down to medieval times led much nearer to the foot of the steep outer hill chain overlooking the flat plain to the east of Kashgar.

Then near Faizabad the eastern edge of the great and fertile oasis of Kashgar was entered, and by the last day of May I passed once more at Chini-bagh under the ever hospitable shelter of the British Consulate General, which ever since the year 1900 had served as the cherished and most helpful base for all my Central-Asian explorations.

CHAPTER XIX

From Kashgar
to the Alichur Pamir

THE HOT WEEKS of June 1915 which followed my arrival at Kashgar saw me kept hard at work at the safe repacking of my collection of antiques, filling 182 heavy cases, for its long journey across the Kara-koram to Kashmir, and at a host of other practical tasks. They were lightened by the kind hospitality afforded to me at my old base by Colonel (since Brigadier General) Sir Percy Sykes, who had temporarily replaced Sir George Macartney as H.B.M.'s Consul General. Though a shooting trip to the Pamirs soon deprived me of the congenial company of this distinguished officer of the Indian Political Department and his sister, Miss Ella Sykes, the gifted writer and traveler, I continued to benefit greatly by all the comfort and aid which I derived from the arrangements kindly made for me at Chini-bagh.

But what helped most to keep my spirits buoyant was the prospect of realizing my long-cherished plan of a journey across the Russian Pamirs and the mountains north of the Oxus. Those great regions of the "Roof of the World" and of the adjoining extreme east of Iran had ever since my youth had a special fascination for me by reason of their varied geographical interest and their ethnic and historical associations. Political conditions seemed for a long time to bar all access to them for British travelers, and in particular for anyone serving like myself under the Indian Government. But the conclusion of the Anglo-Russian agreement reconciling the Asiatic interests of both Empires seemed to encourage some hope that the bar might at least partially be lifted for the sake of my scholarly aims. I accordingly had in the autumn of 1913 addressed a request to the Foreign Department of the Government of India that with the approval of the Foreign Office in London the Russian Government might be approached for permission enabling me to visit the Alai portion of the Pamirs and the mountain tracts westward through which the route of the ancient silk trade from China to Bactria must have passed.

Previous experience had induced me to provide an adequate allowance of time for needful diplomatic procedure and slow postal communications in Chinese Turkistan. All the same, it was a great relief when a mail bag received at Kucha in April 1915 brought cheering demi-official information from Simla that the desired permission had been accorded by the Russian Foreign Ministry. I felt duly grateful for the alliance between Russia and the British Empire, cemented by the war, which was likely to have helped toward securing this concession.

But my hope for the prompt realization of my program, which in the end was to take me through Russian Turkistan to southeastern Persia for the following winter's work, was much damped on my arrival at Kashgar. The Russian diplomatic representative, Consul General Prince Mestchersky, cultivated very friendly relations with his British colleague and accorded me a very kindly reception. But he declared he had received no instructions whatever about the permission required for my entry into Russian territory. On a reference promptly made by him to Tashkent, the Governor General's office declared itself equally ignorant of the grant of the permission in question. The suspense was naturally a cause of serious anxiety for me. But at last a telegraphic inquiry addressed by myself direct to the British Ambassador at Petrograd had brought Sir George Buchanan's assurance that the desired permission had been duly granted by the Imperial Ministry long before. Thereupon Prince Mestchersky very kindly agreed to accept this message to myself as a sufficient authority for issuing the requisite special permit.

I had additional reason to feel very grateful for the consideration thus shown when, on my representing the scientific interests which drew me to that region, that cultured diplomat readily agreed to make the permit apply to the whole of the Pamirs and the adjoining parts of Russian Turkistan. It was no doubt mainly a result of his kind recommendations to the Russian authorities across the border and in the protected State of Bukhara that I enjoyed their most effective help all through my travels of the following three months. When I think of the suspicion with which British visitors to Russian Turkistan used to be treated in former years, and the still more adverse conditions prevailing since in those parts, I must indeed give thanks for the kindly Fate which facilitated my long-hoped-for visit just during the favorable interval created by the war.

By July 6 I was able to leave Kashgar for the mountains westward after having completed all arrangements for the safe passage of my eighty heavy camel loads of antiques to India. But the summer floods in the valleys of the K'un-lun would not allow the valuable convoy to be started at once toward the Kara-koram passes. So R. B. Lal Singh, to whose care I had to entrust it, had set out in the meanwhile for a survey of the high snowy mountains which extend the great range of Muztagh-ata northward to the headwaters of the Kashgar river and join it to the T'ien-shan.

Before he rejoined me for manifold final instructions I could enjoy a week of delightful peace, much needed for many urgent writing tasks, in the seclusion of a small fir-clad alp above the Kirghiz camp of Bostan-arche. Lower down in the valley my brave camels, those hardy companions in the wastes of the Lop desert and elsewhere, had enjoyed weeks of happy grazing in coolness. When the time came for my start from that alpine retreat I felt the final separation from them almost as much as the temporary one from devoted Lal Singh. Of my remaining Indian assistants I kept by me only young Afrazgul Khan, whom I knew to be ever ready to make himself useful even where no surveying or digging could be done.

With a delightful sense of freedom regained after weeks of toil I sent off on July 19 my last mail bag, a heavy one, for Kashgar and India from my mountain camp and started for the high Ulugh-art pass and the Pamirs beyond. On the following day we crossed the difficult pass at a height of about 16,600 feet. From the narrow saddle, gained after a very steep ascent, the clouds lifting at intervals revealed a grand view across the broad valley of Moji toward the mighty eastern rampart of the Russian Pamirs. Below the pass there were to be seen the middle and lower reaches of a magnificent glacier some ten miles long descending from an ice-crowned spur to the south.

The descent, difficult throughout and in places impracticable for laden animals, led across a succession of precipitous spurs on the north close to where small glaciers overhang and divide them. By the time we had reached easier ground overlooking the snout of the large glacier I felt duly impressed with the fact that I had passed the great meridional mountain barrier, the ancient Imaos, dividing Ptolemy's "Inner" and "Outer Scythia," as it does now easternmost Iran

from the westernmost marches of China's Central-Asian dominion. The same night, after a thirty-three miles' walk and
ride, I reached the Kirghiz grazing ground of Kun-tigmaz in
the main valley below Moji. There I met Sir Percy and Miss
Ella Sykes returning from the Taghdumbash Pamir, and next
day in their camp enjoyed a happy day of reunion.

Five days of rapid travel then carried me along the
northernmost of the Chinese Pamirs and up the gorge of the
westernmost feeder of the Kashgar river. When crossing the
Kosh-bel pass at a height of some 13,800 feet on the way to
the latter, I gained my first view of the great Trans-Alai
range stretching east to west and rising to peaks of over 20,-
000 feet. While ascending the bed of the Markan-su, which
sends its water toward Kashgar, we passed the unmarked
Russian border. That night we were visited by a snow storm
at a temperature well below freezing point. Next day, on
July 26, we reached the saddle of Kizil-art, where the military
road connecting the Russian posts on the Pamirs and along
the Oxus with the province of Farghana crosses the Trans-
Alai range at an elevation of about 14,000 feet.

It was a strange feeling to find myself after fully two
years once more on a properly made cart road duly marked
with milestones. We had not met a single human being since
leaving a Kirghiz camp above Moji, until descending to the
north the little rest house of Por-döbe was reached the same
evening. There I found a kindly Russian Customs officer, by
birth an Ossete of the Caucasus, just arrived from Irkesh-tam
station on the main Farghana-Kashgar road. From him I
learned that Colonel Ivan D. Yagello, holding military and political charge of the Pamir Division, was expected to arrive
next day on a rapid passage from his headquarters to Tashkent. A day's halt at Por-döbe secured me a meeting with this
distinguished officer, whom a letter sent from Kun-tigmaz by
a fast Kirghiz rider had advised of my coming.

Experience soon showed that even on the Indian side of

the Hindukush I could not have hoped for arrangements more complete or effective than those which proved to have been made on my behalf by Colonel Yagello both on the Pamirs and in the Upper Oxus territories of Wakhan, Shughnan and Roshan included in his charge. He had filled the chair of Oriental Languages at the Military Staff College of Tashkent, and being greatly interested in the geography and ethnology of the Oxus regions, was anxious to aid whatever investigations could throw light on their past. It was due mainly to Colonel Yagello's willing help and forethought that I succeeded in seeing so much interesting ground, far more than my original program had included, within the comparatively short time available, and without the loss of a single day.

One of the chief reasons which had made me eager from the start to extend my third expedition across the Pamirs and the adjacent mountain tracts on the Russian side of the Oxus was the hope that I might thus be able to study on the spot questions bearing on the ancient routes along which the earliest intercourse between China and Western Asia had been carried on. Experience gathered elsewhere in the East had long before taught me the advantages of such study on the ground itself where questions of historical geography were concerned. This explains the special satisfaction I felt when I started to travel down the whole length of that great Alai valley. Fourteen years before, on my return from my first expedition, I had been able to see only its head on my way from Irkeshtam to the foot of the Taldik pass.

Topographical facts, climatic conditions and local resources all support the conclusion that along the great natural thoroughfare of the Alai trough, which skirts the high northern rim of the Pamirs from east to west and is continued lower down by the fertile valley of the Kizil-su or Surkh-āb, "the Red River," there once passed the route which the ancient silk traders coming from China and the Tarim basin followed down to the middle Oxus. Of this route Ptolemy, the great geographer of the second century A.D., has preserved for us an important and much-discussed record of Marinus of Tyre, his famous predecessor. This describes the progress made in the opposite direction by the trading agents of "Maës the Macedonian also called Titianus" as they traveled from Baktra, the present Balkh, to the "country of the Seres," or China, for the sake of their silk.

There is no need here to discuss the details which this record indicates as to the direction followed by the route. That it led up from the Oxus to the Alai had been established long ago by Sir Henry Yule, that great elucidator of early travel, when he proved that "the valley of the Komedoi," through which the ascent toward Imaos is said to have led, could be no other than Kara-tegin, the valley of the Surkh-ab. Medieval Arab geographers still knew it by the name of *Kumedh*. The Kara-tegin valley and its eastern continuation, the trough of the Alai, offer in fact the easiest line of communication from the Oxus to the Tarim basin. But the advantages of the physical features which make the Alai particularly suited to serve as a natural highway between the two were brought home to me best by what the actual journey along it showed most clearly.

For fully seventy miles from where the Russian military road crosses it the open trough of the Alai stretches with an unbroken width from six to eleven miles at its floor down to the Kirghiz village of Daraut-kurghan. Eastward for another twenty miles up to the Taun-murun saddle, where the route from the Kashgar side enters the Alai, the "thalweg" is equally wide and easy. Climatic conditions, moister than on the Pamirs to the south, provide everywhere ample steppe vegetation. Hence the Alai forms the great summer grazing ground for thousands of Kirghiz nomads who annually move up there from the plains of Farghana with their flocks, camels and horses. Well did I remember their picturesque caravans with camels carrying rich carpets, felts and other comfortable possessions of nomadic households as I had met them on their regular migration when I traveled early in June 1901 from Irkesh-tam to Osh and Andijan in Farghana. Now the warmth of the summer had made their camps seek the higher side valleys for the young grass, and thence they would descend later in the season to graze along the main valley. All the way the great snowy range to the south, with Mount Kaufmann rising to close on 23,000 feet, presented grand panoramic views in the distance.

Long before reaching Daraut-kurghan, I came at an elevation of about 9000 feet upon traces of former cultivation and remains of roughly built stone dwellings such as are occupied now by the semi-nomadic Kirghiz lower down during the winter months. Similarly, on the Kashgar side cultivation is to be found at Irkesh-tam and above it to about the same elevation. Thus wayfarers of old could be sure of finding shelter and some local supplies all along this ancient route except for a distance of less than seventy miles on the highest portion of the Alai. Though the snow lies deep on the Alai from December to February, the route would be practicable even then just as the Terek pass (12,700 feet), much frequented from Irkesh-tam to Farghana, is now at that season, provided there were sufficient traffic to keep the track open.

Such trade between the Tarim basin and the middle Oxus as was once served by the route through Kara-tegin and the Alai no longer exists. Balkh and the rest of Afghan Turkistan to the south of the Oxus have long ceased to see traffic passing from China. What little local trade comes up Karategin from the side of the Oxus proceeds from Daraut-kurghan to Marghilan or Andijan in Farghana, while exports from the Kashgar side find their way across the Terek pass to these places on the Russian railway.

Daraut-kurghan, where I was obliged to make a short halt for the sake of arrangements about transport and supplies, is a small place at the point where the Kara-tegin valley opens out toward the Alai. A Russian Customs post here guarded the frontier of Bukhara territory. Three miles farther down lies the village of Chat with a large, well-cultivated area and a ruined circumvallation of some size occupied during the troubled times preceding the Russian annexation of Turkistan. It is a point well suited for a large roadside station, and it is in this vicinity that we may safely locate the famous "Stone Tower" which the classical record preserved by Ptolemy mentions as the place reached from Baktra "when the traveler has ascended the ravine," *i.e.* the valley of Kara-tegin.

It is equally probable that "the station at Mount Imaos whence traders start on their journey to Sera," which Ptolemy's account of the trade route to China as extracted from Marinus mentions on the eastern limits of the territory of the Nomadic Sakai, corresponds to the present Irkesh-tam. This is still a place well known to those who carry on the lively caravan trade from Kashgar to Farghana and who face here the vagaries and exactions of the Chinese and Russian Customs stations, both established close to each other.

From Daraut-kurghan I turned south to strike across the succession of high snowy ranges which separate the headwaters of the Muk-su and the rivers of Roshan and Shughnan from the uppermost Oxus. It was the only route, apart from the well-known one leading across the Kizil-art and past the Great Kara-kul lake, by which it was possible for me to cross the Russian Pamirs from north to south and to see something of the great ranges buttressing them on the west. It was for this reason that I had decided on this route. But it proved one distinctly difficult to follow, even with such exceptionally hardy ponies as Colonel Yagello's orders secured for me at the few Kirghiz camps encountered. There was, however, abundant reward in the mass of interesting geographical observations to be gathered and in the splendid views which it offered into a region little explored and in parts still inadequately surveyed.

As far as the Tanimaz river, a large tributary of the Murghab rising on the Great Pamir, our route led past a grand glacier-clad range which forms, as it were, the north-western buttress of the Pamirs. It is known to the Kirghiz vaguely as Sel-tagh or Muz-tagh, "the Ice Mountain." Rarely have my eyes in the Himalaya, Hindukush or K'un-lun beheld a sight more imposing than the huge glacier-furrowed wall of the Muz-tagh as it rose before me with magnificent abruptness above the wide torrent bed of the Muk-su, after I had crossed the Trans-Alai by the Tarsagar, our first pass from Daraut-kurghan. Its boldly serrated crest line seemed to rise well above 21,000 feet, and individual ice-clad peaks to reach a great height above it.

No approximately exact elevations had up to that time been determined with the theodolite or clinometer for this and some other prominent ranges towering above the western portion of the Pamirs and the valleys draining them into the Oxus. Neither Afrazgul nor I myself could help feeling regret again and again at the obvious considerations which precluded any attempt at survey work on Russian ground, however modest in scope. But even without this it appeared to me that the height reached by the main summit of the Muz-tagh massif was distinctly greater than that of Mount Kaufmann on the Trans-Alai. It was hence a distinct satisfaction to me when I learned that a Russo-German expedition, led by that well-known geographer and traveler, Dr. R. Rickmers, had in 1929 chosen this grand alpine area for the scene of their systematic explorations and determined the height of Muz-tagh as exceeding that of Mount Kaufmann.

The direct route past the Muz-tagh massif would have led up the Muk-su and thence on to the valley by which the Zulum-art and Takhta-koram passes, giving access to the drainage areas of the Great Kara-kul lake and the Tanimaz river, are approached. But the floods fed by the huge Sel-dara or Fedchenko glacier, as it has been named after the Russian explorer who first saw it, completely close this route from springtime until the late autumn. So we were obliged to make our way over a pass, about 15,100 feet high, at the head of the Kayindi gorge. Ancient moraines completely blocked the latter in places and made the ascent very troublesome.

Beyond the Kayindi the ground assumed an easier Pamir-like character and, on descending over a plateau, an extensive panorama opened toward the Sel-dara and the valleys draining into it. Then we crossed the Takhta-koram pass at an elevation of over 15,000 feet after an easy ascent past some beautiful tarns of intense green. The necessity of securing fresh transport and a fresh guide for our further move now obliged me to seek contact with Kökan Beg, the Ming-bashi or headman of the Kirghiz who graze eastward about the Great Kara-kul lake. So next day, August 8, we crossed the Kizil-bel saddle to this summer encampment close on 14,000 feet above sea level and were heartily welcomed by this fine old man. Decked with Imperial decorations and a gorgeous silver belt, he looked quite imposing. Fifteen years later I learned with regret on the Taghdum-bash Pamir how rough Bolshevik treatment had deprived Kökan Beg of almost all his possessions and driven him for refuge into Chinese territory, where he afterward died.

From that capable headman I first learned of the great lake which after a mighty earthquake four years before had formed in the Murghab river valley. Covering what had previously been the Sarez Pamir, this new lake was declared completely to block the route by which I had intended to reach the Alichur Pamir across the Marjanai pass. I did not care to turn to the well-known route past the Russian station known as the Pamirski Post, but decided to move down to Saunab, the last village at the head of the Roshan valley. I hoped for a chance of being thence able to make my way up the Murghab and to find a passage past the great barrage which had created the new lake. Kökan Beg did not believe that with our baggage we could possibly get around it. But then I knew that for Kirghiz, who never will walk if they can possibly help it, a passage would mean one practicable for animals.

A day's halt at Kara-chim was utilized for collecting anthropological measurements from the Kirghiz there encamped, good specimens of that hardy Turkish tribe which in scanty numbers braves the rigors of the Pamir climate with icy blasts in the winter. Then we passed back again toward the Tanimaz river. As we crossed to its right bank some distance below the point where its main feeder from a great glacier of the Muz-tagh massif turns south, we soon found the valley floor completely smothered under enormous masses of rock debris. The same cataclysm which blocked the Murghab valley had thrown them down from the slopes of the spur flanking the valley on the west. They rose in wild confusion up to two hundred feet or more above what had been the once cultivated plain of Palez. Progress for two miles was here very difficult, and I was heartily glad when by the evening of August 12 we reached the few scattered homesteads of Pasor, occupied by Tajik herdsmen and ensconced among luxuriant poplars and willows.

Next day a march along steep cliffs overhanging the river or else over high plateaux brought us to where the Tanimaz joins what had been once the bed of the Murghab, now practically dry. Above it, in the picturesque village of Saunab, the Tash-kurghan, or "Stone Tower," of the Kirghiz, we found ourselves at the highest settlement of those Iranian-speaking hillmen, or Ghalchas, who inhabit the secluded alpine tract of Roshan. They were tall, well-built men, many quite European in looks. Their fair hair, blue or steel-gray eyes and flowing beards distinguished them at a glance from their nomadic Kirghiz neighbors. These hillmen of Roshan, along with those of the valleys of Wakhan and Shughnan to the south, represent the racial type of *Homo Alpinus* in remarkable purity, as found also in parts of Europe. So there

was ample work for me during a day's halt in collecting anthropometrical records and in noting much that alpine seclusion had allowed here to survive in customs, domestic architecture, simple decorative wood carving and the like. It
was delightful, too, to see once more well-tilled patches of
wheat fields and groves of fruit trees, the first met since leaving the Kashgar countryside.

Here we secured a band of load-carrying men indispensable for our further progress. The only route open to us for
reaching the southern Pamirs led up the defiles through
which the Murghab, or Bartang, as the river is known higher
up to the Kirghiz, had cut its way. The passage of these narrow gorges proved exceptionally difficult owing to the results
of the great earthquake of February 1911. The huge land-
slides attending it had in many places completely choked up
the river passage and destroyed what tracks ever existed along
or above it. The big river, once rivaling in volume the Ab-i-
Panja and at one time claimed as the main feeder of the Oxus,
had ceased altogether to flow. Strings of deep alpine tarns,
with colors of exquisite beauty, had here and there replaced
the river and contributed to our difficulties. In some places
detritus was still moving on the slopes like mud and offered no
foothold.

On the second march we clambered up to a steep spur
flanked on the north by a high ridge of shattered rock which
the landslide had bodily carried across from the opposite side
of the valley. On descending, I sighted the narrow fiordlike
lake which had been formed in what was before the mouth of
the Shedau valley by the same huge barrage as had blocked
the Bartang river. Scrambling with much trouble over rock
debris heaped up in wildest confusion, we made our way past
the northern end of the Shedau lake and along the foot of
that enormous barrage.

At last the spur was gained which divides what was the
Shedau valley from what had been the Sarez Pamir. On as-

cending this spur to the southeast, the full extent of that great cataclysm revealed itself. The fall of a whole mountain from the range on the north had converted the Sarez Pamir, once a favorite grazing ground for the Kirghiz, into a fine alpine lake which, according to a Russian account, was already in 1913 over seventeen miles long and had since been spreading up the valley. Enormous masses of rock and detritus had been pushed by the impetus of the landslips up the steep spur flanking the mouth of the Shedau valley. The gigantic dam thus formed seemed even then, four years after the great landslide, to rise some 1200 feet above the level of the new lake. Some portion of the uppermost slopes on the scarred mountainside above the barrage seemed still on the move, and stone avalanches descending from it accounted for the clouds of dust rising in the distance.

At the foot of the above spur I found a small Russian party under Professor J. Preobrazhenski just arrived from the side of the Alichur Pamir for a survey of the great barrage. The Russian scientists had arrived by skin raft from the southern extension of the lake, which they reached across the Langar pass, the same I wished to make for. They gave me a very kindly welcome, but were confident that my intended passage along the precipitous slopes above that inlet would prove impracticable. As, however, the plucky Roshani headmen with us were prepared to make the attempt, the spur was ascended to a height of about 13,200 feet and camp pitched near a small spring.

When next morning a steep descent had brought us down to the dazzling green waters of the Yerkh inlet, I realized the difficulties of further progress along the precipitous rock slopes thrown down by the earthquake and across dangerous debris shoots, in many places still liable to move. Fortunately our Roshanis were all excellent cragsmen, as befits people bred in such mountains as theirs, and quite experts in building *rafaks*, or ledges of brushwood and stones, along otherwise impassable precipices. It was fully five hours before we had crossed the worst of those treacherous scarps; yet the direct distance was scarcely more than a mile.

After reaching the head of the inlet and ascending the valley for a couple of miles, we found a small patch of level ground where cultivation had, since the earthquake, been resumed by a few Roshani families. Even here, some five hundred feet above the level of the lake, dread was felt of the continued rise of the lake's waters. After a day's welcome halt at this pleasant spot, we moved up the valley to the south and, on approaching the Langar pass, were fortunately met by Kirghiz transport which the Commandant of Pamirski Post had kindly sent to assist us. So by August 20 the previously unsurveyed Langar pass, an almost level talus-covered saddle, was crossed at an elevation of about 15,400 feet. Next day we arrived at the western extremity of the great Yeshil-köl lake and gained a fine view of it from the Buruman ridge, which separates the open Alichur Pamir from the head of the main valley of Shughnan. Here we had set foot once more on an ancient route traversing the "Roof of the World."

CHAPTER XX

By the Uppermost Oxus

AFTER ALL THE PASSES and defiles by which our route had led since leaving the Alai, the onward journey seemed easy notwithstanding the height of the ground over which it passed. On moving up the wide trough of the Alichur Pamir for two days, it was easy to realize the advantages which its flat expanse, stretching from east to west for over sixty miles, offered since early times for direct approach to the mountain territory of Shughnan from the side of the Tarim basin. We have direct evidence of the use of this route by those Chinese travelers and troops of whose moves across the Pamirs toward Shughnan and the middle Oxus definite historical record has come down to us.

Thus we know that when Kao Hsien-chih, the Chinese general to whose great exploit in crossing the glacier pass of the Darkot I have already referred in Chapter III, made his famous expedition in A.D. 747 across the Pamirs to oust the

Tibetans from the Oxus, he led first the main column of his force down this way to Shughnan. It was done obviously for the sake of the supplies to be secured there from the side of Badakhshan. Four years later this route had seen Wu-k'ung, a humble Chinese traveler, proceeding to the northwest of India. There he lived for some thirty years as a Buddhist monk. On his way home, among many difficulties and dangers, he regained Kashgar once more through Shughnan, just in time before the final collapse of Chinese rule closed the passage through the Tarim basin.

When nearly nine centuries later the Chinese had again established their power over Eastern Turkistan, it was on the Alichur Pamir that a Manchu force overtook the last Khoja ruler of Kashgar and his retainers on their flight to Shughnan and Badakhshan and defeated them with great slaughter. Nor would Süme-tash, the point where this victory was gained in 1759, have become again in 1892 a scene of bloodshed had its position at the eastern end of the Yeshil-köl not marked it out to the Chinese and then to the Afghans as a suitable place for watching the important route to Shughnan as it leads along the northern shore of the lake.

On the cliff of Süme-tash, which we reached at the end of a day's march along the winding lake, there rises a small shrine. It once sheltered a stele with the Chinese inscription commemorating that victory of 1759. The inscription had been removed to the Tashkent Museum, after Colonel Yonoff's Cossacks, on June 22, 1892, had wiped out the small Afghan detachment which held out to the last in a post close by. But the massive granite base of the stele was still *in situ*, an emblem of that Chinese power which during the last 2000 years had made itself felt again and again even beyond Mount Imaos.

Two marches up the wide, grassy trough of the Alichur Pamir brought us to Bash-gumbaz-aghzi, the chief summer camp of the Kirghiz grazing on this Pamir. Then, after a day's halt, needed for anthropometrical work and securing fresh supplies, we moved south to cross the high chain dividing the Alichur from the Great Pamir. On August 26 we crossed it by the Bash-gumbaz pass, which, in spite of its elevation of about 16,300 feet, was found clear of snow. As we descended toward the glittering expanse of Lake Victoria or Zor-köl, where the Great Pamir branch of the Oxus rises and the Pamir borders of Russia and Afghanistan meet, a grand panoramic view opened across it toward the glacier-crowned range which divides the Great Pamir from uppermost Wakhan.

Ever since my youth I had longed to see the truly "Great" Pamir and its fine lake, of which Captain John Wood, its modern discoverer in 1838, had given so graphic a description. This desire was greatly increased when the closer knowledge since gained of the topography of the Pamir region had confirmed my belief that the memories of those great old travelers, Hsüan-tsang and Marco Polo, were associated with the route leading past the lake.

The day of halt, August 27, spent by the sunny lake shore was most enjoyable, though with an icy wind sweeping along the lake shore at an elevation of nearly 14,000 feet it felt bitterly cold even while the sun was shining from a speckless sky. In the morning the thermometer showed a minimum temperature of 12° Fahrenheit below freezing point. In the peace around, undisturbed by any sign of human activity past or present, it was easy to lose all count of time and to feel as if spiritual emanations of those cherished old patrons of my travels were still clinging to the scene.

As I looked across the deep blue waters of the lake to where in the east they seemed to fade away on the horizon, I thought it quite worthy to figure in old traditional belief as the legendary central lake from which the four greatest rivers of Asia were supposed to take their rise. Hsüan-tsang's narrative reflects this belief in curious mixture with a correct record of locally observed facts. The clearness, fresh taste and dark-blue color of the lake are just as he describes them. What the Kirghiz told us about its shores swarming with aquatic birds in the spring and autumn, and about their eggs then to be found in plenty amidst the thin scrub of the shore, agrees accurately with the pious traveler's account. Nor can it surprise us that the imagination of old travelers passing this great sheet of water at such a height, and so far away from human occupation, should have credited it with great depth and with hiding in it "all kinds of aquatic monsters" such as Hsüan-tsang was told of.

Marco Polo's account of the "Pamier" makes it equally clear that his route led him past the great lake. His graphic description is so accurate in its details that I cannot forgo quoting it in full. "And when you leave this little country [Wakhan], and ride three days northeast, always among mountains, you get to such a height that 'tis said to be the highest place in the world! And when you have got to this height you find a great lake between two mountains, and out of it a fine river running through a plain clothed with the finest pasture in the world; insomuch that a lean beast there will fatten to your heart's content in ten days. There are great numbers of wild beasts; among others, wild sheep of great size, whose horns are good six palms in length. From these horns the shepherds make great bowls to eat from, and they use the horns also to enclose folds for their cattle at night. Messer Marco was told also that the wolves were numerous, and killed many of those wild sheep. Hence quantities of their horns and bones were found, and these were made into great heaps by the wayside, in order to guide travelers when snow was on the ground.

"The plain is called *Pamier*, and you will ride across it for twelve days together, finding nothing but a desert without habitations or any green thing, so that travelers are obliged to carry with them whatever they have need of. The region is so lofty and cold that you do not see even any birds flying. . . ."

Ever since Captain John Wood confirmed all these details, Marco's narrative has been recognized, in the words of Sir Henry Yule, as one of the great Venetian's "most splendid anticipations of modern exploration." So only a few remarks need be added. The sense of this being "the highest place in the world" strangely impressed me also. The excellence of the pasture was attested by reports of big flocks of sheep which were annually brought up to the Great Pamir from the Wakhan side. At the time of my passage they were grazing in the side valleys to the north. Marco's "wild sheep," the *Ovis poli* justly named after him, still have favorite haunts on the heights above the lake. We met a large herd of them close to the Bash-gumbaz pass, and on small grassy patches lower down came upon numerous horns and bones of others where, driven down by the winter snow on the range, they had fallen victims to wolves. During our halt Afrazgul Khan's rifle promptly secured a fine head in one of the side valleys above the lake to serve me as a souvenir. The neighborhood is known to hunters for bears and panthers.

My day's stay by Lake Victoria did not pass without a piece of antiquarian intelligence once more confirming the accuracy of Chinese historical records. In describing Kao Hsien-chih's expedition of A.D. 747 across the Pamirs, the T'ang Annals mention that he concentrated his forces at a point on the uppermost Oxus corresponding to the present Sarhad by three routes, from the east, west and north. The first two obviously lay along the Ab-i-Panja, the main branch of the Oxus. But of the northern route, which must have led from the side of the Great Pamir, no information could be gained by me from maps or books. Now, inquiries from two much-traveled Kirghiz in my party elicited definite evidence as to an old track still used by Tajik herdsmen of Wakhan leading across the high range south of the Great Pamir lake to Sarhad. Through my glasses I could clearly make out the head of the valley, known as Shor-jilja, up which this route leads. But, alas, the valley lay on the Afghan side of the border as determined by the Anglo-Russian Boundary Commission, and hence it was impossible for me to test the information on the spot.

Traveling along the right bank of the Great Pamir branch of the Oxus which forms the boundary between Russian and Afghan territory, I reached the first village in Wakhan by three marches, just as Marco Polo's road estimate puts it. There at Langar-kisht, near the junction of the Pamir river with the Ab-i-Panja, I received a very kind welcome from the commandant of the small post guarding the upper portion of Russian Wakhan. Even before I reached it, my eyes were gladdened by the sight in the distance of the snowy rampart of the Hindukush guarded by needlelike peaks. Its watershed marks the frontier of India.

How near it lies here in Wakhan, separated from Russian territory only by the narrow strip of Afghan soil on the left bank of the Ab-i-Panja, was brought home to me also in other ways. Thus when Sarbuland Khan, the Ming-bashi or head of the Wakhis on the Russian side of the river, came to greet me on the way, I found that it was his son, settled in the Ashkuman valley controlled by the British Political Agent of Gilgit, who had been in charge of the party which two years before had helped me to cross the difficult Chillinji pass into Hunza.

It was a great satisfaction to find myself in Wakhan. Remote as this open valley of the main branch of the Oxus is, and poor in climate, and now also in population and resources, it has claimed importance since early times as the most direct thoroughfare from the fertile regions of ancient Bactria to the line of the oases along the southern rim of the Tarim basin and thus toward China. In May 1906 I had been able to follow only the uppermost course of the river from Sarhad to its source at the glaciers of the Wakhjir. Access to the main portion of Wakhan was barred to me on either side of the river. Now I was able to move down the big valley in a less hurried fashion and at what probably is the most favorable of its seasons.

After the bleak Pamirs, it was refreshing to behold the verdant appearance which the cultivated portion of Wakhan during the first half of September presented, in spite of an elevation from 8000 to 10,000 feet above sea level. Fortunately, too, I was spared the biting-cold east winds which for the greatest part of the year make travel in Wakhan very trying. Crops of wheat and oats were just ripening on carefully irrigated terraces, and the little orchards in more sheltered nooks promised a modest harvest of fruit. Even where the cultivated ground at the valley bottom was broken by steep rocky spurs descending close to the river or by stretches of sandy waste along its bank, the eye could rest with joy on the glorious vistas opening to the south. Towering above narrow side valleys, and seemingly quite near, there showed in magnificent boldness ice-clad peaks of the Hindukush main range rising to 22,000 feet and more. They looked indeed just as Sung Yün, an early Chinese pilgrim who passed here on his way to the Indus, had described them, like peaks of jade.

There offered welcome opportunities for anthropological work by measurements and observations on the Wakhi population. Of ancient stock, it has preserved, like its Eastern Iranian language, also its well-marked *Homo Alpinus* type. The fair hair and fair eyes of the Wakhis had struck already that observant Jesuit traveler Benedict Goës when he passed up Wakhan in 1602 on his way in search of "Cathay" and noted their resemblance to Flemings.

But what claimed my attention most were the ruins of ancient strongholds, some of them of considerable extent and in part remarkably well preserved, to be found on hill spurs overlooking the valley. There was much of antiquarian interest to observe in their plans, the construction and decoration of their bastioned walls. The natural protection afforded by unscalable rock faces of spurs and ravines had always been utilized with skill in these defenses. This is not the place to describe them in detail, nor need I set forth the reasons which even in the absence of direct archeological evidence such as only excavations could produce lead me to believe, that several of these fastnesses go back to a period roughly corresponding to Sasanian domination or possibly even somewhat earlier. Their local attribution to "Kafirs," *i.e.* unbelievers, gives expression to a traditional recollection that they date back to times preceding the introduction of Islam.

Some idea of the labor which the construction of these strongholds must have implied can be formed from the fact that at one of them, known as Zamr-i-atish-parast ("the Zamr of the Fire-worshiper"), the successive lines of walls with their numerous bastions and turrets solidly built with rough stones or large sun-dried bricks ascend the slopes of a precipitous spur over 1000 feet high and have a circumference of more than three miles. The extent and remarkable solidity of such defenses, even though they may have been intended only to afford temporary refuge in times of danger, clearly show that at the time of their erection Wakhan must have possessed a population and resources greatly in excess of those to be found there at present. According to the figures supplied to me, the Russian portion of Wakhan counts about two hundred households; though these are usually large, the total population on that side of the river is not likely to exceed 3000 souls. The need for such places of safety is accounted for by the fact that Wakhan, owing to the openness of the valley and its position on a great line of communication, must have always been exposed to invasion, and particularly, as modern history shows, from the west.

The dryness of the climate explains the remarkable state of preservation of Wakhan's ruins. To what cause the longevity I noticed among its inhabitants may be due, I do not know. A curious instance of this was afforded by the chief "Pir" or spiritual head of the Ismailias, a Mohammedan sect, in Wakhan, whom I met engaged on a visit of faith-healing to a sick devotee. The old man claimed an age well over a hundred years, and looked it. To my surprise, he furnished exact data proving that he had been at his home the host of Captain Wood when in the winter of 1838 he was on his way to the Pamirs. He had clear recollections, too, of the tyrannical rule of Sultan Murad of Badakhshan, whose misdeeds in this region are often referred to in Captain Wood's classical narrative.

Lower down in the valley I passed into the small tract of Ishkashm, which, separated from Wakhan by a succession of rocky defiles, is named as a distinct chiefship both by Hsüan-tsang and Marco Polo. Here I had occasion to survey remarkable remains of an ancient stronghold in the ruined fortress known as the "Castle of Qaʿqa" near the pretty village of Namadgut. Its massive walls, built with sun-dried bricks and in places over thirty feet thick, crown the top of two closely adjoining ridges. These rise precipitously above the deep fosse of the river, here unfordable at all seasons. The isolated rocky eminence close on a mile long which these ramparts enclose is dominated at its western end by a citadel. Here also the extent of the fortifications points to a population and resources far greater than those of today.

Then a day's march brought me to the little Russian post of Nut, which faces the main settlement of Ishkashm on the Afghan side and significantly also the approach from that side of the Oxus to the Dorah, the easiest of the passes into Chitral. There Captain Tumanovich, its commandant, very hospitably received me. It was very pleasant to find in him an officer familiar with both Persian and Turki. Such knowledge of the local languages, unusual at the time among Russian officers of the Turkistan Province, made converse far easier than it could have been for me otherwise with my exceedingly scanty Russian. Nor could I fail to appreciate the homely ways of Madame Tumanovich's household, which would not turn night into daytime by long sittings over tea and cigarettes such as seemed to be obligatory at other Russian outposts. A two days' halt gave me the welcome chance

of taking down specimens of Ishkashmi, one of the Eastern
Iranian languages preserved among the isolated communities
of hillmen on the uppermost Oxus, and one previously un-
recorded. The specimens have since been published by my old
friend, Sir George Grierson, O.M., the great linguistic authority.

From Nut, where the Oxus makes its great bend to
the north, I moved down the river through that very confined
portion of the valley which is known as Gharan. Until the recent construction of a bridle path under Russian orders, it had
been ground most difficult of access both from the north and
the south. The very scanty population of Gharan was then
dependent upon Badakhshan, the fertile tracts of which could
be reached through side valleys leading down from the plateaux to the west. This explains why Marco Polo refers to
"those fine and valuable Balas Rubies," in reality a product
of Gharan, in his account of Badakhshan. Above the little
hamlet of Sist I passed the pits in which they used to be dug
by forced labor as a monopoly of the Mirs of Badakhshan.

The marches through Gharan, with constant ups-and-
downs on a very narrow rocky track along precipices, had
been rather fatiguing. So I was glad enough when by September 12 I reached the mouth of the open valley in which
the considerable river uniting the streams of Shughnan carries
its water to the Oxus. A short distance above the junction I
arrived at Khoruk, the administrative headquarters of the
Russian "Pamir Division." Ensconced among groves of walnuts
and other fruit trees which an elevation of some 6600 feet allows to grow to a good height, Khoruk is an attractive spot,
and the very kind and helpful reception accorded to me by
Colonel Yagello, who had by then returned from his visit to
Tashkent, made my two days' halt there very pleasant and
profitable. The friendly interest shown by this accomplished
officer in the antiquarian and other objects of my journey
made it possible for me to extend my visit to Shughnan far-

ther than I had originally expected. By his effective help he also greatly facilitated my subsequent passage through the hill territories to the north, then under the rule of the Amir of Bukhara.

At Khoruk civilizing Russian influence manifested itself in various ways, including electric lighting of the small cantonment and a well-frequented Russian school. My brief stay there allowed me to collect useful information about the past of Shughnan and the present ways of its population. The Chinese accounts of the territory contained in the T'ang Annals and itineraries of several Buddhist pilgrims agree in ascribing to the people of the "five *Shih-ni*," *i.e.* Shighnan (an alternative form of the local name), a fierce and intrepid character. Hsüan-tsang, who did not visit Shughnan in person, heard them on his passage through Wakhan described as prone to "murder in cold blood and given to theft and plunder." This account of the Shughni people is fully borne out by the reputation for both bravery and violence that they still enjoy among their meeker neighbors both to the south and west. Their raids were still a subject of lively recollection among the people of Wakhan, and the present occupation of Sarikol on the Chinese side of the Oxus headwaters by a population speaking a language which differs but slightly from Shughni supports the traditional belief in conquest from Shughnan.

Raids and invasions had become a matter of the past since first Afghan rule and then Russian power asserted itself along the uppermost Oxus. But the migratory instinct and the spirit of enterprise which the scantiness of arable land and the want of adequate grazing grounds in the narrow valleys engender still manifest themselves. Thus I found that, driven forth by the poverty of their homeland, these fine hillmen annually proceed in numbers to Farghana for temporary work as farm laborers. Plenty of others were used to seek employment as servants at Kabul or in Samarkand and elsewhere in the north. It was amusing to observe at times such traveled men accoutered in old frock coats or odd military garments which evidently had thus found their way from the bazaars of Peshawar via Kabul.

From Khoruk I moved up through Shakh-dara, the southern of the two main valleys of Shughnan, to where its head approaches plateaux communicating with the Alichur Pamir. In numerous places we passed ruins of forts and *chiusas* guarding particularly difficult points in narrow gorges, all reminiscent of the chronic insecurity prevailing in old times. At some of these ruins the massive construction seemed distinctly to support traditions ascribing to them Kafir, *i.e.* pre-Mohammedan, origin. It was the same also in the somewhat wider Ghund valley into which we crossed by the route of Dozakh-dara. It appropriately derives its name, corresponding to the "Höllenthal" so common in the Alps, from the troublesome slopes of rock debris of an old moraine which chokes its head for miles.

Descending then the Ghund-dara from where the Russian cart road connecting Pamirski Post and the Alichur Pamir with Khoruk joins in, I gained some impressions of the middle portion of this great valley of which I had sighted the head just a month before from above the outflow of the Yeshil-köl. There were recollections to be gathered here from graybeards serving as depositories of local tradition about intermittent Chinese control as well as of the severe exactions under which Shughnan had suffered during the last local Mirs, or chiefs. Their practice of selling women and children as slaves to increase their revenue was said to have led to extensive emigration to the Khanates in the north. This accounted for the half-deserted condition of several picturesque villages we passed on the way.

Subsequent Afghan rule and the regime from Bukhara which had followed it for a time had been almost equally oppressive, and though the direct Russian control under "military politicals," as the Indian phrase has it, secured a great improvement, it had not lasted long enough at the time of my passage to repair these ravages. One could hardly then have foreseen how soon the Russian revolution and the rise of the Soviet would carry fresh troubles and sufferings into these secluded alpine valleys of the Oxus region.

CHAPTER XXI

From Roshan to Samarkand

FOR PROGRESS TO ROSHAN, the mountain tract adjoining
Shughnan on the north, it would have been easier to descend
the Ghund valley to the Oxus below Khoruk and then from
opposite Kala-Bar-Panja on the opposite side to have followed
the right bank of the river by the newly made Russian bridle
path down to Kala-i-Wamar, the chief place of Roshan. But I
was anxious to see something of the high snowy range, dividing Shughnan from Roshan and the drainage of the Bartang
river, which I had first reached more than a month before at
Saunab. So I preferred to make my way to Roshan by the
high pass which leads across the range from above the small
village of Shitam. Light as our baggage was, it proved impossible to take it on laden ponies beyond a point about 12,600 feet
above sea level.

On the ascent made next day with load-carrying men, it
was necessary alternately to advance over a much-crevassed

glacier and to climb steep rock *couloirs* before, after six miles
of such trying progress, the narrow arête of rock forming the
pass was reached at an elevation of some 16,100 feet. The
magnificent views opening from this height were a fit reward
for our toil. To the west and northwest they extended over
the heads of fine glaciers uniting below in a large ice stream
which descends far into the Raumedh valley. To the southwest across the boldly serrated crest line of the range, I
could see far away the snow-covered tops of mountains belonging to Badakhshan. This region, toward which I had been
drawn since my youth, was, alas, destined still to remain
closed to me.

A somewhat easier descent over névé beds and then
along the gray ice wall of the glacier brought us after about
seven miles to the latter's snout, and near it to the first
point where it was possible to pitch camp. Thanks to arrangements made under Colonel Yagello's orders, we found
here a posse of strong-limbed Roshanis waiting to relieve our
hard-tried load carriers from Shughnan. So another day's
march down the Raumedh valley over a succession of old
moraine terraces and then through narrow gorges allowed us
to emerge into the Bartang valley close to the hamlet of
Khaizhez.

The two days' journey which thence carried us down to
Kala-i-Wamar sufficed to impress me with the exceptional difficulties offered to traffic by the tortuous gorges in which the
Bartang river has cut its way down to the Oxus. I now un-
derstood why Roshan has always remained the least accessible
of all the valleys descending from the Pamirs, and why in the
stock of its people and in its traditional ways it has retained
most of its early inheritance.

The line of progress lay everywhere through narrow,
deep-cut gorges, between towering mountain masses wildly
serrated above and exceedingly steep at their foot. After
crossing from Khaizhez to the right bank of the river on a

raft of goatskins, there followed a succession of trying climbs up and down precipitous rock faces where the track led along narrow ledges or was represented only by footholds a few inches wide. Glad enough I felt that it was possible for a few of us to avoid some of the worst of these *awrinz* by taking to a small goatskin raft where the absence of dangerous cataracts allowed of its employment. Guided from behind by dexterous swimmers, it let us glide down the tossing river in scenery of impressive wildness. Boldly serrated snowy peaks showed again and again above the high frowning rock walls which, as we rapidly passed them, ever seemed to close in upon us like the jaws of an underworld. Meanwhile the baggage was being carried in safety by sure-footed Roshanis past sheer precipices; seen from the river, the men looked like big spiders.

The hamlets nestling here and there at the mouth of ravines and half-hidden amidst fine fruit trees relieved in pleasant contrast the uniform grimness of these forbidding defiles. The dwellings at the places where we broke our journey looked from outside unpretending rubble-built hovels. But in the interior, smoke-begrimed as it was, there could be seen arrangements indicative of rude comfort and interesting as obviously derived from antiquity. Thus the living hall, in its ground plan and in the arrangement of the skylight ceiling and sitting platforms, invariably showed the closest resemblance to the internal architecture of residences excavated at ancient sites in the Taklamakan and of others still occupied by the living in Hindukush valleys to the south. This small corner of Asia, in its alpine seclusion, seemed indeed as if untouched by the change of ages. I felt inclined to wonder whether it could have presented a very different picture to some Bactrian Greek or Indo-Scythian visitor in the last centuries before Christ.

The same impression was conveyed by the physical appearance of the men I met on the way and subsequently was able to examine anthropometrically at Kala-i-Wamar.

Clean of limb they were, and made wiry by constant movement on such impossible tracks—no cattle or horse could ever
be brought over them. They all showed clear-cut features,
often of almost classical regularity, generally light-colored
eyes and fair hair. Among the Iranian-speaking hillmen of the
valleys I traversed in the Oxus region, the people of Roshan
seemed to me to have preserved the *Homo Alpinus* type in its
greatest purity. The expert analysis which my friend Mr. T.
C. Joyce, Keeper of the Anthropological Department of the
British Museum, has made of the measurements and observations collected by me has since confirmed this impression.

Before reaching the Bartang river's junction with the
Oxus, more forbidding gorges had to be passed where the
track clings to almost vertical rock faces by frail wooden
"Rafaks," or ladders. Then at last a stretch of fairly open
ground gave access to Kala-i-Wamar, the chief place of Roshan. There a day's delightful halt was spent over anthropometrical work in a pleasant orchard adjoining the ruinous
castle from which the Mirs of Shughnan used to rule this dependent tract. It allowed me also to recover some interesting
pieces of old wood carving which for the sake of intended al-
terations had been removed from the Ming-bashi's house and
put away with the lumber. Amidst their ornamentation it was
easy to recognize the survival of decorative motifs, such as
a stylized clematis-like flower, which were familiar to me
from the Greco-Buddhist relievos of Gandhara and the wood
carvings of the Niya and Lou-lan sites.

The interior of the same house afforded a typical illustration of the curiously elaborate arrangement of the hall
which serves as the living room for the whole large household
in the winter. Every one of the wooden pillars supporting the
timber ceiling has its particular name, and each part of the sitting platform as divided by the pillars has its special use. It
was amusing to observe that a raised recess just below the
ceiling serving as the sleeping place for the children was pro-

vided with a kind of hypocaustic heating by the calves being accommodated in a closet below it.

The women of Roshan are said to be famous for good looks and particularly for the fairness of their complexion. I had a wayside chance of verifying this reputation when in company of the village headman I passed three generations of his family gathered in a group near his home. Wife and mother were as fair of face as if they had been ladies of Europe, and the two little girls looked very pretty. In order to increase the attraction of the elder's complexion according to local fashion, her grandmother was just then busily engaged in smearing her rosy cheeks with some wild berries intended to bleach the skin.

On September 27 I left Kala-i-Wamar in order to make my way toward Kara-tegin across the easternmost valleys and ranges of what until 1877 had been the principality of Darwaz and had since passed under the rule of the Amir of Bukhara. The season was now closely approaching when the high passes on the route I had planned to follow might become blocked by snow. So I felt obliged to travel here rapidly. To this I could reconcile myself more readily since a considerable portion of this alpine portion of Bukhara had been described before in publications like Dr. Rickmer's *Doab of Turkestan,* accessible also to readers not acquainted with Russian. For the same reason my account of this part of my journey may be succinct.

Communication between Roshan and Yazgulam, the valley adjoining on the north, was before practically impossible along the Oxus owing to a succession of formidable defiles. The recent construction of a Russian bridle path blasted along the rock faces had changed this. But I preferred to follow the old track and accordingly crossed the range dividing Roshan from Yazgulam over the pass of Adude. The glaciated saddle on the watershed was reached at a hight of about 14,500 feet. The descent thence led by zigzags across a much-crevassed glacier and then over a succession of old moraines into a narrow valley filled at its bottom with thickets of birch trees and junipers. Night overtook us here before the village of Matraun was reached.

The Bukhara officials who greeted me there next morning afforded welcome assurance of the help which Colonel Yagello had provided for me on the Darwaz side. But their gay flowing silk robes and swarthy faces made me realize also how soon the alpine tracts of the Upper Oxus were to be left behind. The people of Yazgulam, reckoned at some 190 households, had for a long time enjoyed the advantage of occupying a kind of no-man's land between the chiefships of Darwaz and Shughnan-Roshan. They had used it to prey impartially, when occasion offered, upon their neighbors on both sides. Though their language is closely related to Shughni, yet more frequent intercourse with Darwaz was reflected both by their physical appearance and the fact that, like all the "Ghalchas," or hillmen, to the north, they are supposed to be Sunnis. No doubt, while the fanatical rule of Bukhara over Shughnan and the other valleys farther south lasted, their inhabitants, too, had to profess this orthodox Mohammedan creed, though all of them belonged to the heretical Ismailia sect which has its quasi-deified head in the Agha Khan, so well known in London and Paris.

After rapidly passing down Yazgulam, I was glad to gain the mouth of the great valley of Wanj by the new bridle path along the bank of the Oxus. As it is almost throughout blasted out of perpendicular rock walls or else carried over boldly built narrow balconies, I could easily realize why the passage of these gloomy gorges was formerly risky even for the local hillmen and impossible for the carriage of loads. After this the open character and abundant cultivation of the Wanj valley afforded a pleasant change. A long but easy march on October 1 up the valley afforded evidence of a moister climate. On the lower hillsides there were to be seen terraced fields tilled without irrigation, and above them plentiful tree growth. Large orchards around the villages and rows of trees between the fields gave quite a parklike appearance to the valley bottom.

In keeping with the altered landscape, there was a change in the look and ways of the population. Like all the Tajiks throughout the hills of Bukhara, they speak only Persian. Though their old Eastern Iranian tongue has been abandoned, yet they probably represent the Iranian race indigenous to ancient Sogdiana in greater purity than the "Sarts" of the plains. The large whitewashed homesteads with their flat roofs also reflected changed conditions of climate and life.

Heavy clouds had hung over the mountains that day and hidden from view the great ice-clad peaks between the Seldara and Tanimaz headwaters which I had seen from the other side on my way south from the Alai. The next day brought heavy rain with fresh snow on the mountains, and obliged me to halt at Sitargh village. The pass named after it was to take us across into Khingab, the head portion of the large hill tract known as Wakhia-bala. The local headmen were apprehensive of risks in attempting the pass under such conditions, but were intelligent enough to accept from me a written statement that they were not to be held responsible if anything went wrong. Fortunately the sky cleared in time to permit us to start for the pass long before daybreak.

The ascent was steep but at first easy, lying over slopes clothed with alpine vegetation. Then the climb led over large snow-covered moraines past a steep glacier, until after seven hours from the start the narrow ridge forming the pass was reached at an elevation of about 14,600 feet. The view from the pass was limited to the head of the large glacier over and past which the descent leads. But when we had made our way over the glacier for about a mile and a half, zigzagging between many long crevasses, a magnificent panorama opened over the huge ice stream and side glaciers of great size which join in from the range to the south. It was not until after a total march of some ten miles from the pass, over trying slopes of lateral moraines, that the snout, some 150 feet high, of the united ice stream was reached. Three miles lower down we were glad to gain a camping place for the night on a small grassy plateau.

On October 4 an easy march brought us to Pashmghar, the highest village in Khingab. The first cultivation was passed at an elevation of about 9500 feet and traces of abandoned fields already three miles higher up. I knew that the considerable Garmo stream we had to ford is fed by the glaciers which clad the western face of the great Muztagh massif which had so much impressed me when approaching it early in August from the north. There was no time available now for getting within sight of it. Instead, I had to descend the main valley of Wakhia-bala by two marches in order to gain access to Kara-tegin in time before early snowfall might block the last high pass remaining to be crossed.

These marches led us past a succession of picturesque villages all ensconced among orchards and arbors. But the effects of maladministration as carried on from Bukhara manifested themselves only too clearly in much good land remaining untilled and in other signs also. The gorgeous silk robes usually combining all the colors of the rainbow in which the headmen even of small places paraded to greet me could scarcely deceive as a mark of prosperity. For I learned soon that the presentation of these "Khillats" was a traditional method of exaction starting from the Amir's court. Favorites of the ruler or else officials whose salaries were overdue would be sent from Bukhara to carry such robes of honor to governors of provinces as tokens of the ruler's special satisfaction. Custom required the person bringing them on behalf of the Amir to be richly rewarded in silver by the recipient. Then the governor would reimburse himself by passing on these precious gifts through his unpaid subordinates to the Amlakdars or heads of subdivisions, and so in turn, until in the end all this display of high favors had served to mulct local headmen and through them the cultivators. What with methods of fiscal administration and justice thoroughly medieval, one could scarcely feel surprised at the indifference or worse with which the Amir's subjects watched the Bukhara regime disappear after the Russian revolution. They could not well foresee what worse misfortunes were in store for them after "liberation" by the Soviet's agents.

Heavy rain obliged me to halt on October 6 at Lajirkh near the dilapidated headquarters of the Amlakdar of Wakhiabala. But luckily the weather cleared again and, in spite of fresh snow in the mountains, allowed us in the course of the next two days to get across first the Girdan-i-kaftar ("the pigeon's neck") pass and then the elevated plateau of Tupchak, in character resembling a Pamir. Dr. Rickmers, who made Tupchak his base for prolonged alpine explorations, has described the imposing series of high peaks and fine glaciers which border it on the south.

When I passed from the plateau across the great range which stretches all along the valley of the Surkh-ab and borders Kara-tegin on the south, I enjoyed a magnificent panoramic view. It extended from the snowy range of Peter the Great in the west past the great Cis-Alai chain to the ice-wall formed far away to the east by the peaks on "Muztagh" which I had first sighted from the Tarsagar pass. Thus two months' instructive wanderings across the Pamirs and the high valleys by the uppermost Oxus had brought me back again to that "Valley of the Komedoi" and the line of the ancient silk trade which I wished to follow from the Alai.

On descending into the open valley over fertile slopes where adequate rain and snowfall permit of cultivation without irrigation, I noticed that harvesting was just proceeding from about 8000 feet downward. Taken in connection with the fact that in Wakhan crops at elevations more than 2000 feet higher had been cut a month earlier, this illustrated the effect of far moister climatic conditions. In Kara-tegin I found myself once again among Turki-speaking people of Kirghiz stock settled in comfortable villages. But there is good reason to believe that the fertility of the land combined with the easy access to rich grazing grounds must have attracted there invaders of Turkish race long before the last wave of migration brought these Kirghiz there.

This early Turkish occupation of Kara-tegin is proved by its present designation and the prevailing local names, which are Turki. It was hence of special interest to observe how the Kirghiz settlers, who had no doubt gained this desirable territory by conquest, just as their predecessors of Turkish stock, were now being slowly ousted again from the land by the steady reflux of Tajiks from Darwaz and from tracts to the west. The Kirghiz of Kara-tegin, who invariably still observe their customary semi-nomadic migration to summer grazing grounds, are obviously unable to extract from their land as much produce as their industrious if meeker neighbors.

The process here observed makes it easier to understand how the original Iranian population of ancient Sogdiana has also in the plains of the present Samarkand and Bukhara managed to regain a prevalent share in the land that had been wrested from it again and again by nomadic invaders. Kirghiz intermarriage with Tajik women, of which I learned on my passage through Kara-tegin, illustrates another potent process by which the old Iranian population has gradually transformed the racial character of its Turkish conquerors if not altogether absorbing them.

At Gharm, the headquarters of the "Mir" administering Kara-tegin, I spent a pleasant day's halt on October 11 encamped in that hospitable dignitary's large garden. It afforded interesting glimpses of the quaint medieval style of official pomp and circumstance then still surviving in these quiet backwaters of Western Turkistan. Thence two enjoyable marches carried me down to the point where the valley of the Surkh-ab turning south greatly contracts and for a considerable distance ceases to be practicable for trade. There near the village of Ab-i-garm, called after its hot springs, our route turned off westward. It was no doubt the same which those ancient silk traders had followed to Baktra.

There I left behind the last of the valleys which descend from the Pamir region and entered the open valley plains of the once independent chiefship of Hissar drained by the Surkhan and Kafirnihan tributaries of the Oxus. It seemed hard to forgo a visit south to the Oxus where it passes nearest to Balkh, the ancient Baktra. But regard for the time needed to reach Sistan, my distant Persian goal, for the winter's work, obliged me to seek the Trans-Caspian railway at Samarkand by the nearest route and that as quickly as possible. So my journey across these comparatively well-known parts of the hill territory of Bukhara was done by nine rapid marches covering altogether some 270 miles.

The fertile region through which the first four of those marches took me must always have offered special attractions to nomadic invaders of Sogdiana. On the way from Ab-i-garm to Faizabad we crossed splendid grazing grounds. They are all held like those of the valleys to the north by the Özbeg landowners of Hissar, who move up there for the summer with their flocks of sheep and large herds of cattle and horses. In the wide fertile stretches of plain which we skirted on the following three days along its northern edge past Doshambe, Kara-tagh and Regar, the most productive lands capable of irrigation were still held by Özbegs. But the labor is largely furnished by Tajiks, and much of the land, too, seemed slowly to be passing into their hands whether as tenants or owners.

The conservative fashion in which the conquering Turkish race still clings to semi-nomadic customs was well illustrated by the portable felt-covered reed huts we found pitched in the courtyards of many Özbeg village homesteads.

They had been brought back from the summer grazing grounds, and the owners still preferred to use them as quarters instead of the mud huts built around them. In spite of the exactions practiced by corrupt Bukhara officials, all I saw of this tract favored by soil and climate suggested a fair degree of rural comfort and flourishing agricultural trade. Little did I foresee all the misery which within a few years a futile Mohammedan rising against the revolutionary Russian regime and its ruthless repression by the Soviet forces were to carry into this peaceable region.

The usual and easier route from the Hissar tract would have taken me southwest to the ancient highroad which passes from Termez on the Oxus through the lower hills and past the old "Iron Gate" to Samarkand and Bukhara, those centers of Sogdiana all through history. But in order to shorten the journey and see something of the mountains which separate Hissar from the arid steppes of Bukhara I chose the track leading northwestward past Tash-kurghan to Shahr-i-sabz. It led first through narrow cañon-like gorges and higher up past picturesque forest-clad mountain slopes up to the Karkhush pass already under snow. Beyond it we descended over downlike plateaux, with rich grazing much frequented by nomadic Özbegs, down into the wide and abundantly irrigated valley which drains toward Karchi. There I reached the large town of Shahr-i-sabz by October 20, and on the following day a long and dusty drive on a jolting Russian tarantass carried me across the Takhta-karacha pass and the wide Zarafshan valley to Samarkand.

In this great busy city I felt that my long journey on ancient Central-Asian tracks had reached an appropriate terminus. There were the huge debris mounds of Afrasiab to be visited to the east of the present city, marking the site of the ancient capital of Sogdiana, the Marakanda of Alexander's historians and well known to the Chinese records. Nearer still were to be seen the noble monuments with which the Emperor Timur had adorned this center of medieval Mughal greatness. But the Russian part of Samarkand appeared to have grown greatly since my first visit fifteen years before and looked even more than before like a town of Eastern Europe.

There was much in the streets of the Russian town to call to mind the sad fact of the great struggle shaking the foundations of modern Europe. There were signs also ominously foreshadowing the upheaval which was threatening the empire of the latest invaders of Central Asia. And here at this ancient historical scene this account of my Central-Asian wanderings may fitly be brought to its close.

ABOUT THE AUTHOR

SIR AUREL STEIN (1862-1943), the great British archeologist, was born at Budapest on November 26, 1862. Educated at Budapest and Dresden and at the Universities of Vienna and Tübingen, he went to England for further study and then to India, where he became principal of the Oriental College, Lahore, and registrar of the Punjab University in 1888. He was appointed to the Indian Education Service, and for the next two years carried out archeological explorations for the Indian government in Chinese Turkistan. In 1906-8 he made further explorations in Central Asia and western China. From 1910 he was superintendent of the Indian Archaeological Survey, and in 1913-16 carried out explorations in Iran and Central Asia, described by him in *The Geographical Journal* (1916). He was created Knight Commander of the Order of the Indian Empire in 1912. In 1926 he continued his explorations on the northwest frontier, identified the site of Aornus, between 1926 and his death explored Iran, Iraq and Trans-Jordan. He died in Kabul, Afghanistan, October 28, 1943.

His writings include: *Chronicle of Kings of Kashmir* (1900); *Ancient Khotan* (1907); *Ruins of Desert Cathay* (1912); *Serindia* (1921); *The Thousand Buddhas* (1921); *On Alexander's Track to the Indus* (1929); *A Catalogue of Paintings Recovered from Tun-huang* (1931); *An Archaeological Tour in Gedrosia* (1931); *Archaeological Reconnaissances in S.E. Iran* (1937); *On Old Routes of Western Iran* (1940). *On Ancient Central-Asian Tracks* was originally published in 1933.